Crime and Consequence in
Early Modern Literature and Law

Edinburgh Critical Studies in Renaissance Culture

Series Editor: Lorna Hutson

Titles available in the series:

Open Subjects: English Renaissance Republicans, Modern Selfhoods and the Virtue of Vulnerability
James Kuzner

The Phantom of Chance: From Fortune to Randomness in Seventeenth-Century French Literature
John D. Lyons

Don Quixote in the Archives: Madness and Literature in Early Modern Spain
Dale Shuger

Untutored Lines: The Making of the English Epyllion
William P. Weaver

The Girlhood of Shakespeare's Sisters: Gender, Transgression, Adolescence
Jennifer Higginbotham

Friendship's Shadows: Women's Friendship and the Politics of Betrayal in England, 1640–1705
Penelope Anderson

Inventions of the Skin: The Painted Body in Early English Drama, 1400–1642
Andrea Ria Stevens

Performing Economic Thought: English Drama and Mercantile Writing, 1600–1642
Bradley D. Ryner

Forgetting Differences: Tragedy, Historiography and the French Wars of Religion
Andrea Frisch

Listening for Theatrical Form in Early Modern England
Allison Deutermann

Theatrical Milton: Politics and Poetics of the Staged Body
Brendan Prawdzik

Legal Reform in English Renaissance Literature
Virginia Lee Strain

The Origins of English Revenge Tragedy
George Oppitz-Trotman

Conceiving Desire: Metaphor, Cognition and Eros in Lyly and Shakespeare
Gillian Knoll

Crime and Consequence in Early Modern Literature and Law
Judith Hudson

Visit the Edinburgh Critical Studies in Renaissance Culture website at edinburghuniversitypress.com/series/ecsrc

Crime and Consequence in Early Modern Literature and Law

Judith Hudson

EDINBURGH
University Press

Edinburgh University Press is one of the leading university presses in the UK. We publish academic books and journals in our selected subject areas across the humanities and social sciences, combining cutting-edge scholarship with high editorial and production values to produce academic works of lasting importance. For more information visit our website: edinburghuniversitypress.com

© Judith Hudson, 2022, 2023

Edinburgh University Press Ltd
The Tun – Holyrood Road, 12(2f) Jackson's Entry, Edinburgh EH8 8PJ

First published in hardback by Edinburgh University Press 2022

Typeset in 10.5/13 Adobe Sabon by
Cheshire Typesetting Ltd, Cuddington, Cheshire

A CIP record for this book is available from the British Library

ISBN 978 1 4744 5435 3 (hardback)
ISBN 978 1 4744 5436 0 (paperback)
ISBN 978 1 4744 5437 7 (webready PDF)
ISBN 978 1 4744 5438 4 (epub)

The right of Judith Hudson to be identified as the author of this work has been asserted in accordance with the Copyright, Designs and Patents Act 1988, and the Copyright and Related Rights Regulations 2003 (SI No. 2498).

Contents

Acknowledgements — vii
Note on Spelling, Citation and Abbreviation — viii
Series Editor's Preface — ix

Introduction — 1

1. 'Vipers in the bosom of our Law': The Emergence of Perjury as a Common Law Offence — 25

2. 'Hollow-hearted angels': Coins, Counterfeits and the Discourses of Treason — 62

3. 'The Woman's *Case* put to the Lawyers': Miscarriage of Justice and the Case of Anne Greene — 97

4. Pardon and Oblivion: Pardon, Benefit of Clergy, *Peine Forte et Dure* — 130

5. 'England's rubidg': Mary Carleton and the Early Use of Transportation — 168

Bibliography — 204
Index — 223

For my parents and for Neil and Lara.

Acknowledgements

This book owes a tremendous debt to the colleagues, friends and family who have supported me throughout the lengthy process of its completion.

First and foremost, I am profoundly grateful to Susan Wiseman for her invaluable insights, her generosity and her support throughout this project, both within and well beyond her role as my PhD supervisor.

Very many thanks to Rosalind Smith and Laura Gowing for valuable thoughts on the shape of the book, and to Lorna Hutson and the Edinburgh University Press readers whose insights have proved enormously helpful in completing it. Thanks also to the EUP team for their helpful advice throughout: Michelle Houston, Susannah Butler, Ersev Ersoy, James Dale, Fiona Conn, Caitlin Murphy and freelance editor Camilla Rockwood. Gratitude also to Rebecca Tomlin, Rachel Holmes, Simon Stern, Derek Dunne and Adrian Streete for input and suggestions along the way.

Thanks are due to all my fellow students and colleagues at Birkbeck College, but particular gratitude to Linda Grant and to my fellow-traveller Samantha Smith for their insight, support and ongoing friendship.

Huge thanks to my whole family and particularly to my parents, who have supported and believed in me throughout my very protracted academic exploits. Finally, to Lara, who has lived with this project her whole life, and to Neil for encouragement, support and all-round excellence; I am incredibly grateful.

An earlier version of Chapter 1 appeared as 'Punishing Perjury in *Love's Labour's Lost*' in Adrian Streete (ed.), *Early Modern Drama and the Bible* (Basingstoke: Palgrave Macmillan, 2012), pp. 118–36.

Material from Chapter 3 was published in '"The nine-liv'd Sex": women and justice in seventeenth-century popular poetry', in Susan Wiseman (ed.), *Early Modern Women and the Poem* (Manchester: Manchester University Press, 2013), pp. 201–19.

Note on Spelling, Citation and Abbreviation

I have retained original spellings and punctuation in quotations from early modern texts, but have followed standard practice in modernising i/j and u/v.

The following abbreviations are used:

Wing   Donald Wing, *Short Title Catalogue of Books Printed in England, Scotland, Ireland, Wales and British America and of English Books printed in Other Countries 1641–1700*, 3 vols (New York: Modern Language Association of America, 1972–94).

STC   A. W. Pollard and G. R. Redgrave, *A Short Title Catalogue of Books Printed in England, Scotland and Ireland and of English Books Printed Abroad 1475–1670*, 2nd ed., revised by W. A. Jackson, F. S. Ferguson and Katharine F. Pantzer, 3 vols (London: Bibliographical Society, 1976–91).

Cobbett   William Cobbett, *Cobbett's Complete Collection of State Trials and Proceedings for High Treason and other Crimes and Misdemeanours from the earliest period to the present time*, ed. T. B. Howell and T. J. Howell, 33 vols (London: R. Bagshaw, Longman & Co., 1809–26).

OBP Online   *Old Bailey Proceedings Online* <www.oldbaileyonline.org>.

OED Online   *Oxford English Dictionary Online* <http://www.oed.com>.

ODNB Online   *Oxford Dictionary of National Biography Online* <http://www.oxforddnb.com>.

Series Editor's Preface

Edinburgh Critical Studies in Renaissance Culture may, as a series title, provoke some surprise. On the one hand, the choice of the word 'culture' (rather than, say, 'literature') suggests that writers in this series subscribe to the now widespread assumption that the 'literary' is not isolable, as a mode of signifying, from other signifying practices that make up what we call 'culture'. On the other hand, most of the critical work in English literary studies of the period 1500–1700 which endorses this idea has rejected the older identification of the period as 'the Renaissance', with its implicit homage to the myth of essential and universal Man coming to stand (in all his sovereign individuality) at the centre of a new world picture. In other words, the term 'culture' in the place of 'literature' leads us to expect the words 'early modern' in the place of 'Renaissance'. Why, then, 'Edinburgh Critical Studies in *Renaissance Culture*'?

The answer to that question lies at the heart of what distinguishes this critical series and defines its parameters. As Terence Cave has argued, the term 'early modern', though admirably egalitarian in conception, has had the unfortunate effect of essentialising the modern, that is, of positing 'the advent of a once-and-for-all modernity' which is the deictic 'here and now' from which we look back. The phrase 'early modern', that is to say, forecloses the possibility of other modernities, other futures that might have arisen, narrowing the scope of what we may learn from the past by construing it as a narrative leading inevitably to Western modernity, to 'us'. Edinburgh Critical Studies in Renaissance Culture aims rather to shift the emphasis from a story of progress – early modern to modern – to series of critical encounters and conversations with the past, which may reveal to us some surprising alternatives buried within texts familiarly construed as episodes on the way to certain identifying features of our endlessly fascinating modernity. In keeping with one aspect of the etymology of 'Renaissance' or 'Rinascimento' as 'rebirth', moreover, this series features books that explore and interpret anew elements of the critical encounter between writers of the period 1500–1700 and texts of Greco-Roman literature, rhetoric, politics, law, oeconomics, *eros* and friendship.

The term 'culture', then, indicates a license to study and scrutinise objects other than literary ones, and to be more inclusive about both the forms and the material and political stakes of making meaning both in the past and in the present. 'Culture' permits a realisation of the benefits to be reaped after two decades of interdisciplinary enrichment in the arts. No longer are historians naive about textual criticism, about rhetoric, literary theory or about readerships; likewise, literary critics trained in close reading now also turn easily to court archives, to legal texts and to the historians' debates about the languages of political and religious thought. Social historians look at printed pamphlets with an eye for narrative structure; literary critics look at court records with awareness of the problems of authority, mediation and institutional procedure. Within these developments, modes of research that became unfashionable and discredited in the 1980s – for example, studies in classical or vernacular 'source texts', or studies of literary 'influence' across linguistic, confessional and geographical boundaries – have acquired a new critical edge and relevance as the convergence of the disciplines enables the unfolding of new cultural histories (that is to say, what was once studied merely as 'literary influence' may now be studied as a fraught cultural encounter). The term 'Renaissance' thus retains the relevance of the idea of consciousness and critique within these textual engagements of past and present, and, while it foregrounds the Western European experience, is intended to provoke comparativist study of wider global perspectives rather than to promote the 'universality' of a local, if far-reaching, historical phenomenon. Finally, as traditional pedagogic boundaries between 'Medieval' and 'Renaissance' are being called into question by cross-disciplinary work emphasising the 'reformation' of social and cultural forms, so this series, while foregrounding the encounter with the classical past, is self-conscious about the ways in which that past is assimilated to the projects of Reformation and Counter-Reformation, spiritual, political and domestic, that finally transformed Christendom into Europe.

Individual books in this series vary in methodology and approach, sometimes blending the sensitivity of close literary analysis with incisive, informed and urgent theoretical argument, at other times offering critiques of grand narratives of the period by their work in manuscript transmission, or in the archives of legal, social and architectural history, or by social histories of gender and childhood. What all these books have in common, however, is the capacity to offer compelling, well-documented and lucidly written critical accounts of how writers and thinkers in the period 1500–1700 reshaped, transformed and critiqued the texts and practices of their world, prompting new perspectives on what we think we have learned from them.

Lorna Hutson

Introduction

Oh England! How is it that after so many Parliaments this most unjust Law is still put in execution in the midst of thee, to take away the life of man for Goods? . . . Oh how this will stink in the Nostrils of the Ages following, when Equity and Righteousnesse shall take place, when Judgement shall be laid to the Line, and Righteousnesse to the Plummet, when men shall be so able to discern of things, as to make the punishment and the crime proportionable![1]

The image of the scaffold looms large in our modern perception of Tudor and Stuart culture, but how was the idea of punishment manifest in contemporary literary and legal thinking? This study, which is situated at the interstices of literature, law and history, investigates the complex and reciprocal relation between the criminal law and the literary text in early modern England, examining specifically the role that literature plays in illuminating the relationship between particular crimes and their punishment. As the words of the Quaker William Tomlinson, above, reveal, in a period in which some three hundred crimes were designated as felonies and punishable by death, a consideration of crime must inevitably lead to a preoccupation with consequences.[2] This work therefore traces the ways in which changing ideas about criminal sanction are reflected in and engage with contemporary literary modes, asking how 'proportionable' punishment was imagined in the early modern period and how the possibility of justice miscarried might influence that imagining.

In this book I consider the ways in which the 'story' of early modern criminal sanction was constructed, both as a work in progress via the accumulation of precedent and statute, and retrospectively via the reflections of later commentators. I suggest that this construction was disrupted at a number of levels. First, at a legal level, it was undermined by certain problematic offences such as counterfeiting and perjury, each of which complicated the relationship between divine and secular punishment. Secondly, at the level of text, the narrative of the law was questioned by those who commented on legal verdicts and sentences, either directly in official treatises and case reports, or more obliquely in contemporary literary works. Finally, and most practically, legal process was disrupted by magistrates, jurors and even offenders themselves, who asserted their ownership of the mechanisms of justice by influencing or returning verdicts and outcomes that reflected their own equitable interpretation of the law. In order to examine this further, this book analyses a range of texts, popular, dramatic and legal, all of which may be said to be engaged in the circulation and exchange of narratives about the place of the subject under the law.

Any study of the legal must necessarily be historicised, but this is perhaps peculiarly true with regard to early modern law. The period of this study is framed by two legal moments: 1562, the date of the coming into force of the first Elizabethan Coining Statute, and 1685, when the miscarriages of justice surrounding the 'Popish Plot' trials were exposed.[3] Holger Schott Syme has claimed that:

> The criminal law has the ... attraction of operating, in the sixteenth and early seventeenth century, largely devoid of significant doctrinal formalization; it thus frequently had to fall back on broader cultural assumptions in its efforts to address problems arising from extra-legal, broader cultural shifts and developments. As a result, the practices of the criminal law arguably come closer to offering a lens on the culture at large than other legal fields.[4]

Such a historicised perspective works both ways. It is impossible to ignore the enormous upheavals enacted upon legal absolutes by contemporary events. If the Reformation effected a dislocation between the temporal and the spiritual, then the separation between the common law and the divine became absolute in 1649 with the trial and execution of a reigning monarch. What followed the death of Charles I – the sweeping but ultimately redundant reforms proposed by the Interregnum Hale Commission, and the complete reappointment of the judiciary following the Restoration – did little to build stability within and across the legal system.[5] Remedies were proposed, but these seemed no more coherent in their enterprise: attempts by religious reformers to introduce a more Scriptural basis for the common law led to calls for abolition of the death penalty for theft, for example, but its introduction for adultery.[6] Historical turbulence was encoding a unique dynamic in seventeenth-century law, enacting ruptures in legal thinking and yet simultaneously preventing positive change via the creation of a climate of extreme opinion. This book, then, seeks in part to explore how the criminal law was understood in this era of upheaval, but also to analyse some of the ways in which it was understood to be deficient. It asks a number of questions: what were the imaginative tools used to think about appropriate punishment? How was the link between crime and sanction conceptualised? In this Introduction, I aim to provide a sense of the contexts, historical, legal and methodological, within which these questions are posed.

Seventeenth-Century Legal Fictions

What were the 'practices of the criminal law' in this period? The seventeenth century represents a peculiar time in the history of English law. This was a legal moment in which significant reforms, such as the abolition of Star Chamber and the 'Englishing' of legal process, could coexist with those strange and anachronistic practices which J. H. Baker has grouped together under the heading 'legal fictions': the sanction of *peine forte et dure*, for example, and the outdated benefit of clergy laws.[7] Within a hundred and fifty years, scholars would have begun to document and fix the rules of judicial process in the legal treatises of the eighteenth century, but in the period in question, these rules were still being formed.[8] Throughout the century there were repeated calls for codification of the common law system and for a rationalisation of the diffuse statute base. In 1616 Francis Bacon proposed a motion for 'the compiling and amendment of the Laws of England', for example, which was echoed variously by a 1641 House of Lords proposal to 'Collect and Digest all the common law, methodically into one body', by the Levellers throughout the 1640s, and by numerous advocates at the Restoration.[9] Yet, as Frances Dolan notes:

> Despite dramatic conflict and change in the course of the century, it did not end with the codification of stable canons of evidence that have since been handed down to us unquestioned. Instead what emerged ... was a clearer sense of what was under debate. ... Uncertainty ... was a crucial part of how the seventeenth century understood itself.[10]

In a common law system underpinned by the accumulation and valorisation of precedent, some of this uncertainty arose from the reading practices of lawyers themselves, and it is instructive to consider how those practices were formed. Although some form of law reporting, most usually contained in yearbooks, had been in existence prior to the fourteenth century, it was at best erratic in coverage and certainly lacked rigour. Indeed, as J. H. Baker notes, 'From the middle of the fifteenth century ... lawyers were finding it necessary to compile commonplace books ... to help them recover material when they needed it.'[11] As well as acting as abridgements of official yearbooks, such works were a repository for 'points encountered in casual reading' and certainly it seems that this reading was much wider than we might expect.[12] Even those texts which would become printed authorities were compiled along similar lines: F. W. Maitland describes the construction of the first of Sir Edward Coke's *Institutes*, the *Commentary on Littleton* (1628), in the following terms: 'he [Coke] shovelled out his enormous learning in vast, disorderly heaps', whilst Baker notes that its subject matter included 'such disparate topics as ... the precedence of earth over the other elements, ... the ownership of the Isle of Man, and the legal status of monsters and hermaphrodites'.[13] Throughout the *Institutes*, Coke draws his thesis from a diffuse range of sources, many of which seem unscholarly at best. His tendency is to relate case law as if it were gossip or fairy tale and to garnish it heavily with his own opinion. Herewith his account of an important legal precedent:

> In the County of Warwick there were two brethren: the one having issue, a daughter ... devised the government of his daughter and his lands, until she came to her age of sixteen years, to his brother, and died. The Uncle brought up his Niece very well both at her Book and Needle &c. and she was about eight or nine years of age: her Uncle for some offence correcting her, she was heard to say, Oh good Uncle kill me not. After which time the child after much inquiry could not be heard of. Whereupon the Uncle being suspected of the murder of her ... upon these presumptions he was indicted, found guilty, had judgement and was hanged. But the truth of the case was, that the Child being beaten overnight, the next morning when she should go to school ran away into the next County ... when she was sixteen years old, at what time she could come to her land, she came to demand it. ... Which case we have reported for a [caveat] to Judges, that they in case of life judge not too hastily upon bare presumption.[14]

This 'storytelling' approach was by no means limited to Coke; later we find the Lord Chief Justice Matthew Hale compiling precedent via a series of accumulated stories and half-remembered anecdotes. Responding to Coke's consideration of the law of *corpus delicti* above, he notes its precedent value, while jovially recalling '[a]nother instance that happened in my remembrance in Staffordshire'.[15] To some degree this was the nature of the construction of precedent, but it seems peculiarly exaggerated in these writings. As Holger Schott Syme comments, '[a]bstracting, excerpting, summarizing, blending personal observation with citation of authorities: these practices shaped the way legal professionals thought, read, spoke and wrote.'[16] While eighteenth-century codification was to do much to remedy and contain this approach, it is worth noting Baker's comment that 'with all its faults, *Coke on Littleton* was the principal textbook on property law until the last [nineteenth] century', and both Coke and Hale enjoyed similar longevity in the criminal field.[17]

What such legal commentators were creating, what Lorna Hutson describes as 'the legal fiction-making that dominated the common-law thinking of the sixteenth and early seventeenth centuries in England', was a narrative in which 'reasoning or judging "equitably"' was central.[18] Drawing on earlier discussions, including Edmund Plowden's 1571 *Reports* and, earlier still, Christopher St German's *Doctor and Student*, Coke and others would position equity as a primary component of the practice of common law.[19] Moving beyond jurisdictional debates which had associated equity chiefly with the courts of Chancery and located its operation solely in the person of the monarch or his Chancellor, common-law scholars presented a broader and more nuanced concept of judgment in practice. Far from being merely the expression of mercy, equity as a model was depicted as honouring its rhetorical analogue, *epieikeia* (defined, in its Aristotelian formulation, broadly as a 'rectification of legal justice'), and encompassing a number of associated activities, including the examination of individual fact and circumstance, the conscientious unearthing of mitigation and the practice of attending to the intent of the law-maker, rather than to the letter of his law.[20] Such activities might, of course, be engaged in by a benevolent monarch, but equally they vested in judges, investigating magistrates and even in the assessments made by assize juries. In this formulation, the common law was, as Alan Cromartie notes, 'partly a method as well as a body of knowledge', and a method that was focused not on shoring up individual authority but on the achievement of the common good.[21] Legal 'fiction-making' was impelled by a desire to reach what Plowden described as 'a right judgement', in which 'the letter of a statute' would be 'enlarged by equity'.[22]

The legal canon, then, was constructed via the efforts of writers who were also voracious and acquisitive readers, readers who found relevance and interest in a wider range of sources than we might perhaps expect. This study necessarily mirrors that generic blurring; it examines the diverse narratives encoded in legal record, from the popular selections of William Cobbett's *State Trials* through to key legislative works and the sessions and assize documents for the period, but it also draws on a range of literary texts, including drama, ballads and popular pamphlets. It contends that the valorisation of early modern literary and legal 'evidence' is far from simple; so, for example, the popular texts that form the pamphlet collection of that other acquisitive reader, the antiquary Anthony Wood, which appear in a number of the chapters that follow, may, at times, seem as important to our consideration of a legal point as the analysis of Coke; indeed, the two may have mutual influence.

'Owning' the Law

J. H. Baker comments pointedly on the 'absence of systematic exposition of the law' prior to the eighteenth century, noting that 'if settled law fared badly, the developing law fared worse'.[23] Among those developments were three that have particular bearing upon this study. The first was really a question of ownership, of where, within a system of multiple jurisdictions and instruments, the law actually lay. Writing in 1601, the playwright and legal scholar William Fulbecke attempted to present the English civil, canon and common law systems as a coherent and harmonious whole: 'it seemed straunge unto me, that these three laws, should not as the three *Graces*, have their hands linked together', but was ultimately forced to acknowledge dissonance, if not full discord: 'like the . . . faces of *Janus* . . . the one . . . turned from the other'.[24] It was the relationship between two of Fulbecke's 'Graces' in particular that came into play in questions of punishment, and this relation, between canon and common law systems, was complex. Post-Reformation, the influence of canon law and the concomitant jurisdiction of the ecclesiastical courts was certainly diminishing in scope, as increasing numbers of offences passed into the purview of the common law or began to be regulated by statute. Bradin Cormack has noted that:

> while at the beginning of the Tudor period it was possible to imagine English law substantially in terms of interrelated spheres of judicial activity, by the mid-seventeenth century the common law of the central royal courts was fully present to the culture as the dominant source of juridical norms.[25]

That is not to say that the church courts were formally in decline in this period; as scholars including Martin Ingram, Laura Gowing and J. A. Sharpe have demonstrated, these courts in fact witnessed an upsurge in activity, 'an explosion in litigation', during the late sixteenth and early seventeenth centuries, particularly in relation to slander and defamation cases.[26] Yet by the early seventeenth century the common law represented a valid alternative for litigants and authorities alike and, as Lorna Hutson has demonstrated, with increased public understanding of 'the evidential processes of the participatory justice system', it began to gain in moral, as well as administrative, authority.[27]

The transition to a more centralised legal structure was not a seamless process; as Ethan Shagan comments, the processes of the English

Reformation did not include the addressing of 'ecclesiastical polity and its awkward relationship to legislation, enforcement and jurisprudence', leaving questions of church law 'frighteningly inchoate'.[28] That the general perception of a 'spiritual' jurisdiction extended far more widely than even the traditional remit of the church courts is evidenced by ongoing debates regarding the adoption of a scripture-based legal system in the period. Crucially, while such debates considered issues of judicial and trial procedure, they were chiefly focused on ideas of appropriate punishment, or at least on the need for an explicable system of sanction, and it is clear that for many legal commentators a powerful momentum towards the *lex talionis* remained. This was not a straightforward transposition; with the exception of the power to excommunicate, the sentencing options available to the church courts were rarely draconian and certainly did not enact the prescriptions of scripture in any real sense. Nonetheless the penitential aspects of such sentences were appealing in their ability to calibrate a particular crime in terms of its sinfulness, an equation that the secular courts struggled to provide.[29] That there was an appetite for such calibration is demonstrated when we look beyond the official record. Appropriate punishment is a constant preoccupation of the writers of popular pamphlets on criminal cases – and where the law cannot provide, providential fantasies are invoked to remedy its shortcomings. So, perjurers are struck dumb, infanticides are driven to self-immolation and murderers are revealed by the bleeding corpses of their victims.[30] In some instances, the narratives of these providential texts became absorbed into the discourses of the law itself, creating a generic blurring that complicates our reading of even the most nominally authoritative of works.

The second consideration relates to the nature of the common law itself, which was being challenged by the growing status of statutory measures in relation to the prosecution of criminal offences. Although its ultimate effect was to centralise legal authority, this is not to say that legislation was suddenly being created and enacted in an orderly and systematic fashion; procedurally, as John Langbein notes, most statutes were introduced into Parliament almost haphazardly, as individual Members' Bills, even into the eighteenth century.[31] Nor was the increasing implementation of statute law an explicitly secularising process; indeed, as Cormack comments, there is a clear link between post-Reformation models of scriptural interpretation and the centralisation of legal practice via statutory mechanisms:

> [S]tatute had a new place in the constitution, and the proliferation of written law in the wake of the Reformation effected a corresponding change in how the central law was understood, since the need to mediate between the

unwritten and written law allowed the law theoretically to take on the shape of its own interpretation in the central courts.[32]

Certainly, a scriptural analogue for the practice of legal interpretation has resonance: Chapter 1 of this study, for example, explores the complex relationship between the 1563 Perjury Statute and its canon law counterpart, Thomas Cranmer's *Homily Against Swearing and Perjury*. In that chapter and the one that follows, I investigate how the interplay between statute and common law – and more pointedly a perceived idea of how the common law should operate that was rooted in ideas of biblical precedent – created areas of dissonance and controversy, both in relation to the implementation of the law and to its consequences. We see this problematic played out in surprising ways in early modern literary texts, where the technical language of statute, indictment and sentence infuses both narrative and structure, and works to reveal deep fissures in the understanding and rationalisation of these measures.

Interpretation, whether of legal jurisdiction or of the appropriate prosecutorial instrument, was therefore peculiarly integral to the operation of the criminal law in this period. The third and final element of this hermeneutic process was the interpretation of evidence, conducted by magistrates as part of the investigation of crime, by the jury during the course of a trial and finally, as I will argue, by those assessing and 'reading' verdicts post-conviction. In order to consider interpretation, we must return to the question of ownership, albeit a question inflected somewhat differently. In the last thirty years, scholars including Barbara Shapiro and Cynthia Herrup have argued persuasively for early modern English criminal procedure as a model of communal participation, opposing this to the Continental prosecutor-driven approach propounded by Michel Foucault.[33] Lorna Hutson has developed this line of reasoning to posit a more active and evaluative role for sixteenth-century juries and magistrates than has previously been considered.[34] In Hutson's thesis, jurors and Justices of the Peace were active participants in the creation and dissemination of emerging discourses of probability and 'circumstance', discourses originating in Latin treatises on rhetoric, discourses that were also seen to operate within the forensic narratives that inform the drama of the period. Most pertinently, Hutson links this model to legal changes in the mid-sixteenth century, which required:

> Justices to take written examinations of those arrested to record the grounds on which they decided to detain a suspect in prison or, alternatively, to grant bail. In order to comply with these statutes, Justices of the Peace had to find ways of weighing likelihoods applicable to all kinds of cases.[35]

This participation, Hutson argues, extended from Justices to jurors, whose task it was to evaluate the rhetorical success of a particular narrative scenario, and indeed to the wider community, who, in the event of a crime's discovery, might participate 'in a process of the following of clues and constructions of narrative'. Nor is such a position irreconcilable with an acceptance of the providential narratives that surround early modern crimes. As Hutson notes, 'the rhetoric of providential disclosure, ... along with frequent recourse to so-called irrational proofs such as cruentation, or the bier-rite, [is] not in any way incompatible with the development of "forensic" or "detective" habits of mind among ordinary people'.[36]

Hutson asks productive questions about the application of a Foucauldian theory of disciplinary power to English judicial practice: 'What, then happens to a Foucauldian reading when we acknowledge the traces of a communal justice system? ... Who decides the "truth" of what happened in a criminal case?'[37] This position has particular resonance when considering punishment, and we might add further questions to these inquiries: how far does communal participation in justice equate to communal responsibility for sanction? And what are the implications when that justice is miscarried? This latter point is a central concern of the third chapter of my study, wherein putative communal 'responsibility' for wrongful executions seems to manifest in a range of different impulses surrounding the writing and reading of the crimes in question.

Writing on the status of felony crimes in the seventeenth century, Abbot Emerson Smith suggests that 'the judge had no alternative. He could condemn to death, or he could reprieve the felon for some good reason, but there was no third course open, and no lighter penalty which he might impose.'[38] The judge had no alternative, perhaps, but the jury might. One corollary of communal participation in justice manifested itself very practically in capital cases, in the conscious manipulation of legal sanction by jurors themselves. In some instances this led to a refusal to return a guilty conviction at all (a practice known as juror nullification).[39] Further, it is now well documented that it was common practice for juries to exploit their knowledge of the law to return so-called 'partial' verdicts, convicting the defendant of a lesser offence, in order to avoid the death penalty or to allow him, or after 1623, her, to take advantage of benefit of clergy.[40] Although most widely practised in cases of theft, where the value of stolen goods would be reduced in order to rewrite the offence as the non-capital petit larceny, partial verdicts also occurred in trials for burglary, which was reframed as the clergyable larceny, and for murder, which might be reduced to manslaughter to permit a similar chance of reprieve.[41] Louis Knafla, analysing J. S. Cockburn's *Calendar of Assize Records for the Home Circuit*, has identified a pattern of cases in which juries returned 'not guilty' verdicts on infanticide, murder and manslaughter charges, asserting that the victim had been killed by divine visitation or a mystery person unknown: 'several synonyms developed for finding the prisoner not guilty because someone else did it. Names such as John ap Noke ... Thomas Staff ... John at Death ... John in the Wind.'[42] Even in the coroner's court, mid-century juries would return *non compos mentis* verdicts in suicide cases, representing the deceased as of unsound mind in order to permit a Christian burial and to prevent forfeiture of property.[43]

We might assume that this activity was simply grounded in a momentum of sympathy for the accused: however, J. M. Beattie has demonstrated that, in certain cases, there may have been a more sophisticated project at work. In his study of the London and Middlesex courts he notes that at one typical mid-seventeenth-century session:

> Thirty eight of the men and six of the women who were whipped for petit larceny had been originally charged with a form of grand larceny for which they might have been granted clergy, branded in court, and released; had that been their punishment they may have preferred it to being returned to gaol and subsequently whipped.[44]

Beattie notes that such a reduction was more common in cases of repeat or 'nuisance' offenders, suggesting that juries were consciously manipulating the penal code in order to increase the eventual penalty.[45] A comprehensive awareness of the implications of the law becomes more credible when we note that, due to the difficulties of jury selection, many jurors sat on multiple trials at multiple sessions, and would have convicted defendants in numerous cases of this type.[46] The causes of such low-level subversion seem to be best sought in the complex nature of the contemporary legal landscape, in a perceived inadequacy in the balance of crime and punishment, and in a sophisticated understanding of the factors that might motivate or even necessitate an offence.

The Debate on Capital Sanction

Death, or clergy: such were the outcomes of a felonious criminal enterprise in the seventeenth century. What was missing was, as John Langbein notes, any real '*via media* between the blood sanctions and the petty sanctions'.[47] It is precisely this movement between extremes that renders punishment so useful as a point of entry into early modern criminal law, yet it is crucial to remember that such polarisation was not necessarily always acknowledged by contemporary commentators. Indeed, prior to the Civil War, there seems to have been no sustained mainstream dialogue on the issue of capital punishment in England. Individual concerns were expressed – Henry Finch, serjeant-at-law to James I, wrote in his legal treatise *Nomotechnia* that 'our law making the stealth of 12d value a capital and deadly crime, is without all question a cruel and deadly law' – and research has indicated that, from the 1630s onwards, there was a decline in numbers of executions.[48] As noted above, partial verdicts were recorded by juries seeking to manage the outcome of a guilty verdict. Yet it is not until the mid-century that we witness a robust engagement with the issue.

The challenge came initially from politically radical sources. The Levellers explicitly addressed the question of capital punishment in their *Large Petition* of March 1647, requiring that it might only be imposed following the testimony of 'two witnesses at least, of honest conversation' and that any punishment, corporal or capital, be wholly proportional to the offence at law – '[that] no man's life may be taken, his body punished ... but upon weighty and considerable causes'.[49] The same themes were reiterated to Parliament in September 1648, in the *Humble Petition of Thousands wel-affected persons*, a statement of growing dissatisfaction:

> We have long expected: ...
> 15. That you would have proportioned Punishments more equal to offences; that so mens Lives and Estates might not be forfeited upon trivial and slight occasions.[50]

The subject was again addressed in the second *Agreement of the People* at the end of 1648, which advocated limiting capital punishment to the offences of murder and treason.[51] By this point, individual petitioners and pamphlet writers had also begun to discuss the death penalty. In general, their theme was not total abolition, but a review of those crimes that attracted capital punishment, and in particular a revision of the felony status of property crimes, this 'most unjust Law ... to take away the life of a man for Goods', as William Tomlinson described it.[52] This latter point was explicitly related to a wider problem of want, which was figured as addressable – the words of the army preacher, Hugh Peters, are typical:

> that poore Thieves may not be hang'd for 13 d. ... but that a Gally or two may be provided to row in the River or Channell, to which they may be committed, or employed in drayning lands, or banished.[53]

In a survey of death penalty debates, Robert Zaller notes that the attitude of the Levellers and other writers on this issue was clear: 'society had a special obligation to those in want, an obligation that precluded it from considering as enemies those driven by such want to crimes against property'.[54] A petition of 1653 made this explicit: 'Nor should Death be inflicted for a trifle of five shillings ... whilest vast sums are taken from the Commonwealth, without any accompt, by Committee men, and others.'[55] Not only were there explicit accusations of hypocrisy here, but connotations of tyranny.

The contemporary sectarian position on legal matters owed much to a perception that a return to a notion of divine or Mosaic law was the only route to reform, and scriptural sources were readily invoked to support this stance. Scripture advocated that the convicted thief should make restitution of four (or sometimes seven) times the value of the goods or money stolen, or be imprisoned or otherwise bound in servitude. The pamphleteer Samuel Chidley was perhaps the most active proponent of such reform: in *A Cry Against a Crying Sinne* (1652) he articulated the claims of equity – 'how unjust it is to kill a Man for stealing xiiii d, let all Men reasonable judge' – in terms of an absolute adherence to the limitations of divine law as expressed in the Bible: 'all laws which are not according to God's Law, and pure Reason, are null and void'.[56] However, a scriptural justification of capital punishment was obviously problematic for those who saw equity as a measure of reason and who hoped to limit the application of capital punishment to the most serious of crimes. The claims of the *lex talionis* were not exactly innocent of blood and, as Zaller points out:

> [I]n addition to murder, treason, kidnapping, bearing false witness in a capital case and adultery, the Bible demanded death for blasphemy, wilful profaning of the Sabbath, idolatry or inciting to idolatry, witchcraft, the cursing of God, one's mother or father, and the ruler, 'Unnatural Copulations, whether Sodomy or Buggery', and 'Whoredome of a maid in her Fathers house'.[57]

Some commentators saw no contradiction in this; Finch, for example, was an advocate for the death penalty for dishonouring one's parents, and, as Barbara Shapiro notes:

> [M]any of the most vocal critics emphasized the unscriptural nature of the penalties, motivated in their desire to change the penalty for theft from death to restitution ... less by humanitarian impulses than by Biblical conviction. The same motive prompted the introduction in 1650 of the scripturally required death penalty for incest and adultery.[58]

As we will see in relation to perjury in Chapter 1, concerns about the proportional nature of punishment by no means always tended to leniency. For those less comfortable with the sweeping proscriptions of scripture, however, the general response to this difficulty was to suggest that Mosaic law represented merely the outer boundaries of what was permissible, as the Leveller John Cook commented:

> Moyses lawe, thoughe it were ungentle and sharpe ... yet it punished thefte by the purse, and not wyth deathe. And let us not thynke that God in the newe lawe of clemencie and mercie ... hath geven us greater scoupe and license to execute crueltie one upon another.[59]

The Commonwealth's position on the debate was complex. Whilst Cromwell expressed reservations about the erratic application of capital sanction – 'to hang for a trifle and to acquit murder ... This is a thing God will reckon for' – the fundamental obstacle to any sweeping reform lay, as Zaller notes, in 'the circumstances of the English Commonwealth itself ... founded on an act of such punishment'.[60] Nonetheless, whilst abolition of capital sanction may have seemed too great a step, there were mitigations already in existence that could be explored. As discussed in Chapter 5, the most promising of these was the growing trade in transportation of vagrants, convicts and others to settle the land in the Americas. This route was already being used on an ad hoc basis, but it was a cumbersome and protracted process for the judiciary. In an oblique gesture towards the capital punishment debate, then, in 1654 the Interregnum government authorised a change to this procedure, which allowed judges to pardon a convicted felon without (as previously required) the intervention of the Privy Council. Whilst on the surface this change seemed merely administrative, it represented a breakthrough in expediting and systemising what was really the only credible alternative to the death penalty then in existence. Pardon for transportation was perhaps the ideal compromise: abolitionists such as Peters had already expressed support for 'banishment' as an alternate punishment for theft, and Chidley suggested that offenders might 'be transported to some of our owne Plantations', yet, by retaining transportation as a mechanism of reprieve rather than a direct sentence, the sanction maintained the deterrent properties of the death penalty.[61]

Although the dialogue on abolition diminished at the Restoration, Charles II also recognised the expediency of the conditional pardon system, as an approach 'that might become our royal clemency and be likewise an advantage to the public', and the process remained the chief means of mitigating capital penalty until the formalisation of transportation as a direct sentencing option in 1718.[62] Reform was thus encoded in seventeenth-century legal procedure as part of a system of compromise, of negotiation, a means by which the judicial establishment, and indeed the state, could circumvent the prescriptions of the law without formally undermining them: a practice that was ultimately not too different in intent from the activities of early modern juries.

Law and Literature; Literature and Law

What were the claims of literature upon the debate around early modern sanction? In Act 4 of Shakespeare's *Love's Labour's Lost*, Berowne acknowledges his guilt, and that of his friends and sovereign, in breaking their oath of chastity. His reasoning leaps immediately from crime to consequence:

> BEROWNE: He, he and you – and you, my liege – and I
> Are pick-purses in love and we deserve to die.[63]

For many in the period the moral schema of the criminal law was most acutely imagined via the mechanisms of punishment, and this is clearly manifest in the literary representation of that punishment, in accounts of cases both real and fictional.

Academic study of the relationship between literature and law is a field that, in the early modern arena at least, stands in complex relationship to its component discourses. In a 2005 essay, Julie Stone Peters identified that field as predicated 'not so much [upon] the shared content of law and literature, as its shared longing'.[64] In this formulation, she argued, each discipline has 'in some way fantasized its union with the other: law would give literature praxis; literature would give law humanity and critical edge'.[65] Peters' analysis, which suggested that in seeking to operate across boundaries, law and literature had inadvertently recreated and reinforced those boundaries, represented a challenge to a model that had hitherto dominated the field. Peter Goodrich describes that model thus: 'They argue . . . that literature represents a fracture, a crisis, a puncture of the legal restraint of the text.'[66] If the law can be 'punctured' then it is figured as distinct, self-contained; to the literary practitioner, law is seen as being, or presenting itself as, a monolith, a univocal authority. In such a formulation, as Richard Posner termed it in his 1988 study, law 'appears a solid ground'.[67]

Scholarship has positioned law as hugely influential in the early modern period: in the research of Shapiro and others, the epistemological, 'fact-finding' methods of early modern legal process are presented as underlying the knowledge-making practices of a range of contemporary fields of learning: scientific, philosophical, literary.[68] Erica Sheen and Lorna Hutson term the relationship thus: 'The habits of interpretation and expectations of genre which more or less define the reception of Anglophone literary and popular culture are profoundly indebted to developments in Anglo-American common law.'[69] However, whilst ostensibly privileging the solidity and 'restraint' of law, this paradigm may also be seen to undermine it. Goodrich's 'fracture' is in this sense morally freighted; as Subha Mukherji suggests:

> [I]mplicit in the polarisation that most of us [scholars of law and literature] have tried to resist to a greater or lesser extent is the problematic assumption that literature is an equitable corrective to law ... the temptation is to think that literary uncertainties are more complex than legal certainties, and that this makes literature more ethically satisfying.[70]

When considering ideas of punishment, it can be tempting to read literary renderings of legal scenarios in terms of this 'equitable corrective' to the law's rigour. Yet investing that notion of equity in the reader of a literary text or the audience of a play is problematic. In many early modern instances, such an impulse within the literary was merely the expression of the lived experience of early modern law. Moreover, the seventeenth century sits uneasily with any notion of the legal as solid and knowable; rather, it offers us a problematic model of disrupted justice and abortive reform. Rather than positioning literature as an agent of unbinding, we must recognise that in certain periods, law was already unbound, openly so; its fractured origins of church, king and community exposed, it was being made and remade by contemporary events. The monolith law, which the paradigm of 'law and literature' exhorts us to seize and dismantle, did not really exist. We cannot have a practice of law and literature in this period without the claims of historical specificity.

Inevitably, this raises questions: what sort of model *can* work for a study of the legal and the literary in the English seventeenth century? Recent scholarship in the field has, to varying degrees, sought distance from any conception of law as 'solid ground', recognising what Mukherji describes as the 'productive instabilities of early modern legal process and even theory'.[71] Much thought-provoking work has been published on the law's relation to early modern dramatic form in particular. Mukherji's own scholarship has sought to interrogate the reasons for the prevalence of the 'theatre-as-court metaphor' in early modern plays, asking whether 'the analogy between the two ... amount[ed] to a substantive connection rather than a mere literary commonplace'.[72] In particular, what this study shares with Mukherji's is an understanding that any analysis of the period requires a broad and inclusive approach to texts: 'where legal documentation is insufficient or non-existent, there is a case to be made for using literary material to reconstruct certain aspects of the experience of law' – an approach that implicitly recognises historical reality, but also the 'patchwork' nature of early modern law.[73]

That nature is an explicit concern of Bradin Cormack's work, which uses a very specific model of jurisdiction to counter the binaries of law and literature. Cormack, responding to Giorgio Agamben's theorisation of the relationship between 'sovereign power and bare life', proposes jurisdiction as a primary 'principle of analysis', a means of exploring the fluid boundaries between the legal and wider early modern culture, as it is manifested in literature.[74] Emphasising the peculiarly heterogeneous nature of jurisdiction in the Tudor and Stuart periods, he focuses on the 'impact of the legal threshold on the constitution and configuration of meaning', challenging Agamben's concept of the 'state of exception', the idea that there exists a 'discursive position beyond law'.[75] Cormack regards the work of literature in relation to law as similar to that of jurisdiction, 'because it is implicated in the same process of shaping unruly practice for which jurisdiction itself stands' and is at pains to discredit the idea of a monolith law:

> students of literature ... have often looked to the law of a given historical period as though it were already coherent, whether as a storehouse of categories and norms that the culture at large might re-present by absorbing or resisting them, or as a stable constitutional reality rather than a set of constitutional hypotheses.[76]

In the context of this study, jurisdiction provides a powerful tool for thinking through the factors influencing the punishment – and the conceptualisation of that punishment – of offences that seem to exist on the boundaries of secular and religious censure, as well as a reminder of the multiple manifestations of 'law' that were experienced by early modern subjects.

It is of course important to remember that that experience of law was far from passive. As discussed above, Lorna Hutson's *The Invention of Suspicion* explores the relation of the law and the subject by positing a model that has wide-ranging implications for the literary: 'the possibility that participation in the justice system diffused concepts of fact-finding and evaluation of narrative through the culture'.[77] In considering such narrative, Hutson is careful to reject any assumptions about 'the natural inevitability of ideas like sequential and circumstantial coherence of plot', demonstrating how these mimetic elements were 'among the far from inevitable new products of the transformation of dramaturgy', by playwrights drawing upon the forensic rhetoric of new Roman comedy.[78] Such an approach has been used productively by other scholars, including Virginia Lee Strain in exploring ideas of legal reform, and Derek Dunne in examining the investigative modes of revenge tragedy. It also seems to bear useful application to a wider consideration of early modern texts, illuminating the constructed nature, the 'far from inevitable' status of those narratives we find in popular pamphlets about legal cases, for example, and dismantling any notion of the psychological inevitability of a particular narrative dynamic.[79]

The works above, amongst others, have opened up the study of early modern literature and law to permit an acknowledgement of the 'vast, disorderly heaps' of contemporary legal process, whilst also finding meaning in that instability. As will be evident, this book owes much to this approach, but seeks to channel it into new and productive spaces by foregrounding a consideration of consequences rather than legal process. The work of legal historians and historians of crime, including John Langbein, J. M. Beattie, Laura Gowing, Cynthia Herrup and Malcolm Gaskill, is therefore also particularly relevant to my analysis.[80] Not only have these scholars questioned and disrupted received assumptions about seventeenth-century legal practice, they have, in many cases, proposed productive methodologies for the study of criminal activity. Gaskill, for example, is explicit in his mentalities-based approach to early modern crime, drawing on a tradition of microhistorical interpretation to write 'history from within', as he terms it.[81] 'It may be helpful to think of mentalities as a bridge between social history and intellectual history,' he writes, but equally his work creates a formal link between historical and literary modes, in his consideration of the 'striking similarities' between court depositions and popular literature, and his discussion of contemporary investment in providential narratives as a means of 'ordering' experience.[82] Gowing also considers legal testimony in its relationship to narrative, usefully demonstrating the breadth of possible influences, literary and otherwise, 'the variety of strands in popular culture', operating in the constructions of such depositions.[83] These approaches enable us to start thinking about the ways in which a variety of generic modes were valorised and deployed alongside the more obvious narratives about punishment.

Last, and perhaps most significant, is Herrup's proposal of an analysis of criminal law motivated not by a desire to reconstruct the truth about a case, but by a deliberate stance of 'agnosticism on the verdict'.[84] For Herrup, 'law is a cultural dialect', influential, but with no inherently superior truth-value; that value inheres in the ways in which narratives about the law are constructed and rendered – 'the story of this trial is not recoverable; many of the stories about the trial, however, are'.[85]

Through the lens of sanction, then, I hope to demonstrate not only the value of Herrup's 'stories', but the way in which, at times, such stories actually become constitutive of the law itself.

The Structure of This Book

Crime and Consequence therefore seeks to examine the relationship between the early modern law, literature and history as it is illuminated by considerations of crime and its punishment. While similar themes, questions and indeed personalities are present throughout, the book is broadly constructed in two parts. The first section considers the evolving nature of the law itself, asking what constituted a felony crime and how, in relation to individual offences, that status might reflect or oppose wider perceptions of appropriate sanction. The opening two chapters examine two problematic, but relatively underworked, crimes – perjury and counterfeiting – to consider what a perceived gap between crime and consequence can tell us about the idea of sanction in early modern England. Each chapter traces a long trajectory, from the late sixteenth century through a hundred years. Chapter 1 considers the crime of perjury, which, though not a capital offence in the period, was at times conceived of in those terms. Biblically proscribed – 'thou shalt not bear false witness' – an act of perjury could have the most extreme consequences, undermining both the force of the law and the link between truth and testimony. This was to be seen most clearly in the Popish Plot trials of the 1680s, when the crimes of Titus Oates and others, in the words of one commentator, 'unhing[ed] the whole society of the World'.[86] Yet an unease with the disjunction between the sin of false witness and the crime of perjury is evident far earlier, manifesting itself in a popular concern with the appropriate punishment of the offence.

The peculiar nature of perjury as a secular crime involving the breach of a religious oath makes it particularly fruitful subject matter when considering sanction, and a useful starting point for this study. Perjury was undergoing a change in legal status in the period, as the 1563 Elizabethan perjury statute passed the power to punish false witness from the ecclesiastical to the secular courts. This chapter maps the tensions inherent in the reformulation of an Old Testament commandment as a temporal and secular offence, examining the progress of the statute and some key contemporary cases, but also reading that anxiety in providential pamphlets and contemporary drama, most notably Shakespeare's *Love's Labour's Lost*. As such, it seeks to illuminate both the limitations of the common law's control and the degree to which those boundaries could be conceived of as permeable.

Chapter 2 inverts this model of inadequate punishment to consider a crime that was not popularly perceived as a sin, yet was punished by the most extreme sanction available to the English courts. Counterfeiting had been a capital offence since a statute of Edward III, and from 1562 onwards, Elizabeth I's legislative programme reaffirmed and extended its status as high treason.[87] Yet, unlike other 'treasonous' crimes of the period, the severity of punishment decreed for coining and counterfeiting seemed to have little moral force behind it, and crucially in post-Reformation society, it was absent from the proscriptions of the biblical Decalogue. Counterfeiting, as William Fleetwood put it in his 1694 *Sermon Against Clipping*, was an 'unfixed evil', which seemed to do little harm: 'a crime, by which we know of none that are undone, or greatly injured'.[88]

With the exception of Gaskill's study of the offence, scholars have neglected the subject of counterfeiting in the sixteenth and seventeenth centuries, focusing rather on the prosecution of large coining rings in the eighteenth.[89] And yet questions of coining and counterfeiting were intimately bound up in the discourses of mercantile worth and personal profit that permeate contemporary drama. Much of this concern with coining evinces knowledge of the severity of its penalty, yet it also points up the ambiguity of the offence, its existence as a part of everyday experience. This chapter, then, considers the dramatisation of the idea and the reality of counterfeiting in a number of Middleton's plays – *The Revenger's Tragedy, A Chaste Maid in Cheapside, The Roaring Girl* – asking how far that representation can be said to replay or reject the 'official' discourses of treason. It also interrogates the representation of the offence in legal record and popular print, seeking the traces of a counter-discourse on coining that may or may not exist.

Chapter 3 continues the discussion of appropriate sanction, reflecting on the types of evidence that writers and readers of accounts of criminal cases evaluated in search of what Shapiro has termed 'the satisfied conscience'.[90] It focuses on miscarriage of justice, in particular in relation to the crime of infanticide, and explores the popular, legal and scientific discourses that surrounded that offence during the seventeenth century. The chapter discusses the 1650 case of Anne Greene, an Oxfordshire servant who, having been made pregnant by her employer's grandson, was subsequently tried and condemned to death for the murder of her stillborn child. Greene was hanged, but she revived shortly before her body was due to be dissected as part of an anatomy demonstration. She was subsequently pardoned – her survival of the gallows being regarded as a signifier of her innocence – and found herself at the centre of a seventeenth-century sensation, a focus of immense public interest and support.

This chapter, then, takes as a starting point a single early modern case of capital sentencing. We must be cautious in extrapolating certainties from such limited evidence, attempting, as Cynthia Herrup puts it, 'to contemplate the impact of a narrative, rather than surrender to it'.[91] The Greene case has been discussed as an example of the popular providential narrative at its most vivid; indeed it has been suggested that the exemplary nature of the case is such that it may even have been a convenient fiction. I suggest that the case is notable not merely for its literary qualities, but for the picture it, and its surrounding literature, gives us of popular interaction with the legal in the period, and of the evolving influence of scientific evidence upon the law's ability to determine the 'truth' of a set of facts. As English criminal process moved away from earlier models of 'self-informing' neighbourhood juries to approach a fully realised system of trial, the problem of what could be known about a past event came sharply into focus. Greene's case exposes the anxiety of the jury's interpretative act, enacting what might be seen as a fantasy of its erasure, in the literal reversal of her conviction that is effected by her survival. Using popular accounts of the affair, as well as parallel cases in France, the chapter examines the possibility that this fantasy crystallises a growing public concern about the unstable nature of 'knowing' and its implications for the deployment of death as legal process.

An emerging theme of each of these chapters is the 'ownership' of the law discussed earlier in this Introduction, in particular the agency displayed by judicial officers, jurors and observers in subverting verdicts, influencing sentencing and mitigating the literal application of the legal. The second section of the book moves to focus specifically on such interventions to examine the ways in which they presaged genuine change, exploring the alternatives to a capital sentence in the period and asking how clemency was valued and deployed within the early modern justice system. Considering a range of contemporary literature, including Shakespeare's *Measure for Measure*, Chapter 4 focuses on the temporal space between conviction and execution. Within that space, it explores the alternative consequences of prosecution in the period, interrogating the mechanics of royal clemency, the questionable outcomes of benefit of clergy and the penalties associated with a refusal to plead. The chapter asks questions about the uses of pardon in early modern society, about the jurisdictional interaction of pardon and penance in a landscape of secularised justice and about the influence of political forces on the debate around capital punishment, analysing whether what appears to be disruptive and dramatic may in fact be considered and transactional. Further, it examines the ways in which alternative outcomes become part of a metaphoric landscape, at times a structuring principle, in contemporary dramatic works.

Finally, Chapter 5 considers how the English criminal law system at last began to address the extremes of the 'death or clergy' paradigm, via the early use of transportation as a mechanism for pardoning offenders in capital cases. While, as noted above, the 1718 Transportation Act is often regarded as marking the inception of this remedy, the practice of transportation to America was already functioning as a means to reprieve those convicted of capital offences.[92] As the Act itself acknowledges, however, this could be a problematic endeavour: it comments pointedly upon the fact that many such offenders 'have often neglected to perform the said condition [i.e. of transportation], but returned to their former wickedness'.[93] One such was Mary Carleton, 'commonly stiled the German Princess', the adventurer, thief and polygamist, whose cheating of justice kept the courts and scandal-mongers of Restoration England occupied for more than a decade.[94] Carleton met her judicial fate only after a conviction for theft caused her to be sentenced to transportation in Barbados – from which she returned, illegally, only to be recaptured and hanged. This discussion of Carleton is focused chiefly on that experience, examining what the texts that chronicle her exploits tell us about the use of transportation as a system of pardon and correction, marked by anxieties around verdicts and their consequences. Her progress through the courts also illuminates another form of 'ownership', demonstrating the ways in which offenders themselves could manipulate the mechanisms of reprieve in order to influence their judicial destiny.

In summary, then, this study seeks to present a number of perspectives on the relationship between crime and sanction, as part of a wider exploration of the interaction between the law and the literary text in the early modern period. In a field that has, to date, focused largely – and productively – on issues of legal process, it aims to demonstrate the further potentialities inherent in an analysis of consequences. Of course, from a distance of four hundred years or more, consequences are always already known, the 'denouement' is never a surprise; and perhaps this is the point. Our position as modern readers of early modern legal experience is, in this regard, a privileged one. If we are able to think beyond the requirement to reach a verdict, to resist the compelling narrative dynamic of the criminal trial, then there are rich possibilities to be explored. If, as Cynthia Herrup terms it, 'we are willing to find a balance on less solid ground', then the interaction of offence and sanction, with all its uncertainty and inconsistency, becomes a viable model for analysis, a model that at once illuminates and complicates the relationship between early modern legal sanction and literary print culture.[95]

Notes

1. Tomlinson, *Seven Particulars*, f. 11.
2. See Smith, 'Transportation of Convicts', p. 233.
3. 5 Eliz. 1, c. 11.
4. Syme, *Theatre and Testimony*, p. 18.
5. See Shapiro, 'Law Reform in Seventeenth-Century England'.
6. See the 1650 Commonwealth Adultery Act, Firth and Rait (eds), *Acts and Ordinances of the Interregnum, 1642–1660*, pp. 387–9.
7. Baker, *Introduction to English Legal History*, p. 230.
8. See, e.g., Blackstone, *Commentaries on the Laws of England*; Gilbert, *The Law of Evidence*.
9. Bacon, *The Works of Francis Bacon*, xiii, p. 71; *Harleian Miscellany*, 8 vols (London: 1744–6), MSS.6424, p.1. On the Levellers' proposals, see Wolfe, *Leveller Manifestoes*. See also Shapiro, 'Law Reform', p. 287.
10. Dolan, *True Relations*, p. 5.
11. Baker, *Introduction to English Legal History*, pp. 211–12.
12. Ibid. p. 212.
13. Maitland, *Collected Papers*, vol. 2, p. 484.
14. Coke, *Third Part of the Institutes*, p. 232. For further discussion of this case, see Hudson, 'Seventeenth-century legal fictions'.
15. Hale, *History of the Pleas of the Crown*, vol. 2, p. 190.
16. Syme, *Theatre and Testimony*, p. 107.
17. Baker, *Introduction to English Legal History*, p. 218.
18. Hutson, 'Imagining Justice', p. 123.
19. St German, *The dyaloges in Englishe*.
20. See further Cromartie, '*Epieikeia* and Conscience'.
21. Cromartie, 'The Constitutionalist Revolution', p. 84.
22. Plowden, *Commentaries or Reports*, vol. 2, p. 167.
23. Baker, *Introduction to English Legal History*, p. 214.
24. Fulbecke, *A parallele or conference*, p. 3.
25. Cormack, *A Power to Do Justice*, p. 27.
26. Ingram, *Church Courts, Sex and Marriage*; Gowing, *Domestic Dangers*; Sharpe, *Defamation and Sexual Slander*, p. 3.
27. Hutson, *Invention of Suspicion*, p. 45.
28. Shagan, 'The Ecclesiastical Polity', pp. 337, 344.
29. See Hutson's discussion of the canon law obligation of restitution: *Invention of Suspicion*, pp. 49–63.
30. See, e.g., Munday, *A View of sundry Examples*; Bicknoll, *A Sword Agaynst Swearyng*.
31. Langbein, 'Albion's Fatal Flaws', p. 118.
32. Cormack, *A Power to do Justice*, p. 33.

33. Shapiro, *A Culture of Fact*; Herrup, *The Common Peace*; Foucault, *Discipline and Punish*.
34. Hutson, *Invention of Suspicion*; see also Hutson and Kahn (eds), *Rhetoric and Law in Early Modern Europe*.
35. Hutson, *Invention of Suspicion*, p. 2.
36. Ibid. pp. 82, 272.
37. Ibid. pp. 68–70.
38. Smith, 'Transportation', p. 233.
39. Green, *Verdict According to Conscience*, p. 140.
40. See Beattie, *Policing and Punishment*. In 1623, women convicted of theft of goods valued at less than 10 shillings were granted clergy; full implementation followed in 1691.
41. J. S. Cockburn, 'Twelve Silly Men? The Trial Jury at Assizes, 1560–1670', in Cockburn and Green (eds), *Twelve Good Men and True*, pp. 171–2.
42. Knafla, '"John at Love Killed Her"', p. 314.
43. Macdonald and Murphy, *Sleepless Souls*, p. 15.
44. Beattie, *Policing and Punishment*, p. 304.
45. Ibid.
46. See Langbein, 'The Criminal Trial before the Lawyers', p. 274.
47. Langbein, 'Historical Origins of the Sanction of Imprisonment', p. 55.
48. Finch, *Nomotechnia*, STC (2nd ed.)/10871, f. 25. Finch approves the death penalty for adultery, which 'breaks holy bonds', and for dishonouring of parents: see Prest, 'The Art of Law and the Law of God'. On execution levels, see Sharpe, *Crime in Seventeenth-Century England*, pp. 141–2.
49. Wolfe, *Leveller Manifestoes*, p. 140.
50. *To the right honourable the Commons of England*, p. 6.
51. See Wolfe, *Leveller Manifestoes*, p. 302.
52. Tomlinson, *Seven Particulars*, f. 20. The only vocal advocate of total abolition in the period was Gerrard Winstanley, who wrote in *The New Law of Righteousness*: 'if I kill you I am a murderer, if a third come, and hang, or kill me for murdering you, he is a murderer of me' (p. 41). Even Winstanley did not sustain this position, later readmitting the death penalty for certain crimes.
53. Peters, *A Word for the Armie*, p. 12.
54. Zaller, 'Debate on Capital Punishment', p. 130.
55. Pendred, *The humble remonstrance of many thousands*, p. 3.
56. Chidley, *Retsah*, p. 8.
57. Zaller, 'Debate on Capital Punishment', p. 136.
58. Shapiro, 'Law Reform', p. 296.
59. Cook, *Unum Necessarium*, p. 43.
60. Quoted in Veall, *The Popular Movement for Law Reform*, p. 1; Zaller, 'Debate on Capital Punishment', p. 142.
61. Peters, *A Word for the Armie*, p. 12; Chidley, *Retsah*, p. 16.
62. Royal Proclamation, 1663, quoted in Beattie, *Crime and the Courts*, p. 473; Transportation Act 1718, 4 Geo. 1, c. 11.
63. Shakespeare, *Love's Labour's Lost*, IV.iii.204–5.
64. Peters, 'Law, Literature and the Vanishing Real', p. 448.
65. Ibid. p. 448.
66. Goodrich, 'Endnote: Untoward', p. 161.

67. Posner, *Law and Literature*, p. 15.
68. See, for example, Shapiro, *A Culture of Fact*, ch. 1.
69. Sheen and Hutson, *Literature, Politics and Law in Renaissance England*, p. 1.
70. Mukherji, '"Understood Relations"', p. 710.
71. Ibid. p. 719.
72. Mukherji, *Law and Representation*, p. 1.
73. Ibid. p. 16.
74. Agamben, *Homo Sacer*; Cormack, *A Power to Do Justice*, p. 4.
75. Cormack, *A Power to Do Justice*, p. 4.
76. Ibid. pp. 3–4, 24.
77. Hutson, *Invention of Suspicion*, p. 80.
78. Ibid. pp. 2, 106.
79. Strain, *Law Reform in English Renaissance Literature*; Dunne, *Shakespeare, Revenge Tragedy and Early Modern Law*.
80. See, e.g., Langbein, *Prosecuting Crime in the Renaissance*; Beattie, *Crime and the Courts*; Gowing, *Domestic Dangers* and *Common Bodies*; Herrup, *The Common Peace* and *A House in Gross Disorder*; Gaskill, *Crime and Mentalities*.
81. Gaskill, *Crime and Mentalities*, p. 4.
82. Ibid. pp. 7, 222.
83. Gowing, *Domestic Dangers*, p. 56.
84. Herrup, *A House in Gross Disorder*, p. 6.
85. Ibid. pp. 6, 7.
86. *True Narrative of the Tryal of Titus Oates for Perjury*, f. 1.
87. 25 Edw. 3, st. 5, c. 2; 5 Eliz. 1, c. 11.
88. Fleetwood, *A Sermon against clipping*, p. 21.
89. Gaskill, *Crime and Mentalities*, chs 4 and 5.
90. Shapiro, *A Culture of Fact*, p. 22.
91. Herrup, *A House in Gross Disorder*, p. 8.
92. See, e.g., Beattie, *Crime and the Courts*; Langbein, 'Historical Origins'; Coldham, *Emigrants in Chains*.
93. 4 Geo.1, c. 11.
94. *Memoires of Mary Carleton*, title page.
95. Herrup, *A House in Gross Disorder*, p. 6.

Chapter 1

'Vipers in the bosom of our Law': The Emergence of Perjury as a Common Law Offence

LONGAVILLE: Ay me, I am forsworn!
BEROWNE: Why he comes in like a perjure, wearing papers.[1]

Berowne's wry observation on Longaville's appearance in Act 4, scene 3 of *Love's Labour's Lost* refers explicitly to the sixteenth-century penal sanction for the criminal offence of wilful perjury. As part of their punishment, convicted perjurers were to be set 'on the pillory in some market-place within the shire, city or borough', wherein the offence had been committed.[2] Standing exposed to the public gaze, they wore a paper, fixed either to their head or their back, on which was inscribed the details of their offence. Longaville's 'perjury' consists in breaking his scholarly oath by falling in love with Maria, and Berowne's depiction thus enacts public justice upon him precisely at the moment of his admission of guilt. When his co-offender, Dumaine, enters the scene a moment later, he unwittingly invokes the image once again: 'O would the King, Berowne and Longaville/ Were lovers too! Ill, to example ill/ Would from my forehead wipe a perjured note' (120–2).

Shakespeare's play is considered to have been written between 1594 and 1595. Three decades earlier, in 1563, royal assent had been given to 5 Eliz. 1, c. 9, the first English statute to legislate for the trial of perjury cases at common law.[3] Whilst many of Shakespeare's works, most notably the history plays, exhibit what Tom McAlindon describes as an 'almost obsessive' interest in issues of swearing and forswearing, in *Love's Labour's Lost* the breaking of oaths becomes the play's organising principle.[4] Although critics have noted the profusion of vows, made and broken, in the play, what a closer study reveals is that in fact the text is suffused with the precise terms of the perjury statute, demonstrating just how far its language had permeated in late Tudor England.[5] Yet, throughout the play there are also multiple references to the sanctions for perjury as 'penance', to the crime itself as 'eternal shame'. In this ambiguous presentation of perjury and the punishment thereof, *Love's Labour's Lost* gradually reveals the issues of definition and determination surrounding the contemporary understanding of a crime that is also a sin.

This study asks how the link between crime and sanction was conceptualised in the early modern period, and how literary texts can illuminate this connection. In the case of perjury, we find this conceptualisation underpinned by a nexus of biblical, legal and literary relationships operating in complex ways. Prior to the Act's coming into force in 1563, contemporary thinking around the offence had centred on the logic of the 1547 State *Homily Against Swearing and Perjury*, which asserted that:

> Almightie God to the intent his moste holy name should be had in honor, & evermore be magnified of the people, commaundeth that no man shoulde take hys name vainly in his mouth, threatenyng punishmente unto hym that unreverently abuseth it, by swearyng, forswearyng, and blasphemy.[6]

Drawing on the book of Jeremiah, early modern perjury (or false swearing of any kind) was constructed as an assault not only upon the name, but upon the very existence of God – 'as surely as the Lord lives, still they are swearing falsely' (Jeremiah, 5:2).

If perjury was a crime against God, then punishment would come from Him; via the workings of divine providence or, more prosaically, through the censure of the ecclesiastical authorities. Accordingly, prior to the Act, crimes of perjury were explicitly punishable only by the church, or by conciliar courts, most notably Star Chamber. In some cases, a perjury conviction could be grounds for excommunication.[7] The Elizabethan statute, however, created a crime that could be tried in the common-law courts; in effect passing the power to punish perjury into the hands of the state. The ambiguities of the Act and of its attempt to provide a coherent and prosecutable definition of perjury – and an appropriate sanction for that crime – contributed to a landscape of transition and uncertainty around the nature of the offence in the period.

Those uncertainties were to persist across a hundred years, coming into focus once again as the seventeenth century drew to a close. In 1685 Titus Oates, the infamous perjurer of the Popish Plot, was sentenced to a fate not dissimilar to that of the perjured lovers of Navarre. Oates was to 'stand in the *Pillory* before *Westminster-hall gate* . . . one hour . . . with a Paper on his Head writ *Perjury, Perjury*, twice; and walk around the Hall with the said Paper on his Head'.[8] The shocking nature of Oates' crime and its consequences prompted an outpouring of contemporary comment on perjury as an offence. Whilst, in addition to his pillory sentence, Oates was defrocked, whipped, fined and imprisoned for life, there was a popular sense that no sanction could be severe enough for the man whose crimes had, in the words of one commentator, 'unhing[ed] the whole society of the World'.⁹ The anonymous author of *The Third Commandment*, a pamphlet issued in the year of Oates' conviction, decried the paucity of the sentence pronounced upon the man he describes as Titus 'Oat[h]es':

> And what can deter them from the villany? Alas the greatest punishment our Laws inflict will be very insignificant, they will no more fear a Pillory, than Crows a Man of Clouts... And indeed what has a Pillory formidable in it? If an uneasie posture for a time, a being exposed to the derision and reproaches of the Multitude, and perhaps the enduring a little pelting with rotten Eggs and Turnips...
>
> Can a Pillory be sufficient to punish the contempt of God, the violation of the Religion of an Oath, the perverting Justice, and disappointing the excellent design of wholsome Laws?¹⁰

Over the course of a century, the popular, and indeed the legal conceptualisation of perjury had been shaped by a series of tumultuous upheavals, both religious and political; yet it remained in transition. This chapter investigates that transition via a study of forswearing and perjury in a variety of early modern texts, ranging from the Homily and its imitations, through the 'taffeta phrases' of *Love's Labour's Lost*, the Judas-iconography of contemporary providential pamphlets and back to the statute itself. In so doing it seeks to demonstrate how the concern with an active 'punishment' of forswearing in these texts maps the tensions inherent in the reformulation of an Old Testament commandment as a temporal and secular offence.

'The pit of perdition': Lawful Oaths and the *Homily Against Swearing and Perjury*

In their writings on society and power, Carl Schmitt and Giorgio Agamben propose a model of sovereignty based on the concept of the 'state of exception', the suspension of law creating a movement outside its boundaries into a realm of situational judgment, a process not unlike the equitable reasoning advocated by Plowden, Coke and others.¹¹ A modified version of this framework may offer some useful points in a consideration of early modern perjury. Agamben writes:

> The law has a regulative character, and is a 'rule' not because it commands and proscribes, but because first of all it must create the sphere of its own reference in real life and *make that reference regular*.¹²

Perjury, it seems, is constantly in a 'state of exception' in this period; the law functions only in the knowledge of the existence of a wider structure of censure, which simultaneously supports and undermines its application. This is less the creation of the sovereign will, however, than of the peculiar status of perjury as an offence, in transition between the operations of canon and common law. As such, Bradin Cormack's reformulation of Agamben's theory in jurisdictional terms is also of relevance. Cormack writes that:

> [A]lthough jurisdiction belongs to the law in the sense of defining its operations, it remains a powerful index of just how unstable those operations are ... For the law functions by keeping the source of its authority in fixed view as, insistently, the merely technical (and for that reason discursively unassailable) image of its own jurisdictional scope and operation.[13]

Cormack's positioning of the 'Tudor and Jacobean periods as a transitional moment ... a moment in which, necessarily, the question of jurisdictional heterogeneity was messier' has particular resonance for the history of perjury across those periods.[14] As we have seen, the 1563 Act attempted to formalise (and indeed to expedite) the transition of that offence from ecclesiastical to secular jurisdictions. Yet that transition, I would argue, was far from linear. While Cormack's work foregrounds what he describes as 'jurisdictional complexity', that complexity is ultimately part of a process, in which the common law – and, by extension, the legislative measures that underpin that law – takes a dominant ideological position: 'the common law came to see alternative legal frameworks as possessed of an authority that could be said to be valid just to the extent that the common law itself acknowledged and controlled those alternatives'.[15] That process is undeniably the aim of the Perjury Statute; yet such a power relationship seems far from clear. As Ethan Shagan writes of the early modern period: '[t]heology mattered in the enforcement of law, because the law itself was in some sense an act of exegesis.'[16] What actually surrounds, and at times opposes, the common law conception of perjury is not merely the prior jurisdiction of the church courts, but a wider accretion of ideas about the offence, fuelled by a biblical discourse of sermons, providential tracts and lurid pamphlet exemplars, existing both in the popular and (crucially) the legal imagination. Further, it would seem that this competing discourse holds sway over a significant time period, without a clear trajectory towards resolution. Finally, it is specifically in relation to the punishment of those who bear false witness that this accumulation of ideas becomes most apparent.

Underlying this discourse is the *Homily Against Swearing and Perjury*. The author of the *Homily* places considerable emphasis upon St Paul's use of the particular form, 'I call God to witnesse'.[17] Writing a century later, John Tillotson, the then Dean of Canterbury, expands upon the implications of this form of oath-taking:

> An *Oath* is *an invocation of God, or an appeal to him as a witness of the truth of what we say* . . . whether the Name of God be expresly mentioned in it or not . . . in all these cases a man doth virtually call God to witness; and in so doing, he doth by consequence invoke him as a Judge and an Avenger, in case what he swears be not true. And if this be expresst, the oath is a formall Imprecation; but whether it be, or not, a curse upon our selves is always implyed in case of perjury.[18]

Tillotson's sermon, which has its genesis in the 1547 text, expresses perfectly the conflation of legal and sacred that is central to the debates on perjury and oath-taking in the period. It was preached at the Assizes at Kingston and York, ostensibly glossing a secular legal proceeding, however for Tillotson, the oath, 'whether the Name of God be expresly mentioned in it or not', is a religious speech act, which explicitly invites the Divine into the courtroom. This elision of human and divine account is also a commonplace of the literary representation of oath-taking. In *Love's Labour's Lost*, for example, when Berowne takes an oath to study 'three years' term' at the Court of Navarre, he sees his oath as weighted in both senses: 'so to the laws at large I write my name/And he that breaks them in the least degree/Stands in attainder of eternal shame' (I.i.153–5).

Tillotson takes as the central premise of his sermon St Paul's statement 'An Oath for confirmation is to them an end of all strife' (Heb. 6.16). In this he is unusual. Earlier writers, including the author of the *Homily*, struggled to reconcile the swearing of oaths with New Testament teaching, specifically due to the – seemingly – explicit prohibition upon swearing made by Christ in Matthew 5:34–7:

> But I say unto you, Sweare not at all, neither by heaven, for it is God's seate: nor by the earth, for it is his footestoole . . . /But let your communication be yea, yea; nay, nay: For whatsoever is more then these, commeth of evyl.[19]

Even *Love's Labour's Lost* encodes this proscription; we hear Christ's words echoed in Berowne's challenge to the terms of his sworn oath: 'By yea and nay, sir, then I swore in jest' (I.i.54).

Although the publication of the *Articles* of the Church of England in 1563 seemed to resolve this anxiety, the thirty-ninth article asserting that, despite the prohibition, 'a man may sweare when the Magistrate requireth, in a cause of faith and charitie', disputes around the legality of oath-taking continued.[20] Whilst religious groups such as the Quakers took a visible stand against swearing, it is clear that this remained an area of unease even among the more orthodox. In his 1644 sermon, preached to the Royalist Court at Oxford, William Strode drew on Luther to endorse oath-taking, noting that Luther:

> hath well endeavour'd to clear this point, by comparing Christ's Sermon together with his Auditors: here he instructs not the *Maegistrate*, but the *People*, and divers things are unfit for them in their own Persons, which may become fit under the Magistrates command.[21]

Similarly, John Gauden's 1662 treatise, *A Discourse Concerning Public Oaths*, which explicitly sets out to challenge 'the scruples of the Quakers' and other 'sober dissenters', engages in a tortuous justification of Matthew 5:34–7 as a statement aimed specifically and solely at the practices of the Jews, who had 'much *depraved* both the true *nature* and *use* of Oaths'.[22]

Writing some fifteen years before the publication of the *Articles*, the author of the 1547 *Homily* is in fact quick to point out that Christ himself engaged in a form of assertory oath-taking – 'thus did oure saviour Christe swear diverse tymes, saying: verely' (sig. Gii). His chief texts, however, are drawn not from the New Testament, but from the prophets of the Old. Central to this is the message of Jeremiah 4:2:

> God by the prophet Jeremie saieth: thou shalt sweare the Lord liveth, in truth, in judgement, in righteousnesse. So that whosoever sweareth when he is required of a Judge, let hym be sure in his conscience, that hys othe has these three condicions, & he shall never nede to be afraied of perjurie. (sig. Gii)

For the author of the *Homily* the 'lawfull' oath, conforming to 'these three condicions', is indubitably a valid and godly endeavour: 'a parte of God's glory' (sig. Giii).[23] 'By lawfull othes, which Kynges, Princes, Judges, and Magistrates doo sweare,' he asserts:

> common lawes are kept inviolate, Justice is indifferently ministered ... malefactors are searched out, wrong doers are punished, and thei whiche sustein wrong, are restored to their righte. (sig. Giii)

This was by no means wholly original; John Spurr has noted that:

> The clerical concern to control and curb the oath clearly has a long history. If one goes back no earlier than the fourteenth century, the catechisms and preachers are recognisably pursuing the same goals as those of the seventeenth.... Jeremiah iv.2 is quoted by Chaucer's Parson and Pardoner in the 1380s.[24]

Nonetheless, this concern was becoming more formalised than ever before, as the State *Homilies* became required reading in churches across the nation. The argument of the *Homily Against Swearing and Perjury* undoubtedly reflects a culture wherein, as Spurr comments, 'oaths were becoming a favoured tool of the secular authorities'– from Henry VIII's 1534 Act of Succession onwards, the Tudor regime had begun to invest in the potential of oaths to shackle souls as well as bodies.[25] Oaths both assertory (making a statement of fact or belief) and promissory (stating a future intention) were being woven into the fabric of what it meant to be an English subject. The argument for lawful swearing appears repeatedly in subsequent sermons and tracts on oath-taking. One of the stated objectives of Edmund Bicknoll's 1579 pamphlet work, *A Sword Agaynst Swearyng*, for example, is to demonstrate that 'there is a lawful use of an oth, contrary to the assertion of the Manichees & Anabaptistes'.[26]

Yet this is after all a *Homily* Against *Swearing and Perjury*, and what is most notable in the context of this study is that its author devotes some two-thirds of his text to what might be described as *un*lawful swearing and the consequences thereof. The original proscription on swearing is, of course, contained in Exodus 20, and key to our understanding of the *Homily* is an awareness of what we might describe as the tendency in this period to conflate the third commandment ('thou shalt not take the name of the Lord thy God in vaine') and the ninth ('thou shalt not beare false witnesse against thy neighbour').[27] As Frances Shirley asserts, 'the third and the ninth commandments were really together in the minds of many ... and the old worry recurs that the habitual swearer would be less apt to think seriously about a formal oath'.[28] Even in 1685, the anonymous author of the Titus Oates pamphlet addresses the 'extream mischiefs of perjury' he witnesses under the auspices of 'The Third', rather than the ninth 'Commandment', noting that '[perjury] being expressly forbid by God in the Third and Ninth Commandments, but chiefly in the Third, and that under a penalty too. For that the words of taking *God's name in vain*, are especially meant of false Swearing.'[29]

In fact, in the *Homily*, the third commandment encapsulates far more than simple blasphemy – all those who swear oaths 'often, unadvisedly, for trifles, without necessitie, and when thei should not sweare ... do *take Gods most holy name in vain*' (sig. Giii, my emphasis). It is thus a short step from swearing oaths 'unadvisedly', in matters of commerce, for example, to wilfully breaking them. All this is 'perjury'. The author links such sinners in an ongoing progression of offence, from malicious oath-takers, such as Herod in his promise to Salome, to rash and foolish swearers like Jephthah.[30] This parade of oath-takers and forswearers culminates in a final condemnation of those who bear false witness under oath: 'how great and grievous an offence against God thys willful perjurye is' (sig. Hii). Edmund Bicknoll, who is clear that 'common or usual swearing leadeth into perjurie', offers a similar vision of the inevitable progress of sin:

> So, of the often naming of God, much more often swearing by his name, there ariseth a vaine abuse, an unhonourable derogation, a path-way to the palace of perjury, an open accesse, or rather a compulsion to the pit of perdition.[31]

It is apparent that perjury as a term had a far wider application than in its modern legal sense of bearing false witness under oath.[32]

'Nor God nor I delights in perjured men,' the Princess tells the King of Navarre as he pursues his suit to her in Act 5 of *Love's Labour's Lost* (V.ii.346). The *Homily* is equally vehement upon the divine 'hatred' of perjury, and upon the enormity of the 'punishment God hath prepared for false swearers and perjured persons' (sig. Hi). A litany of Old Testament vengeance follows this assertion: the people of Israel who broke their oath of 'frendshippe with the Gabaonites' are punished with 'an universall famine, upon the whole countrey, whiche continued by the space of three years'; Jephthah is forced to slay his only daughter; and Sedechias, who reneged upon his oath of fidelity to 'kyng Nabugodonosor', sees his land invaded, his sons slain and is blinded and 'led . . . prisoner miserably into Babilon' (sig. Hi).

The most enduring image of the *Homily*'s depiction of the consequences of perjury comes, however, from the prophet Zachariah (Zach. 5:2):

> [W]hich thing to the prophet Zacharie, god declareth in a vision, wherein the prophet saw a book flying, which was twenty cubites long, and ten cubites brode, god saying then unto hym. This is the curse that shall goe forth upon the face of the earth, for falsehoode, false swearing and perjury. And this curse that entre into the house of the false man, and into the house of the perjured man, and it shal remain in the middest of his house, and consume hym, the timber, and stones of his house. (sig. Hii)

The flying book, or flying 'roll' as it is elsewhere glossed, and the 'curse' it delivers, represents an unequivocal statement of abhorrence – 'thus you se, how much God doth hate perjury'. The perjured man will be destroyed from within, and for generations to follow, for God will be a 'swifte witness and a sharpe judge upon' him (sig. Hii). Bicknoll gives this biblical curse another name, more familiar and immediate for an early modern audience, drawing on Ecclesiasticus 23:11: 'A man that useth much swearing, shalbe fylled with iniquitie, and the plague shal never go from his house.'[33] In *Love's Labour's Lost* this connection is notable in multiple references to illness and contagion; John Kerrigan has written persuasively about the fear of plague and infection in the play, a fear particularly immediate in 1590s London.[34]

And yet, as we have seen, the *Homily Against Swearing and Perjury* was in many respects as much a tool of the state as of the divine. What happened when that state wished to indicate a similar level of displeasure? In order to address this question, we should consider the intricacies of perjury's status under law.

'[A]n othe, before a judge, upon a boke': the 1563 Perjury Statute

The early modern crime of perjury existed in complex relationship to a number of prior ideas and definitions of the offence and was positioned within a nexus of discourses – religious, cultural and legal – surrounding the concept of false swearing. Nonetheless, the mid-sixteenth century saw a significant legislative attempt to surmount those complexities, and an examination of the context of that attempt allows us to understand more about the secular legal response to perjury in that period and through the century that followed.

On 18 February 1563, the *House of Commons Journal* reports the first reading of the 'Bill for Punishment of Perjury and suborned Witnesses'. It was introduced to the chamber by Walter Haddon, a former Regius Professor of Civil Law at Cambridge and a Master of the Court of Requests.[35] The Bill's passage through Parliament appears to have been relatively smooth; it was read again on 6 March, and for a third time on 18 March, at which point it was passed in the Commons. The *Journal* records themselves enact the pattern of confusion we have identified around the terminology of the crime: at its second reading the Bill had become the 'Bill for the punishment of Perjury and false Witnesses'; by its third it was merely the 'Bill against wilful Perjury'.[36] It was subsequently passed in the House of Lords and became the statute of 5 Eliz. 1, c. 9, 'An Act for the Punishment of Such as Shall Procure or Commit Any Wilful Perjury'.

Little is known about the reason for the Bill's introduction at this time. Its post-Reformation context may give us some clue: Walter Haddon was a staunch Protestant, with connections to John Foxe, and he may have had the heresy trials of Mary I's regime in mind when seeking to reinforce the penalties for suborning witnesses – equally, as a lawyer, his interest may have been of a purely administrative nature, as witness testimony in court began to increase.[37] Significantly, a decade earlier he had been closely involved in an attempt to formulate the *Reformatio Legum Ecclesiasticarum*, a new canon law code, which would, its authors asserted, be significantly more 'consistent with the common law and the statutes of the realm' than the existing regime.[38] The treatment of perjury within that code, in particular its proposed punishment by a system of fines, looked ahead to the 1563 statute. The *Reformatio* was never adopted, but it may be that the aspiration towards cross-regime consistency remained. As noted, 1563 was also the year of publication of the *Articles* of the Church of England, which effectively authorised oath-taking in the service of the law for English Christians, but there is no explicit connection made between that text and the Act.

Haddon's final statute provided explicitly for the punishment of perjury committed by witnesses under oath and for those who suborned those witnesses to perjure themselves. It also provided – for the first time – for a subpoena process, which would legally compel witnesses in a case to attend court. What was the significance of these measures? It is generally considered that, prior to the statute's enactment, only juror perjury – that is, the giving of demonstrably false verdicts – had been punishable at common law, a process known as 'attaint', although it is arguable that perjury had effectively been tried in the common-law courts under the mantle of other offences, such as maintenance.[39] George Fisher has suggested that denying the existence of witness perjury had hitherto been 'convenient for the system', for 'it avoided the damage that a perjury prosecution might have caused to the public's confidence in the accuracy of jury verdicts'.[40] However, as the role of the juror became increasingly focused on the evaluation of evidence, including witness testimony, a requirement to shore up the value of that testimony became more compelling. The preamble to the statute does in fact refer to an earlier act, of Henry VIII's reign (most likely 32 Henry 8, c. 9), which addressed itself to the subornation of perjury, claiming that the penalty imposed under that act was 'so small towards the offenders in that behalf, the said offence ... hath greatly increased and augmented', confirming that there had been previous attempts to address that particular problem.[41] Indeed, the question of whether perjury had been punishable at common law at all prior to 1563 is a vexed one: certainly it would appear that there had been little coherence of approach. As we have noted, pre-statute, perjury was largely punishable in the ecclesiastical courts or in Star Chamber, but exactly *what* was being punished was fundamentally unclear. Michael D. Gordon has stated that:

> [Pre-1563] There were a variety of crimes which were identified and defined as perjury and these crimes were under the jurisdiction of various English courts. For example, perjury could encompass petty debt litigation and be handled by ecclesiastical courts. Or it could encompass false returns by sheriffs and be dealt with by conciliar courts.[42]

Unfortunately, the advent of the statute was to do little to remedy this confusion. The reasons for this were fourfold. First was the ongoing ambiguity surrounding the offences that might constitute perjury. Conal Condren comments on the implications for those taking professional oaths ('oaths of passage'):

> [P]erjury was not a statutory offence until 1563, but its meaning was often wider than it is now. According to John Selden, it ought to apply only to assertory oaths. Nevertheless, after an oath of passage any failure in office could be construed as perjury.[43]

Indeed, Gordon cites a 1597 case wherein two goldsmiths, tried as practising forgers, were subsequently also charged with perjury, because they were deemed to have violated the terms of their professional oath, in the taking of which they had sworn never to commit forgery.[44] Obviously this could not have been a prosecution under the terms of the statute, which explicitly restricted itself to witness perjury. It follows then that there was a perception that an offence of perjury existed outside the terms of the statute as well as within its definition. The ambiguities inherent in 5 Eliz. 1, c. 9 seemed implicitly to create that offence, a catch-all for all those instances problematised by the opaque nature of the Act.

The second factor complicating the implementation of the statute was the question of jurisdiction. As noted above, in the sixteenth century, punishment of perjury was most closely associated with the church courts and the statute itself explicitly protected the jurisdiction of those courts over perjury committed as part of their own proceedings: 'This act ... shall not extend to any spiritual or ecclesiastical court or courts.'[45] It also, seemingly, preserved the jurisdiction of 'the court in Westminster commonly called the star-chamber', with an ambiguous reference to the 'authority given by act of Parliament in the time of King Henry the Seventh, to the lord chancellor of England, and others of the King's council ... to examine and punish riots, routs, heinous perjuries and other offences'.[46] Such vagueness seems to imply that the 'act of Parliament', and thus the terms of Star Chamber's authority over perjury, was well known. That in fact they were not was evident almost immediately; three years after the coming into force of 5 Eliz. 1, c. 9 the issue of jurisdiction was being furiously debated in the courts in *Onslowe's Case*.[47] This involved the question of whether perjury allegedly committed at the King's Bench (a common-law court) could be punished by Star Chamber. The judges in the case concluded that it could not. They referred to the new statute and tried in vain to establish to which Act of Henry VII it referred – 'all the Judges were assembled at Serjeant's Inn and perused the statutes of 3 Henry 7, c. 1 and 11 Henry 7, c. 25 and the *proviso* for the starchamber in the act of perjury' – before reaching their decision.[48] This decision crystallised all of the uncertainty surrounding both the offence and the law's jurisdiction over it and exposed the oddly disjointed nature of the previous Tudor legislation. As Michael Gordon notes:

> The reasoning seems to be that perjury was nowhere punishable [in common-law courts] before 5 Elizabeth I, c. 9; hence the court of Star Chamber had never had jurisdiction 'of right' over perjury. And thus, because the proviso in 5 Elizabeth I, c. 9 for the Star Chamber was one which saved existing jurisdictions and did not confer new ones, the Court of Star Chamber had no authority over perjury cases.[49]

The decision was challenged by commentators, including Edward Coke, who claimed that the judges in *Onslowe's Case* needed only to have referred to 'Ancient Authors and Records' to have found instances of perjury as a crime prior to the 1563 statute.[50] Perjury cases continued to be heard in Star Chamber, as well as the common-law courts, throughout the sixteenth century, including, somewhat oddly, cases involving perjury in the ecclesiastical courts.[51] Confusion over jurisdiction, both spiritual and temporal, was a manifestation both of the general uncertainty around the nature of perjury, but also, it seemed, of a vague and undefined legal 'memory' of a history of perjury as an offence that stretched back over centuries.

The third problem surrounding the Perjury Statute was that the mechanisms of the law that were required to permit its successful implementation remained decidedly inconsistent. Prior to the sixteenth century, witnesses had not been a regular part of the jury trial process. Although the degree to which the medieval jury was truly 'self-informing' has been a subject of debate, nonetheless it seems to have been the case that, as Daniel Klerman notes, '[t]he jurors themselves were considered the witnesses – not necessarily eyewitnesses, but witnesses in the sense that they reported facts to the judges.'[52] Gordon contends that witnesses were giving testimony under oath by the mid-fifteenth century and that by 'a century later witnesses seem to have been cross-examined regularly'.[53] Other evidence, however, suggests that this transformation was a much slower process. In the 1618 edition of *The Countrey Justice*, Michael Dalton's comments on witness swearing suggest that this was best practice rather than a matter of course:

> Note that in these former Cases, and all other Cases where the Justice of P. is to take such examination of witnesses, or such accusation or proof, as aforesaid, though the statute doth not expressly set down that it shall be upon oath, yet it seemeth fit that the Justice doth it upon oath.[54]

Dalton later cites an attempt by Coke to clarify this issue: 'And so was the direction of *Sir Edward Coke*, late Lord Chief Justice ... upon the triall of a felon; For (said he) in case of trespasse to the value of two pence, no Evidence shall bee given to the Jurie, but upon oath, much lesse where the life of a man is in question.'[55] Even once witnesses did begin to appear regularly in court, those testifying for the defence in felony and treason cases (including defendants themselves) were not permitted to do so under oath. Barbara Shapiro comments that '[t]he rationale for denying the oath to defence witnesses ... was not obvious', but notes Parliamentary debate on the issue in 1607, during which a direct link was made between perjury and capital sanction: '"men will be more prone to forswear themselves" in cases of life'.[56] In fact it was not until 1702 that statutory provision was made for defence witnesses to testify on oath.[57]

The final and perhaps the dominant factor compromising the Act's implementation was the enduring investment in the idea of perjury as a moral and a fundamentally religious crime. As the *Homily* indicated, if all crime was inherently sinful, then perjury, with its implicit attempt to implicate God in the transgression, was exceptionally so. Frances Shirley notes that, in tracts which engage with the order of the Ten Commandments, it is stressed that 'taking "the name of the Lord in vain" does precede murder, theft and adultery' – all offences that, at one time or other during the early modern period, were capital crimes.[58] This valorisation persisted well beyond the statute's coming into force. Thus, in *Love's Labour's Lost* the Princess warns the King of the eternal consequences of the vow he has made: ''Tis deadly sin to keep that oath, my lord /And sin to break it.' (II.i.105) – a vow that was signed in a firmly secular, quasi-legal setting, and which required Ferdinand 'to keep those statutes/That are recorded in this schedule here' (I.i.17–18). Similarly, the author of the *Homily* describes the taking of a legal oath – in almost exclusively religious terms:

> I wyll shewe you, what it is to take an othe, before a judge, upon a boke. Fyrst, when they layng they hands upon the Gospell boke do sweare trewely to enquire, and to make a trewe presentment of thinges wherewith they be charged, and not to let from saying the trueth, and doing trewely, for favour, love, drede, nor malice of any person, as God maye helpe them, and the holy contentes of that boke. They moste considre that in that boke is contained, gods everlasting trueth, his moste holy and eternal worde.   (sig. Hii)[59]

At this point, it is worth reflecting on one of the ideas underlying the use of statute law in the period. Post-Reformation concepts of authority as vested in the interpretation of the written word (Scripture) opened up the possibilities of the text as an instrument upon which to build national legal autonomy. Cormack, for example, notes the 'proliferation of written law in the wake of the Reformation ... the early Tudor state's increased use of interpretation as the principal means of legal centralization and control'.[60] In the case of perjury, this dynamic evinces a doubleness, however, a tension between the biblical and the statutory interpretations of the offence, in which the legal text is often undermined.

From a legal standpoint, uncertainty around perjury had a long history. The origin of the term itself lay in the Latin word *perjurium*, which was defined as the invocation of a god to witness the truth of a statement, in the knowledge that that statement was false. *Perjurium* was originally conceived as a sin, rather than a crime to be punished by the state. Under Roman law, there was, however, a separate offence of making a false statement (or withholding a true one) when acting as a witness under oath. This crime was punishable by banishment or death. The dual approach of Roman law to the act of false witness has a clarity that its sixteenth-century analogue does not. To some degree the separation of the idea of *perjurium* from the law of the state had been maintained into the early modern period, by the prosecution of perjury cases primarily in the church courts. Indeed, John Spurr notes that 'originally the medieval church embraced existing oaths, oaths inherited from Roman law, rituals of fidelity and fealty, and elsewhere'.[61] As we have seen, offences constituting or similar to perjury occasionally broke through into the secular legal domain via juror attaint, or those cases tried in Star Chamber. In explicitly making 'perjury' punishable by the state, however, the 1563 Act sought to reframe *perjurium* as a secular crime – an endeavour particularly fraught in a post-Reformation landscape saturated with the language and imagery of the *Homily* and similar works.

Whilst problematic in scope and in its definition of perjury as an offence, the Act nonetheless represented a step forward in terms of punishment. What it provided was a clear system of sanction for the crimes it did address, and it was the appropriateness or otherwise of these sanctions that was to preoccupy legal and popular thinking well into the seventeenth century. It was, after all, an Act explicitly concerned with 'Punishment' and it explicitly gave common-law courts the right to punish perjury. Those convicted under the statute would:

> [F]or his or their said offence lose and forfeit twenty pounds, and to have imprisonment by the space of six months with bail or mainprize; (2) and the oath of such person or persons so offending, for thenceforth not to be received in any court of record within this realm of England or Wales, or the marches of the same, until such time as the judgment given against the said person or persons shall be reversed by attaint or otherwise ...

VII. And if it happen the said offender or offenders so offending not to have any goods or chattels to the value of twenty pounds: that then he or they to be set on the pillory in some market-place within the shire, city or borough, where the said offence shall be committed, by the sheriff or his ministers, if it shall fortune to be without any city or town corporate; (2) and if it happen to be within any such city or town corporate, then by the said head officer or officers of such city or town corporate, or by his or their ministers, and there to have both his ears nailed, and from thenceforth to be discredited and disabled for ever to be sworn in any of the courts of record aforesaid.[62]

For those convicted of suborning perjury, the fine was doubled to forty pounds.[63] It is suggestive that, whilst the Act provides for either a fine *or* the pillory, it is the latter penalty, what J. M. Beattie describes as 'a form of public penance' – recalling a church court sentence – which seems to catch the imagination of contemporary commentators.[64] Beattie records use of the pillory for perjury cases through the eighteenth century, and this was to endure: even when, in 1816, the statute of 56 Geo. 3, c. 138 set out 'to abolish the punishment of the pillory except in certain cases', perjury was notable amongst those exceptions.[65] Similarly, whilst the terms of the Perjury Statute represent a fairly early use of the sanction of imprisonment, this is rarely commented on.

One of the most notable terms of the sanction is that the oath of the convicted perjurer is 'thenceforth not to be received in any court of record within this realm'. This proscription echoes the words of the *Homily* – 'for truthe it is . . . that no man is lesse trusted, than he that useth much to sweare' (sig. Giii) – and it would be quoted repeatedly well into the seventeenth century. At the 1680 treason trial of the Earl of Castlemaine, the Lord Chief Justice, Sir William Scroggs, restated the law for those present, emphasising the irrevocable nature of the offence:

> In this I am clear; if a man were convicted of perjury, that no pardon will make him a witness, because it is to do the subject wrong. A pardon does not make a man an honest man.[66]

Moreover, in this issue of credence we find one example of the wider cultural circulation of the statute's terms. Certainly, it is a repeated motif of the ladies' reasoning in the final scene of *Love's Labour's Lost*. 'Yet swear not, lest ye be forsworn again,' Katherine tells Dumaine as he tries to pledge his service (V.ii.820), whilst the Princess reminds Ferdinand that 'your oath once broke, you force not to forswear' (440). The men's forswearing undermines even the value of their written testimony – when Dumaine, protesting at the ladies' lack of trust, complains that 'Our letters, Madam, showed much more than jest,' Rosaline dismissively responds 'We did not quote them so' (778, 780). In fact, Shakespeare's play draws repeatedly upon the terms of the statute, demonstrating just how much its language had come to be absorbed into thinking around perjury. As noted above, the double image in IV.iii of 'a perjure wearing papers/a perjured note' directly recalls the Act's recourse to the pillory, and in the ladies' scepticism here is encoded its subsequent injunction upon future credit. Even the forfeiture provisions are replayed, as Berowne discusses the effects of love upon the men of Navarre:

> BEROWNE: Our states are forfeit. Seek not to undo us.
> ROSALINE: It is not so; for how can this be true,
>   That you stand forfeit, being those that sue.   (V.ii.425–7)

The multiple associations of 'states'– our single, bachelor states, our honour, our material estates – are here crystallised by the legal (as well as romantic) implications of 'sue'. It is hardly surprising, then, that when judgment is finally pronounced upon the men by the Princess and her ladies, the duration of their punishment is 'a twelvemonth and a day' (865), a term which occurs not only in folktales, but also in legal contracts.

Strictly speaking, of course, the protagonists of *Love's Labour's Lost* are incorrect in their application of the terms of the statute to the crimes of forswearing committed in the play. As noted, the Act applied only to 'wilful' or suborned witness perjury and not to the type of oath-breaking, foolish swearing and 'maggot ostentation' indulged in by the courtiers of Navarre (V.ii.409). That they nonetheless conceptualise their crimes and their consequences in such terms is symptomatic of the ongoing state of confusion surrounding penalties for these 'other' manifestations of perjury. The problems of scope and jurisdiction inherent in the statute are thereby revealed as a feature of a much broader cultural model of perjury, a model that informs both the structure and the language of Shakespeare's play.

'Juste and visible punishment': Perjury and Providence

As Andrew Hadfield comments, even following the 1563 Act, the difficulty of proving perjury meant that, as now, accusations and prosecutions 'were relatively rare. To compensate it was sometimes imagined that God, who could see what humans could not, would inflict terrible punishments on perjurers.'[67] The decades following the statute's coming into force saw the publication of a suite of lurid providential texts on blasphemy, oath-breaking and malicious false-swearing. Notable amongst these are Bicknoll's aforementioned *Sword Agaynst Swearyng*

(1579) and Anthony Munday's *A View of sundry Examples* (1580).[68] Bicknoll's work, which ostensibly sets out to demonstrate the lawful and unlawful uses of oaths, concludes with a number of 'Examples of Gods juste and visible punishment upon blasphemers, perjurers, and such as have procured Gods wrath by cursyng and bannying'.[69] This procession of exemplars opens with classical and historical images: Bicknoll describes the fate of Sir Roger Mortimer, for example, who broke his oath of allegiance to Edward II and was drawn and quartered as punishment for his 'perjury'. However, for Bicknoll the real interest lies in the possibility of divine and providential punishment, particularly that associated with cases which might be – however tenuously – located in the contemporary scene. 'How many corrected in Gods mercifull judgement for our example have we known,' he declares:

> some punished by losse of their goods, some by fire, some by strange sicknesses, some with tongues as black as coale, some with such hot tongues, that they could not in any case close their mouthes again, which before they had opened to the dishallowing of Gods most blessed name.   (sig. Ci)

As we might expect, Bicknoll and Munday's cautionary examples span the range of swearing offences, from blasphemy through to witness perjury, with scarcely a distinction made between these crimes. So, 'Widdow Barnes' of London, having been 'rebuked for swearing', is providentially compelled to self-murder – 'within foure dayes after cast her selfe out at a window in Cornhill and brake her necke', and 'one Berry', on trial for perjury, takes his life by cutting his own throat.[70] Clearly, the reader is being cautioned about the power of language and the consequences of its abuse, and this is a recurrent theme of such texts. Alexandra Walsham, writing on Thomas Beard's *Theatre of God's Judgements* (1598), notes that Beard devotes 'an entire chapter to the macabre deaths of individuals whose habitual expletive was "the devil take me"'.[71] What is most notable about the cases of Barnes and Berry is that both Bicknoll and Munday assign very specific, and recent, dates to them – 1574 and 1575 respectively. Whether these dates were randomly attributed to give an appearance of veracity, or were provided by sources, is difficult to discern (Munday seems to take his cue on dating directly from Bicknoll); however, their inclusion seems to suggest a felt need for recent, resonant examples.

What the cases have in common is that they are played out beyond the realm of state-administered punishment. As such, their function would appear to be twofold. First, they address a requirement for the capability to punish the broader range of offences which, in the minds of Bicknoll, Munday and their readers, were linked to, and were manifestations of, perjury. Secondly, and most specifically, they create sanctions for that crime that better reflect the weight of transgression against the divine, filling a perceived gap in the secular administration of justice. As Agamben writes, '[L]aw is made of nothing but what it manages to capture inside itself,' and it is clear that for the writers of pamphlet literature the current legal scope of perjury was far too narrow.[72] These texts remodel the punishment of perjury in a way that exposes the limitations of legislation in relation to a much more extensive cultural understanding of the offence, whilst also offering a commentary on its perceived seriousness. Where the statute's work ended, providence began.

This is particularly evident in Bicknoll and Munday's 'showpiece' cases. The story of Anne Averies, which covers four pages of Bicknoll's text, is not only attributed to a year but to a specific day, 11 February 1575. On this date, Averies, a widow residing in 'Ducke Lane without Aldergate', entered the shop of one Richard Williamson, a flaxe and tow merchant in the City. Having agreed to purchase six pounds of coarse tow '(a very small value)', Averies, 'perceyving the servauntes in the shop busie aboute other customers', left without paying for the goods.[73] Confronted by a member of the merchant's staff, 'perjouriously she forsware the fact (viz. that she departed without payment)', desiring 'vengeance at the Lordes handes and that he would openly shewe upon her in his just judgement' of her innocence. Having uttered these words she was immediately struck down 'speachlesse', and to the horror of the gathering spectators, she began to 'voyde at her mouth' her own excrement: 'that which nature would have cast downward at the bottom of the belly'. Two days later she was dead.

Averies' story is carefully affirmed as fact by Bicknoll, who cites six respectable witnesses by name and refers the reader to an original account of the incident 'imprinted by John Alde in 1576'.[74] The story was hugely popular with the compilers of anthologies in the period, appearing regularly in providential collections.[75] Perhaps most significantly, it was revived in the aftermath of the Popish Plot, in Thomas Doolittle's *The Swearer Silenc'd,* where it is reported alongside another case, concerning:

> [A] certain Maid, that had stoln and pilfered many things away out of her Mistresses house; of which being examined, she forswore them, and wisht *that she might rot*, if she ever touched them or knew of them: But notwithstanding she was carried to prison; and there presently began so to rot, and stink, that they were forced to thrust her out of Prison, and to convey her to the Hospital, where she lies ...[76]

Both Anne Averies and the anonymous 'Maid' are perjurers in their own defence, but Bicknoll and Munday also pair the Averies case with an example of perjury committed against another, the story of Father Lea, set some two years later in January 1577.[77] Lea, 'a man of almost foure score yeares, in Foster Lane in London', had previously borne false witness against another man. Encountering his victim one day, he was overwhelmed with guilt and 'with a rusty knife, rypped his owne belly, and griped his guts with his owne handes', disembowelling himself.[78] 'And so ended his life,' Munday states, although in Bicknoll's version Father Lea's wife summons a surgeon who stitches up his wounds, and he survives, presumably in some lasting discomfort.[79]

These images of disembowelment and of punishment coming from the deepest recesses of the body are particularly suggestive in the context of perjury. On the one hand, the filth that is associated with Averies' demise is a simple metaphor for her poisoned words; on the other, the idea of destruction from within has echoes of the curse of Zachariah, that 'will enter into the house of the perjured man, and it shal remain in the middest of his house, and consume hym'.[80] Father Lea's fate similarly evokes this image, and in a legal sense, it is also a self-inflicted version of the drawing and quartering traditionally suffered by traitors – the most shameful penalty available to the English courts.

The image has intriguing associations with another quasi-historical figure, of course: Judas Iscariot, whose betrayal of Christ is frequently figured as a form of perjury. This notion of betrayal as a key element of perjury figures significantly in early modern literary renderings of oath-breaking, exposing the persistence of biblical discourse in conceptualising the offence.[81] Moreover, it bears a direct relationship to ideas of appropriate punishment. Judas traditionally hanged himself in remorse for his great sin; his fate is described twice in the New Testament. First in Matthew 27:3–10, thus:

> Then Judas, whiche had betrayed him, when he sawe that he was condemned, repented himselfe, and brought agayne the thirtie sylver peeces to the cheefe priestes and elders./Saying, I have synned, in that I have betrayed the innocent blood . . . And when he had cast down the peeces of sylver in the temple, he departed, and went his way, and hanged himselfe./And the cheefe priestes tooke the sylver (peeces,) and sayde, It is not lawfull for to put them into the treasurie: because it is the price of blood./And when they had taken connsayle, they bought with them the Potters feelde, to burie strangers in./Wherefore, that feelde was called, The feelde of blood, unto this day.[82]

The story is recast and developed further in the Acts of the Apostles (1:16–19):

> For he was numbred with us, and had obteyned felowship in this ministerie./ And the same hath now purchased a feeld with the reward of [his] iniquitie.

And when he was hanged, he burst asunder in the midst, and al hys bowels gushed out.[83]

Annette Weber has demonstrated how a new iconography of the hanged Judas gained cultural currency in thirteenth- and fourteenth-century Europe, disseminated by the vernacular preaching of mendicant friars, using texts such as Jacobus de Voragine's *Legenda Aurea*.[84] The *Legenda*'s retelling of the Judas story develops the symbolism of his fate. His death by hanging signifies his utter damnation:

> Judas perished in the air, so that the one who had offended the angels in heaven and men on earth was kept out of the regions belonging to angels and to men, and was left in the air in the company of demons.[85]

It is also fitting that 'the bowels which had conceived the betrayal should burst and spill out, and that the throat from which had emerged the voice of the traitor should be strangled by a rope'.[86] Unlike Anne Averies, whose inner filth emerges from her perjured lips, Judas' mouth 'was spared defilement . . . for it would have been incongruous that a mouth which had touched the glorious lips of Christ should be so foully soiled'.[87] That the traitor's kiss is here sanctified is symptomatic of the complex oversignification of the medieval image as whole, and perhaps goes some way to explaining the multiple and varied allusions to the hanged Judas that arise in later renderings of the perjurer, as we will see below.

Drama also promulgated biblical exempla, and the story of Judas was a popular subject for the medieval stage. Weber notes that:

> [A]ccording to the directions of the medieval passion plays from Donaueschingen and Freiburg, the young priest who played the role of Judas first had to be sewn into a cowhide. Underneath, onto his chest, were to be placed the intestines of a sheep together with a live blackbird, or even a live black squirrel, symbolizing the damned (i.e. black) soul. During the act of hanging . . . the cowhide had to burst from the priest's chest downwards in order to let out the blackbird or squirrel and to show the intestines.[88]

There is a similar reference to Judas 'burst in the middle' in a pageant forming part of the York Mystery Plays.[89] The desired effect of such graphic imagery, which was similarly rendered in sculptures, reliefs and illuminated manuscripts, was of course to point up the hanged Judas as the ultimate example, a warning of the consequences of sin. But of what sin, precisely? For Weber, the dissemination of this image was part of a movement of 'new ideas about heresy, usury and avarice which became increasingly associated with Jews'.[90] However, two hundred years later, we find English writers deploying the hanged Judas as part of an alternative set of associations surrounding treachery and bearing false witness. In his 1598 poem *The Betraying of Christ*, for example, Samuel Rowlands presents Iscariot's despair thus:

> End traitors life, begin a hangmans part,
> Let hangmans part performe thy desp'rate mind,
> Thy desp'rate mind be witnesse th'art accurst,
> Rent heart, drop blood, gush bowels, belly burst.[91]

It is precisely this Judas motif that recurs in one of the most complex of the perjury exemplars circulating in the period, the case of William Grimwood. Bicknoll includes this case in his collection; his source is John Foxe's *Acts and Monuments*.[92] Foxe's own interest in perjury was specifically in relation to its part in the conviction of a number of the Marian martyrs, and the Grimwood case is no exception. William Grimwood had been one of the prosecution witnesses in the trial of John Cooper, a carpenter from Wattisham in Suffolk, a man 'of honest conversation and good lyfe'.[93] Cooper, who had made an enemy of a neighbour called Fenning, had been accused by Fenning of treason, in speaking against Queen Mary. On the strength of the testimony given by Fenning, Grimwood and another, Cooper was convicted and sentenced to be hanged, drawn and quartered.[94] As Bicknoll (after Foxe) relates, at the next harvest following Cooper's execution, Grimwood, 'feeling no paine, complaining of no disease', set forth to stack the corn, when, 'sodenly his bowels fell out of his body and immediately he died moste miserably'.[95] Once again we see the image of the perjurer destroyed from within, this time – with particular poetic justice – in an effective re-enactment of the fate of his victim.

And poetic justice was precisely what this was. Grimwood's case had appeared in the first edition of *Acts and Monuments* in 1563, the same year that the Perjury Statute passed into law. Almost immediately, however, Foxe received correspondence questioning the veracity of the episode, including the fact of Grimwood's providential demise.[96] The account was withdrawn from the second edition. However, it was mysteriously restored and indeed updated in the third edition, which, published in 1576, would have been an obvious source for Bicknoll. Its validity was finally, and sensationally, disproved in 1585 when, as Thomas S. Freeman notes:

> John Prick, the rector of Kettlebaston, Suffolk, preached a semon denouncing perjury. In the course of his sermon, Prick related a story from John Foxe's *Acts and Monuments* [concerning] William Grimwood of Hitcham (a village about a mile and a half north east of Kettlebaston) ... Prick's sermon was probably very edifying and would have been even more edifying were it not

for the inconvenient fact that Grimwood was not only alive but among the rector's congregation that Sunday.[97]

Grimwood went on to sue Reverend Prick for slander.

When we know that Grimwood's providential punishment was in essence a fiction, the whole issue of the nature of that punishment comes into focus. Whatever the provenance of the Averies case, and the story of Father Lea, Grimwood's 'fate' had been specifically selected for him by his slanderers, and this fate was deemed to be exemplary for a perjurer. In fact, Grimwood's punishment replays the fate of Judas in almost literal terms, recreating the 'feelde of blood' in the contemporary Suffolk countryside. This idea of suitability, of appropriateness of punishment, an unspoken but powerful momentum towards the *lex talionis*, recurs repeatedly in representations of perjury.

The case, and most particularly the controversy surrounding Grimwood's alleged providential punishment, was to have a remarkable afterlife. Anthony Wood, the antiquary and pamphlet collector, included Grimwood in his *Athenae Oxonienses* (1691–2) as part of a general attack on Foxe's work, which prompted a number of subsequent defences and reappraisals of the case.[98] For Wood, Foxe had committed 'a most egregious falsity' in reporting the case, in effect a perjury of his own mandated role as chronicler of the Marian martyrs. His literary testimony could no longer be trusted.[99]

Even more important to the legacy of the Grimwood case, however, was the fact that Prick's defence counsel in the slander proceedings was a youthful Edward Coke. The case was an early success for the future Attorney General, the judge finding that Reverend Prick's rendering of the tale was merely storytelling and not, as such, malicious. For Coke the case was not only a career-boosting victory but also an important legal precedent, which he cited in detail twenty years later, in 1605, when acting for the defendant in the case of *Brook* v. *Sir Henry Montague*:

> And Coke cited a case 27 Eliz. where Parson Prick in a sermon recited a story out of Foxes Martyrologie, that one Greenwood, being a perjured person, and a great persecutor, had great plagues inflicted upon him, and was killed by the hand of God; whereas in truth he never was so plagued, and was himself present at that sermon.[100]

Obliquely, then, a perjured tale of a perjured man, a tale more fit to be told in a pamphlet text, was making its way into the heart of common-law authority.

'[H]er Scull, and the Feet, and the palms of her Hands': Subornment of Perjury

The progress of *Love's Labour's Lost* is directed by a legal arrangement, driven by the Princess's diplomatic mission to reclaim her father's title and, as Lorna Hutson notes, by 'the deferral of a process of litigation over [his] debt' to Navarre, a negotiation which, with its questions of good faith, calls into play 'the language of the spiritual courts and the equity courts (or courts of conscience)'.[101] Most specifically, the play evinces a peculiar concern with the nature and appropriateness of the penalty for perjury. There are multiple comic references to the appropriate punishment for crimes of love and desire, for example. Berowne's perjury is repeatedly likened to 'treason' in Act 4 (IV.iii.187–9), and he himself sees the portentous shape of 'Love's Tyburn' (the London gallows) in the three-cornered 'triumviry' of his friends' forswearing (IV. iii.50–1). When his own guilt is ultimately revealed Berowne reinforces this image of a capital crime:

> BEROWNE: He, he and you – and you, my liege – and I
> Are pick-purses in love and we deserve to die.   (IV.iii.204–5)

The play repeatedly and fretfully engages with ideas of law and consequence, both religious and secular. Much of this struggle is couched in the language of contemporary penal sanctions. As the King expounds his new 'schedule', the terms of contract to the 'acadame', in scene 1, this becomes clear:

> BEROWNE [Reads]: *Item, That no woman shall come within a mile of my court* – Hath this been proclaimed?
> LONGAVILLE: Four days ago.
> BEROWNE: Let's see the penalty – *On pain of losing her tongue.* Who devised this penalty?
> LONGAVILLE: Marry, that did I.
> BEROWNE: Sweet lord, and why?
> LONGAVILLE: To fright them hence with that dread penalty.
> BEROWNE: A dangerous law against gentility.
> *Item, If any man be seen to talk with a woman within the term of three years, he shall endure such public shame as the rest of the court can possible devise.*
>   (I.i.119–30)

The man who contravenes the terms of the 'schedule' to speak to a woman must endure a sentence of 'public shame', a pillory, as it were. The woman, however, who defies the injunction to stay away from court – and thus presumably creates the possibility that the man may break his oath – faces a more severe, and more specific punishment. This is interesting: the proposed penalty may be merely a simple comment upon woman's supposed garrulousness – it certainly looks ahead, obliquely, to Boyet's comment at V.ii.257–8: 'the tongues of mocking wenches are as keen/as is the razor's edge invisible'. Yet there are other, intriguing, associations here. In the 1685 perjury trial of Titus Oates, the then Lord Chief Justice gave the court what was apparently a history of the penalties for Oates' crime:

> In former Ages, *Perjury* was present Death; But after (for some reasons,) was mitigated to *cutting* the *Tongue*, &c. But since That, it was again mitigated, not but the Crime was as great as ever.[102]

Whilst Roman law might have decreed death for some cases of lying under judicial oath, the mention of '*cutting* the *Tongue*' is more perplexing. There is no clear evidence to indicate that such an early sanction had existed for perjury, records of the ecclesiastical courts suggesting that excommunication was the severest sentence imposed, yet the Justice's comments are suggestive. As seen in the controversy surrounding *Onslowe's Case*, the crime of perjury came with a weight of perceived historical precedent attached. If there was a popular, even quasi-legal perception that the loss of the tongue was a penalty deemed appropriate for perjury 'in former Ages', then it casts Navarre's dictat in an intriguing light. The graphic aptness of the punishment recalls the themes of the providential pamphlets – yet at the same time, its potential application to those women who approach the court, who have sworn no oaths themselves to stay away, is unsettling. Implicitly, the woman is cast as the suborner of perjury, a crime that, as we have seen, is punished with greater severity in the statute than the actual bearing of false witness.

The chief biblical exemplar of the suborner of perjury is also a woman. In his 1685 pamphlet *The Swearer Silenc'd*, Thomas Doolittle notes that 'In Scripture there are many instances' of perjury. He cites only one 'instance' of subornation, however:

> Jezebel [for] suborning false Witnesses against *Naboth*, 1 *King.* 21.9, 10 was eaten by dogs, that there was nothing of her found, but *her Scull, and the Feet, and the palms of her Hands*. 2 *King.* 9. 35, 36, 37.[103]

The biblical episode of Naboth's Vineyard (I Kings 21) is the story of Ahab, King of Israel, and his desire to acquire a vineyard, which had been owned for many generations by the family of Naboth. To Ahab's displeasure, Naboth repeatedly refused his offers to purchase or exchange the land. Vowing that she would obtain it for him,

Ahab's wife Jezebel convened an assembly of the kingdom's elders and suborned two men to testify falsely that they had witnessed Naboth speaking against God and the King. Naboth was accused of treason and stoned to death outside the city walls. The prophet Elijah was sent by God to reproach Ahab and to pronounce sentence upon him: 'This sayeth the Lorde, In the place where dogges licked the blood of Naboth, shal dogges licke even thy blood also.'[104] Ahab repented and survived, whilst Jezebel did not and suffered the fate reported so eagerly by Doolittle.

Naboth's Vineyard was the subject of one of the early literary attacks on the perjurers of the Popish Plot. John Caryll, a recusant nobleman, produced his mock-biblical epic *Naboth's Vineyard, or The Innocent Traytor* in 1679, whilst imprisoned in the Tower on treason charges relating to the Plot.[105] The work, which its author describes, somewhat disingenuously, as 'copied' from the biblical episode, is a carefully constructed assault upon the legal and political forces at work in the Plot convictions. A number of figures who are merely mentioned in I Kings are developed by Caryll into fully formed characters with identifiable counterpoints in Restoration England. Significantly, he devises names – Malchus and Python – for the two perjurers employed by Jezebel. Malchus, whose portrayal as a 'puny Levite, void of sense/And Grace, but stuffed with Noise and Impudence' (231–2), firmly aligns him with Titus Oates, also has another biblical referent. In the Gospel, Malchus is the High Priest's servant who loses an ear to Peter when he arrests Christ at Gethsemane. He is the instrument of Judas' perjury and the Jewish elders' plotting; in linking the Old Testament perjurer with the New, Caryll draws on a rich vein of allusion, which ultimately figures the alleged conspirators of the Plot as Christ-like in their sacrifice. Similarly, Python seems to be a representation of William Bedloe, Oates' fellow witness in the earliest of the Plot's trials. Michael Suarez comments that: '"Python" should be understood as the spirit or demon who speaks from within one who is possessed.'[106]

Much of the satire of the piece is directed at Malchus and the erratic 'Romance' that he produces in lieu of evidence against Naboth (350), which Caryll knowingly peppers with allusion to Oates' own testimony.[107] The perjured witnesses are described as 'Vipers in the bosom of our Law' (398) and, as we might expect, Caryll is quick to point up the conflation of their crime against the state with their sin against God:

> For when with artificial Perjury
> They make God's Sacred Name espouse their Lye,
> Forthwith, that Lye Omnipotent becomes,
> And governs all below.   (400–3)

Yet there is also a dark strain of censure directed at the law itself. Caryll's other addition to the plot is a formal trial for Naboth, presided over by the new character of Arod the judge, a man who weighs 'his Causes not by Law but God' (154). Although Caryll writes in the Preface that no 'Honourable and just Judge can be thought concern'd in the Character of Arod', this is indubitably a portrayal of Sir William Scroggs, the Lord Chief Justice.[108] Caryll satirises the relationship between Scroggs and Oates, particularly Scroggs' desire to believe his star witness, despite the many inconsistencies in his testimony: Arod requests a 'perfect narrative' (334) from Malchus, much as Scroggs defended Oates' 'True Narrative' when it was challenged in court.[109] More directly, Jezebel dismisses the law as a 'poor, dumb thing' (160) when she sets out to manipulate it, and Naboth condemns his fate as a 'Legal Massacre' (407). It is only when divine law is invoked, in the person of Elijah, that the poem suggests that any appropriate level of justice or redress has been achieved:

> Naboth! Though cast thou art by Humane Laws,
> Heaven's Writ of Errour has remov'd thy Cause.
> And judg'd it so, that it shall stand from hence
> A lasting record of wrong'd Innocence.   (462–5)

Perhaps understandably, Caryll withholds any direct political identification of the characters of Jezebel and Ahab. Instead, the King, and more specifically, the Queen of Israel become representatives of the state in general. Caryll specifically excludes Ahab's repentance from his narrative and closes on Elijah's declaration of God's judgment against the pair: 'And so he left them Thunder-struck and dumb/Stung with their present Guilt; and fate to come' (496–7).

The only charge of subornation of perjury recorded in *State Trials* for the period is also a charge against a woman, a charge made in the same year that Caryll produced his text, but emanating from, not aimed against the Popish Plot witnesses. In late 1679, in the aftermath of the 'first wave' of Plot trials, Stephen Dugdale, another amongst the 'King's Evidence' group whose perjured testimony had condemned five Jesuits the previous year, had a charge of subornation of perjury brought against Ann Price, a former fellow servant in the home of Lord Aston.[110] Dugdale alleged that Price, a Catholic like himself, had tried to dissuade him from testifying against Harcourt and indeed had drafted a letter of retraction for him to sign, offering him £1,000 and a safe passage to Flanders in return for his complicity. According to court record, Price was a troublesome defendant; she attempted to cross-examine Dugdale herself and was at one point threatened with having her 'mouth …

stopped' if she was not quiet.¹¹¹ As with the hypothetical woman of *Love's Labour's Lost*, it was Ann Price's speech that was regarded as most threatening. Price and a co-defendant, John Tasborough, were both fined and imprisoned.

'Our faith not torn': the Redemption of the Perjurer

Love's Labour's Lost being – primarily – a comedy, when a woman does, inevitably, come to court, she is 'The French King's daughter . . . /A maid of grace and complete majesty' (I.i.133–4). Indeed, the play's female characters prove rather redeemers than suborners of perjury. The Princess, who derives much amusement from the King's dilemma – 'I hear your grace hath sworn out housekeeping' (II.i.104) – has come to Navarre because of a dispute about another, seemingly broken, oath, an oath concerning payment of a debt of war between her father and Ferdinand. It is notable however that whilst the Princess' 'embassy' is introduced with all urgency in the opening scene of Act 2, it then disappears from the action almost entirely, meriting only a passing reference at the end of Act 5 to 'my great suit so easily obtained' (V.ii.733). Far more pressing is the immediate likelihood of the broken vow occasioned by the presence of the women. Navarre resigns himself to the collapse of his pompous 'schedule' of penalties:

> KING: We must of force dispense with this decree.
>   She must lie here on mere necessity.
> BEROWNE: Necessity will make us all forsworn. (I.i.145–7)

However, upon arrival, the Princess immediately moves to reinforce the schedule, pointing out to the King that 'you'll prove perjur'd if you make me stay' (113) and agreeing without rancour to remain outside the city gates. Whilst, as John Kerrigan suggests, this may be a tactical play in her role as ambassador for her father's suit, drawing attention to the King's perjury 'for diplomatic or competitive advantage', the Princess's elegant manoeuvring nonetheless allows Navarre to maintain the rituals of hospitality without compromising his earlier avowals.¹¹² Indeed all the women of the play, as James Calderwood notes, 'despite [a] very considerable talent for bandying words, have a great[er] respect for language' – they are cautious in their interpretation of the lords' love letters, they exchange favours in order to disrupt the signs that mark them out to their suitors.¹¹³ The ladies understand the importance of word and meaning – and so, when at the end of Act 5 they are called upon to pronounce 'sentence' on their forsworn lovers, they prove able judges.

Just as the King's strict schema of punishment begins to unravel with the arrival of the Princess, so, throughout the play, ideas of punishment are anxiously reworked and sometimes undermined. Such subversion seems linked to a tension between the rigidity of Navarre's proclaimed law on oath-breaking and the ambiguity of its interpretation, a tension that mirrors the fraught implementation of the 1563 statute. The first instance of this comes in the opening Act, when Costard is delivered to the King by Constable Dull, having been 'taken' in flagrante with Jacquenetta. Having, with much hilarity, deciphered the nature of Costard's crime from Armado's 'fire-new words', Ferdinand confronts the offender with the prospect of his punishment:

> KING: Did you hear the proclamation?
> COSTARD: I do confess much of the hearing it, but little of the marking of it.
> KING: It was proclaimed a year's imprisonment to be taken with a wench.
> (I.i.270–4)

As soon as the sentence of imprisonment is suggested, however, Costard begins to cavil at the language of the statute:

> COSTARD: I was taken with none, sir; I was taken with a damsel.
> KING: Well, it was proclaimed damsel.
> COSTARD: This was no damsel neither, sir; she was a virgin.
> KING: It is so varied too, for it was proclaimed virgin.
> COSTARD: If it were, I deny her virginity; I was taken with a maid.
> KING: This maid will not serve your turn, sir. (I.i.275–83)

Whilst he can find no loophole in the proclamation, Costard does achieve his mitigation and his final punishment is to 'fast a week with bran and water' (285), a penalty quite remote from the prescribed sanction – and as seemingly arbitrary in its signification. The scene contrasts the closed language of the statutory regime – resistant to Costard's attempt to destabilise it with wordplay – with the chaos of interpretation that exists outside it. As soon as the King moves beyond the simple application of the law, he is incapable of determining an apt level of punishment. In this sense Navarre seems to invert the willed 'state of exception' proposed by Schmitt and Agamben; when he moves outside the law it is an act of impotence, rather than a manifestation of sovereign power.[114]

Costard's failed defence looks ahead to the complex 'salve for perjury' that Berowne attempts to construct in Act 4, once the collective nature of the men's shame has become clear – 'that you three fools lacked me fool to make up the mess' (IV.iii.203). In this scene, the men are revealed to be the type of the rash or foolish swearer exemplified by Jephthah in the *Homily* and although their fate will not be so severe, their anxiety to justify themselves indicates that they fear some form of retribution. As the King directs: 'good Berowne, now prove/Our loving lawful and our faith not torn' (IV.iii.280–1). The justification subsequently produced is a feat of sophistry which displays the full power of Berowne's rationalising wit, and rouses the men to a martial fervour: 'advance your standards and upon them, lords!' (341) Over the course of some fifty-five lines, he transforms 'perjury' into a holy 'charity' and broken oaths into 'religion':

> BEROWNE: It is religion thus to be forsworn,
>   For charity itself fulfils the law,
>   And who can sever love from charity? (337–9)

In so doing he draws upon Romans 13:8 and 10 – 'he that loveth another, hath fulfilled the lawe ... charitie woorketh no yl to his neighbour, therefore the fulfylyng of the lawe is charitie'.[115] It is testament to Berowne's agile and irreverent mind that he turns to biblical sources to release him from his 'attainder of eternal shame' (I.i.155).

Exoneration will not prove so easy, however, and judgment comes swiftly. The final scene of the play, which progresses from the masque of the Muscovites through the play of the Nine Worthies, is brought up sharp by the sudden announcement of the death of the Princess's father. This sobering news disperses the 'incensed Worthies' and terminates their torment by the King and his men. As the Princess prepares to return to France, the men, shaken into action by their realisation of the 'extreme parts of time' (V.ii.734), make a final attempt to confess their love. Once again, Berowne endeavours a redemptive transformation of their perjured state: 'And even that falsehood, in itself a sin, /Thus purifies itself and turns to grace' (769–70). The Princess, however, understands the terms of purification and absolution more clearly. Reminding the King of his 'dear guiltiness' (785), she sets him a penance which will effect a surer form of redemption:

> PRINCESS: ... go with speed
>   To some forlorn and naked hermitage,
>   Remote from all the pleasures of the world,
>   There stay until the twelve celestial signs
>   Have brought about the annual reckoning. (788–92)

The King will, in effect, unbreak his oath, keeping the terms of his original vow to retire from the world, albeit with a somewhat reduced 'sentence'. As if in mitigation of her clemency, the Princess will take upon herself the same term of retirement: 'And, till that instance, shut/ My woeful self up in a mourning house' (801–2). Thus, as upon their first meeting at the gates of the court, the Princess will 'salve' the King's perjury far more effectively than could Berowne's 'tricks' and 'quillets' (IV.iii.279).[116]

Longaville and Dumaine receive a similar penance of retirement and fortitude, but Rosaline's judgment upon Berowne is more complex. His sentence is not to curb his tongue, but to use his wit more wisely:

> ROSALINE: You shall this twelvemonth term from day to day
>   Visit the speechless sick and still converse
>   With groaning wretches; and your task shall be
>   With all the fierce endeavour of your wit
>   To enforce the pained impotent to smile.   (838–42)

Berowne, the foolish oath-taker, who admitted in Act 1 that he 'swore in jest' (I.i.54), will now put that 'gibing' to better use and 'jest a twelvemonth in a hospital' (V.ii.859).

What Philippa Berry describes as this 'ambiguous' deferral of resolution at the end of *Love's Labour's Lost* returns us to the idea of the forfeiture of credit figured in both the *Homily* and the statute.[117] 'Until such time as the judgement shall be reversed', the statute cautiously qualifies its own sanction, thereby acknowledging the possibility of remedy. Shakespeare's play concludes on a similar note: 'your oath I will not trust', the Princess tells the King (788), but in rejecting his oath, she offers him something of her own – 'by this virgin palm now kissing thine, /I will be thine' (800–1) – not, she acknowledges, a 'world-without-end bargain' (783), but at least a small hope of deliverance. Over the course of the drama 'oaths' and 'vows' have been replaced by 'bargains', speech-acts that have not yet become devalued by the traffic of the play.[118]

In its final glimmer of salvation *Love's Labour's Lost* anticipates the punishment of perjurers in Shakespeare's later comedies – perjurers who seem to correspond far more clearly to the figure within the statute. Perhaps the most intriguing of these is Iachimo in *Cymbeline*, who confirms his malicious slander of Imogen with an oath: 'Hark you, he swears, by Jupiter he swears' (II.iv.122).[119] Earlier in the play he has goaded Posthumus into swearing a wager on Imogen's virtue with the words 'I see you have some religion in you, that you fear' (I.v.134). Iachimo's oath is at once compelling and deeply problematic in Posthumus' eyes; when later in the same scene he attempts to reaffirm it 'I'll be sworn', he is met with the response:

> POSTHUMUS: No swearing:
>   If you will swear you have not done't, you lie,
>   And I will kill thee if thou dost deny
>   Thou'st made me cuckold.   (II.iv.143–6)

This exchange captures what Tom Flanigan describes as the 'profoundly de-stabilizing effect of perjury in social terms', and in *Cymbeline* such instability is already endemic.[120] The play represents a nation's body politic fractured, seemingly irrevocably, by a single act of false witness, leading to Belarius' banishment. All of *Cymbeline*'s subsequent acts of perjury derive directly or obliquely from this one wilful act. In this climate it is perhaps unexpected that Posthumus believes Iachimo's false words so readily; nonetheless he does so, and it is only as the play closes that the 'Italian fiend' (V.v.210) is brought to justice. What justice this is, is even more surprising, for despite his malicious intent, Iachimo receives even less punishment than the foolish Lords of *Love's Labour's Lost*: 'Live/And deal with others better', are the words with which Posthumus 'nobl'y doom[s]' his former friend (V.v.420–1).

Yet Iachimo does, after all, repent, and revokes his perjured words –

> IACHIMO: *[Kneeling]* I am down again;
> But now my heavy conscience sinks my knee,
> As then your force did. (V.v.413–15)

– and in some sense, perhaps, his 'heavy conscience' returns us not to the common law, but to the realm of the church courts. In setting what constitutes a penance, almost a blessing ('live . . . better') rather than a punishment, for Iachimo, then, does Shakespeare's later play tentatively restore perjury to its ecclesiastical origins? The text remains open regarding the final fate of the perjurer.

Conclusion

In 1628, in his third *Institute*, Edward Coke made an attempt to define, once and for all, the crime of perjury:

> Perjury is a crime committed, when a lawful oath is administered by any that hath authority to any person, in any judicial proceeding, who sweareth absolutely and falsely in a matter material to the issue or cause in question by their own act or by the subornation of others.[121]

By this time the 1563 Act was fully embedded within English legislative structure. It had been reinforced eight years after its first passing by the statute of 13 Eliz. 1, c. 25, section 14, and had been made 'perpetual' by 29 Eliz. 1, c. 5, sections 1–2.[122] In the first year of James I's reign it was 'revived and continued' (1 James 1, c. 25, s. 29) and was again – without any particular rationale – made 'perpetual' by 21 James 1, c. 28. In fact, whilst a statute of George II increased the penalties for the various crimes addressed by the original Act, it remained largely unchanged from this point on into the nineteenth century.[123]

Nonetheless it is evident that, to some degree, the Act remained a partial measure, an unsatisfactory means of dealing with such an over-determined offence. In moving the sin of *perjurium* into the domain of the state, it went too far; yet in a context of punishment it could not go far enough. In his speech at the 1606 trial of the Jesuit Henry Garnet, for conspiracy in the Gunpowder Plot, the Earl of Northampton attempted to summarise the distinction between the unlawful oath of the Plot conspirators and the righteous oaths of the Old Testament:

> [W]hen we take an oath advisedly and freely, according to the measures and conditions limited and expressed in the law of God, that is, according to judgment, righteousness and truth; yes, though it be by duty to a wicked prince, Ezekiel will teach us by the warrant of the holy spirit, that God himself will nail upon the head of the perjurer, the oath which he hath set light, and the covenant which he hath perfidiously broken.[124]

This strange conflation of secular and divine justice, with God as the executor of the penalty imposed by the Act, points up the issue at the heart of the perjury debate. If an oath invites the Divine into the courtroom, where does that interaction end? 'Can a Pillory be sufficient to punish the contempt of God . . . ?' asked the author of *The Third Commandment*, and yet the state clung to the pillory as an expression of its own contempt for perjury, for almost three hundred years.[125]

This chapter, then, has examined the crime of perjury, in relation to texts both literary and legal, in order to explore the ways in which the link between crime and sanction was imagined in the early modern period. As the analysis above has attempted to demonstrate, the dialectic between the 'contempt of God' and the legislative sanction for the secular offence was deeply problematic across the sixteenth and seventeenth centuries and, despite reaching a crisis point with the Popish Plot trials, remained fundamentally unresolved. Even with, and perhaps because of, the statute, the common-law courts struggled to reconcile the two. God could not nail the papers to the perjurer's forehead, desirable as that might be; divine and common-law conceptions of perjury could not be wholly and neatly reconciled. The two stood apart, and the uncomfortable space that resulted was filled not by legal debate, but by a far more curious mixture of alternative responses: the flawed fairytale endings of Shakespeare's texts, the visceral horrors of the providential tracts and, inevitably and repeatedly, a return, via the all-pervading language of the *Homily*, to the terrible 'flying' vengeance of an Old Testament God.

The Emergence of Perjury as a Common Law Offence 57

In his presentation of the law-literature paradigm, Bradin Cormack is clear that the value of literature inheres in its power to reveal and expose, its function as a 'mode of attention':

> [A] close engagement with literary texts can help us track for a particular historical moment the cultural usefulness of the discovery that law is constituted, at limits at once necessary and contestable, as the processing of an unruliness it cannot quite put in order.[126]

Reading *Love's Labour's Lost* alongside the *Homily*, with its rationalisation of biblical decrees upon swearing, and alongside the statute, which seeks to create a space for perjury as a secular crime, does seem to perform this function of exposing and illuminating the limitations of the law's control – albeit often by default, as we witness the play repeatedly and sometimes wilfully misunderstanding the nature of perjury and its punishment. Equally, I would suggest that such a reading also goes some way to explaining the unexpected and unsettling conclusion of a Shakespearean comedy that does not end with a betrothal, and which in fact leaves its characters stranded in a transitional world, a world wherein 'Jack hath not Jill' (863).

There is one last perjurer to be punished in *Love's Labour's Lost*, however. The central episode of the protracted last scene of the play is the performance of the Nine Worthies, with Armado, Costard, Nathaniel, Holofernes and Moth in starring roles. Among Holofernes' multiple representations is the Jewish military hero Judas Maccabaeus, although he is not permitted to play his part for long. Repeatedly, the mocking lords transform Judas Maccabaeus into Judas Iscariot, the warrior into the perjurer – 'a kissing traitor' (V.ii.594) – tormenting the flustered Holofernes to the point of bewilderment: 'you have put me out of countenance' (615).

'What mean you, sir?' Holofernes finally asks of his tormentors, frustrated in his attempts to continue the masque. 'To make Judas hang himself,' Boyet replies (597–8).

Notes

1. Shakespeare, *Love's Labour's Lost*, IV.iii.44–5. All references in this chapter are to the Arden edition (ed. H. R. Woudhuysen).
2. *Act for the Punishment of Such as Shall Procure or Commit any Wilful Perjury*, 5 Eliz. 1, c. 9, s. vii.
3. Ibid.
4. McAlindon, 'Swearing and Forswearing', p. 208.
5. See Shirley, *Swearing and Perjury in Shakespeare's Plays*; Berry, '"Salving the mail"'.

6. Cranmer, *Certayne sermons or homilies*, sig. Gii. The state homilies had multiple authors; authorship of this Homily is most often ascribed to Cranmer himself, however.
7. Gordon, 'Invention of a Common Law Crime', p. 159.
8. *An Account of the sentence which past upon Titus Oates*, p. 2.
9. *A True Narrative of the Tryal of Titus Oates*, p. 1.
10. *The Third Commandment*, pp. 10, 19.
11. Schmitt, *Political theology*; Agamben, *Homo Sacer*. See also Hutson, 'Imagining Justice', Cromartie, '*Epieikeia* and Conscience'; and the Introduction to this work.
12. Agamben, *Homo Sacer*, p. 26.
13. Cormack, *A Power to Do Justice*, p. 7.
14. Ibid. p. 27.
15. Ibid. p. 27.
16. Shagan, 'The Ecclesiastical Polity', p. 341.
17. *Homily*, sig. Gii.
18. Tillotson, *The lawfulness, and obligation of oaths*, p. 5.
19. Parker, *The Holy Byble* (Bishops' Bible), 5:34–7.
20. *Articles*, p. 25. Seventeenth-century texts which engage with the prohibition upon swearing include Strode, *Sermon concerning swearing*, and Gauden, *A discourse concerning publick oaths*.
21. Strode, *Sermon concerning swearing*, p. 10.
22. Gauden, *A discourse concerning publick oaths*, pp. 1, 29.
23. The 'three condicions' of the *Homily* were to go on to form a part of the authorisation of oath-taking in the *Articles* – 'so it be done according to the prophetes teaching in justice, judgement, and truth' (p. 25).
24. Spurr, 'A Profane History of Early Modern Oaths', p. 58.
25. Ibid. p. 40. The *Homily* was overtly a tool of the Protestant state – Edward VI's Council of Regency had prohibited the preaching of sermons, instead sending copies of *Certayne sermons* to all parishes in England. For discussion of oaths and vows elsewhere in Shakespeare, see Stacey, '"The Vow is Made"', and Kerrigan, *Shakespeare's Binding Language*.
26. Bicknoll, *A Sword Agaynst Swearyng*, title page.
27. Parker, *The Holy Byble*, Exodus 20:7 and 20:16.
28. Shirley, *Swearing and Perjury*, p. 11.
29. *The Third Commandment*, pp. 1, 7–8.
30. See Parker, *The Holy Byble*, Mark 6:21–29 and Judges 11:1–40.
31. Bicknoll, *A Sword Agaynst Swearing*, title page, sig. Cv.
32. The *Oxford English Dictionary* entry for 'perjury' asserts that 'from at least the 12th cent., perjury constituted the offence under ecclesiastical law of breaking an oath, irrespective of whether this had been taken within or outside judicial proceedings'. *OED Online* (last accessed 26 November 2019).
33. Bicknoll, *A Sword Agaynst Swearing*, sig. D3 (my emphasis).
34. Kerrigan, *Shakespeare's Binding Language*, pp. 72–3.
35. *House of Commons Journal*, vol. 1: 1547–1629 (London: 1802), pp. 65–6, 18 February 1563, available at <http://www.british-history.ac.uk> (last accessed 4 May 2019).
36. Ibid. pp. 67–70, 6 and 18 March 1563. Michael D. Gordon describes the

statute's legislative history in 'The Perjury Statute of 1563: A Case History of Confusion'.
37. Notably, Foxe's *The actes and monuments of these latter and perilous dayes* was first published in 1563.
38. Spalding, 'The *Reformatio Legum Ecclesiasticarum* and the Furthering of Discipline in England', p. 163. See further Bray (ed.), *Tudor Church Reform*.
39. For discussion of juror attaint, see Mitnick, 'From Neighbor-Witness to Judge of Proofs'.
40. Fisher, 'The Jury's Rise as Lie Detector', p. 607.
41. 5 Eliz. 1, c. 9, s. ii.
42. Gordon, 'Invention of a Common Law Crime', pp. 149–50.
43. Condren, *Argument and Authority in Early Modern England*, p. 248.
44. Gordon, 'Invention of a Common Law Crime', p. 152.
45. 5 Eliz. I, c. 9, s. xi.
46. Ibid. s. xiii.
47. *Onslowe's Case*, Court of King's Bench, 1 January 1564. Reported in 73 E.R. 532; (1564) Dyer 242.
48. (1564) Dyer 242 at 242b. 3 Hen. 7, c. 1 is most usually thought to be the Act in question.
49. Gordon, 'The Perjury Statute of 1563', p. 439.
50. Coke, *Third Part of the Institutes*, p. 164.
51. Gordon, 'The Perjury Statute of 1563', p. 443.
52. Klerman, 'Was the Jury Ever Self-Informing?', p. 123.
53. Gordon, 'The Perjury Statute of 1563', p. 445.
54. Dalton, *The countrey justice*, STC (2nd ed.)/6205, pp. 125–6.
55. Ibid. p. 264.
56. Shapiro, 'Law and the Evidentiary Environment', p. 259.
57. 1 Anne, c. 2, s. 9.
58. Shirley, *Swearing and Perjury*, p. 10.
59. Whilst swearing on objects other than the Bible (e.g. holy relics or the consecrated host) was still known by the sixteenth century, swearing 'on a boke' was by far the predominant model.
60. Cormack, *A Power to Do Justice*, p. 33.
61. Spurr, 'A Profane History', p. 56.
62. 5 Eliz. 1, c. 9, ss. vi–vii.
63. Fines collected under the statute (via 'money, goods and chattels') were forfeit to the Queen, although provision was made for half to be paid to any person who sued successfully on the basis that they had been 'grieved, hindred or molested' by the crime.
64. Beattie, *Crime and the Courts*, p. 464.
65. Ibid. p. 465. Pillory Abolition Act 1816, 56 Geo. 3, c. 138. The pillory remained a punishment for perjury until 1837; see 7 Will. & 1 Vict., c. 23.
66. Cobbett, VII, p. 1083.
67. Hadfield, *Lying in Early Modern English Culture*, p. 39.
68. Munday, *A View of sundry Examples*.
69. Bicknoll, *A Sword Agaynst Swearing*, sig. Ai.
70. Ibid. sig. Eii; Munday, *A View of sundry Examples*, sig. Biii.
71. Walsham, *Providence in Early Modern England*, p. 84.

72. Agamben, *Homo Sacer*, p. 27.
73. Bicknoll, *A Sword Agaynst Swearing*, sig. Eiii.
74. Ibid. sig. Eiii.
75. See Walsham, *Providence*, p. 64, n. 1.
76. Doolittle, *The Swearer Silenc'd*, p. 64.
77. In the 1595 pamphlet *A World of Wonders* the Lea case is positioned as earlier than Averies': T.I., *A World of Wonders*, sig. Ei.
78. Munday, *A View*, sig. Biii.
79. Bicknoll, *A Sword Agaynst Swearing*, sig. Ev.
80. *Homily*, sig. Hii.
81. See, e.g., the pamphlet *A fearefull example, shewed upon a perjured person*, where a convicted perjurer is described as sinning 'for a little peece of Silver, like *Judas*' (p. 5).
82. Parker, *The Holy Byble*, Matthew 27:3–10.
83. Parker, *The Holy Byble*, Acts 1:16–19.
84. Weber, 'The Hanged Judas of Freiburg Cathedral'.
85. De Voragine, *The Golden Legend*, vol. 1, pp. 168–9.
86. Ibid. p. 169.
87. Ibid.
88. Weber, 'The Hanged Judas of Freiburg Cathedral', p. 182.
89. 'Suspensio Jude' pageant, *Memorandum Book A/Y*, Records of Early English Drama, York, 1:48, trans. 2:733.
90. Weber, 'The Hanged Judas of Freiburg Cathedral', pp. 166, 183.
91. Rowlands, *The Betraying of Christ*, sig. Dii.
92. Bicknoll, *A Sword Agaynst Swearing*, sig. Ci.
93. Foxe, *The Actes and monuments of these latter and perilous dayes*.
94. For a fuller account of the Cooper case, see Mozley, *John Foxe and his Book*, pp. 194–6.
95. Bicknoll, *A Sword Agaynst Swearing*, sig. Ei.
96. On the challenges to Foxe's book, see Freeman, 'Fate, Faction, and Fiction'.
97. Ibid. pp. 601–2.
98. Wood, *Athenae Oxonienses*, II, cols 789–90.
99. Ibid. II, cols 789–90.
100. Croke, *The second part of the reports of George Croke*, p. 90.
101. Hutson, *Invention of Suspicion*, p. 17.
102. *An Account of the sentence*, p. 2.
103. Doolittle, *The Swearer Silenc'd*, p. 69.
104. Parker, *The Holy Byble*, I Kings 21.
105. Caryll, *Naboth's Vineyard*.
106. Suarez, 'A Crisis in English Public Life', p. 535.
107. Caryll, *Naboth's Vineyard*, see note at p. 94.
108. Ibid. p. 83.
109. *The Trial of Thomas White*: 31 Charles II. A.D. 1679, in Cobbett, VII, p. 312.
110. *The Trial of John Tasborough and Ann[e] Price*: 32 Charles II, A.D. 1680, in Cobbett, VII, pp. 882–926.
111. Ibid. p. 920.
112. Kerrigan, *Shakespeare's Binding Language*, p. 121.
113. Calderwood, '*Love's Labour's Lost*: A Wantoning with Words', pp. 325–6.

114. See also Kerrigan, *Shakespeare's Binding Language*, pp. 81–4, on contemporary discussion of a monarch's capacity to abrogate the law.
115. H. R. Woudhuysen notes the first reference to Romans (p. 222), but see also Shabeen, 'Shakespeare and the Bishops' Bible', and Streete, 'Charity and Law in Love's Labour's Lost', for discussion of the latter reference.
116. Kerrigan proposes an alternative reading of this, that the Princess's dictat is a reinstatement of Costard's penalty, now imposed on 'the King, not his put-upon subjects': *Shakespeare's Binding Language*, p. 121.
117. Berry, '"Salving the mail"', p. 95.
118. See also Kerrigan, *Shakespeare's Binding Language*, pp. 107, 122.
119. All references to *Cymbeline* are to the Arden edition (ed. J. M. Nosworthy).
120. Flanigan, '*Cymbeline* and the Sermons *Against Strife and Contention* and *Against Swearing and Perjury*', p. 96.
121. Coke, *Third Part of the Institutes*, p. 164.
122. See Gordon, 'Invention of a Common Law Crime', p. 150.
123. 2 Geo. 2, c. 25, s. 2.
124. *The Trial of Henry Garnett, Superior of the Jesuits in England: 4 Jac. I. 28th of March, A.D. 1606*, in Cobbett, II, p. 330.
125. *The Third Commandment*, p. 19.
126. Cormack, *A Power to Do Justice*, pp. 21–2.

Chapter 2

'Hollow-hearted angels': Coins, Counterfeits and the Discourses of Treason

In scene eight of Middleton and Dekker's *The Roaring Girl* (1610), Moll Cutpurse, the play's eponymous heroine, is put to the test by its villain, Sir Alexander, who seeks to remove his son from her influence.[1] Having unsuccessfully attempted to entrap Moll into the theft of 'a German watch' (8.8), a 'gold chain' (8.12) and his own 'ruff band with the diamond at it' (8.30), Sir Alexander's final assay on her reputation comes in the form of four 'marked angels' (counterfeit ten-shilling coins), which are given to Moll in payment for her musical services:

> I'll make her policy the art to trap her.
> Here are four angels marked with holes in them
> Fit for his cracked companions, gold he will give her,
> These will I make induction to her ruin,
> And rid shame from my house, grief from my heart.   (8.207–11)

This is no mere cozenage; Sir Alexander intends a deliberate entrapment here and he is well aware of the likely outcome. No-one living in London or any assize town would have been ignorant of the penalties associated with being in possession of counterfeit coin. In the same year that Middleton's play was first performed, at the Middlesex sessions, Thomas Madockes was sentenced to death for coining 'fourteen pieces of money in the likeness and similitude of the good current moneys called King James shillings', whilst the Essex assizes records note the case of John Davies and Thomas Carter of Brentwood, convicted of counterfeiting '8 King James shillings and 6 Elizabeth sixpences from base metals' and condemned to the same fate.[2] In the eyes of the law, these crimes were not merely economic offences, but high treason, and punishable as such. Sir Alexander's earlier exchange with Trapdoor makes the threat to Moll very clear:

> SIR ALEXANDER: Play thou the subtle spider, weave fine nets
>   To ensnare her very life.

TRAPDOOR: Her life?
SIR ALEXANDER: Yes, suck
  Her heart-blood if thou canst: twist thou but cords
  To catch her, I'll find a law to hang her up.
TRAPDOOR: Spoke like a worshipful bencher. (2.228–33)

The positioning of coinage offences as crimes of treason offers further insight into the central issue of this study, the link between crime and sanction in the early modern period. This chapter will focus on that positioning, therefore, and will explore the consequent impact on the political, legal and literary rhetoric surrounding crimes against the coin. In particular, it will examine the representation of coining in early seventeenth-century drama, a representation which demonstrates the influence of those state discourses of treason, but also opposes them with a more pragmatic and realistic attitude to the punishment of such crimes. Within the scheme of this study, the crime of coining represents, of course, the obverse of the narrative surrounding perjury. A capital offence that is also, on the surface, a victimless crime, coining seems to subvert the moral paradigm associated with biblical proscription and Old Testament vengeance. In any survey of the seventeenth-century discourse on coining, however, we find repeated and determined attempts to impose just such a moral paradigm upon the offence. Those attempts are countered by other, more complex representations that point up the constructed nature of coining as treason and seek to diminish and mitigate the available sanctions. If the providential fictions that surround perjury constitute what Bradin Cormack describes as 'a utopian fantasy of an order of justice beyond law', a stepping outside legal boundaries, then, the popular and literary narratives that accompany coining seek to expose the artificial nature of those boundaries: the dislocation between sign and meaning, coin and value, offence and sanction.[3] It is this disjunction that renders coining so complex and therefore so valuable as a subject for research.

It is also a subject that merits further exploration within the period of this study. Malcolm Gaskill comments that 'Coining has been neglected by historians of crime and the law in early modern England.'[4] This is certainly true with regard to the early and mid-seventeenth century. Both Alan Macfarlane and John Styles have written useful case studies of large-scale coining operations in and around Yorkshire and Lancashire. However, MacFarlane's is an account of a very specific 1680s prosecution, whilst Styles' work is a discussion of the 'yellow trade' (coining in gold) in the 1760s.[5] Prior to Gaskill's own 'mentalities'-based study of seventeenth-century coiners, scholarly consideration of the offence focused either on such isolated instances or on the post-1690 period, when the state of the national currency became part of a narrative of war and the maintenance of the military. In part, such an approach is an account of the evidence available; even Gaskill's analysis draws most frequently upon the much richer archive of surviving trial records from the late seventeenth century, and these are an important part of the story of counterfeiting in England. However, as we shall see, the reasons for this 'neglect' may also be linked to the problems that arise when considering the crime as a capital offence, problems that may in some part be illuminated by a closer focus on the ways in which legal and literary representations of coining interact.

Strictly speaking, we have only one side of the conversation in the extant documents; little or no anti-judicial polemic appears to survive, if indeed it existed. We can judge the prevailing mood only oppositionally, in the tone of the pro-treason discourse, which is prolix, circuitous and, at times, a little uncertain in tenor. Contemporary drama, however, does offer us a little of that 'other side'; analysis reveals that issues of false coin and counterfeits were closely bound up in the discourses of transaction, value and mercantile worth that dominate the stage in the period, most notably in the works of Middleton, Dekker and their contemporaries. Most obviously, this manifests itself in the form of slang, punning and financial metaphor, deployed by characters with an ease and liberality that confirms just how integral the workings of the money market were to seventeenth-century life. Thus, Webster and Dekker's *Westward Ho* imagines the world in terms of a mint – 'we are no sooner cast into the fire, taken out agen, hamerd, stampt, and made Currant, but presently we are changde' – whilst their later work, *Northward Ho*, develops a trope of minting into a universal metaphor: 'silver is the King's stampe, man Gods stampe, and a woman is mans stampe, wee are not currant till we passe from one man to another'.[6] Of course, the very practices of drama are intimately bound up with ideas of counterfeiting, as players 'coin' new characters on stage, and the unstable representation this creates is both underscored and heightened by the language of false monies. This chapter focuses on three works by Middleton (one in collaboration with Dekker) which seem to engage particularly with the rhetoric and issues surrounding false coin and its consequences: *The Revenger's Tragedy*, *A Chaste Maid in Cheapside* and *The Roaring Girl*. The circulation of coin provides a controlling metaphor in these plays, even a verbal architecture, and so the question of illegitimate currency occupies a particular discursive space: sometimes operating as a marker of societal decay, yet just as often functioning to maintain equilibrium. Perhaps most importantly, coining was a metaphor universally accessible to the audience of any Jacobean drama, and to every member of that audience – for, as we will see, the practice of coining was uniquely wide-ranging. That this may have had implications for the way in which coining was prosecuted is a point worthy of further investigation.

This chapter, then, does not seek to perform statistical analysis on coining cases, nor to recover mentalities from archival reports, although it does draw on the records of the Middlesex sessions and the Home Circuit assizes for the first half of the seventeenth century, the closest we have to a legal analogue for those city comedies and court tragedies.[7] What it does attempt to establish, by interrogating coining both literary and legal, is the role played by this unique offence in the period in question, asking how we should read the evidence that surrounds it, and how far its punishment was embedded into the discourses of the time.

'[A] law to hang her up': the Elizabethan Statutes

The law that Sir Alexander now finds 'to hang [Moll] up' is contained in the first Elizabethan anti-coining statute of 1562.[8] The 'Acte agaynst clypping washing rownding or fylyng of Coynes' represented the culmination of several centuries of concern about coinage offences. The making of counterfeit currency was a practice with a long history, as were its 'sister' offences: clipping, the paring off of small amounts of precious metal from true coins for resale; washing, the use of acid to remove that same metal; sweating, the vigorous shaking of coins to produce metal dust; and uttering, the dissemination of false monies.[9] At the heart of the matter lay the issue of the precious metal content of the national currency, and the consequent question of where 'value' really lay. Valerie Forman makes a key point about what counterfeit coin might mean in the seventeenth century:

> Today, counterfeit money is artificial, completely fabricated: it has no value as soon as its status is discovered. In the seventeenth century, however, counterfeit coins were not merely fraudulent imitations; they were often authentic coins which had been altered or adulterated. What made these coins counterfeit was that the amount of gold or silver in the coin had been diminished so that it was less than it was supposed to be for the corresponding face value.[10]

The relationship between a coin's intrinsic worth and its 'face' value was integral to a whole range of circulation issues, from day-to-day transactions to, crucially, international exchange. The intrinsic value of a coin as object was measured by the number of coins coming from a standardised weight of one pound and the fineness of the precious metal therein. By the early modern period, the gold or silver content of each denomination was prescribed and controlled by the state, as was the official bimetallic ratio of value between gold and silver, which both determined and reflected the scarcity or otherwise of each metal.[11] One problem with the idea of 'intrinsic' value was that it could, and often did, carry emotional associations, which could lead to erroneous assumptions about coin, in state policy and beyond.

In 1352 a statute of Edward III had first specifically declared coining to be treasonable, articulating a view long held in common law.[12] This was reinforced by legislation issued by Henry V, which extended this status to clipping, and again by Mary I in 1555.[13] It was under Elizabeth, however, that a wider range of offences were rendered acts of treason. Despite a full reissue of the coin by Henry VII, the national currency was in a particularly deplorable state by Elizabeth's accession, having been repeatedly debased – that is, reduced in value by a diminishment of the precious metal content – by her father's attempts to fill his war coffers.[14] This had consequences both domestic and international: at the start of Elizabeth's reign, Thomas Gresham wrote to the Queen to alert her to the fact that the exchange rate 'is only keppt up by artte and Godes providence; for the quoyne of this your realme doeth not corresponde in finnes not x s. the pounde'.[15] Shortly after coming to the throne, then, Elizabeth set about comprehensive reform, ordering a complete recall and reissue of currency and even visiting the London Mint herself to strike the first of the new coins. In 1562 she sealed this effort by issuing legislation which declared almost any offence against her new coin to be high treason.[16] The substance of the 1562 Act is expressed neatly by William Fulbecke:

> [C]lipping, washing, rounding or filing, for wicked lucre or gaine sake, of any of the proper money or Coyne of this Realme, or the dominions therof, or of any other Realme, or the dominions therof &c., shall be taken and adjudged to be treason by vertue of this Acte.[17]

The Act was reinforced and extended by statutes of 1572 and 1575, and later restated under James I's rule.[18]

Despite his predecessor's efforts, by the time James came to the throne, problems of circulation and value had become particularly acute. Craig Muldrew estimates that 'by the end of the sixteenth century the demand for money had probably increased by something like 500 per cent, while the supply had expanded by only 63 per cent'.[19] This was in part due to population growth and rising prices, but also linked to the economic structure of the money mints themselves. As C. E. Challis notes, 'the moneyers received a flat-rate payment to cover the cost of striking coins ... with the result that it was to the moneyers' advantage to make up their journeys with [larger] coins of high denomination'.[20] James' own policy did little to remedy the situation. In 1604 he issued his first proclamation on the state of the national economy, decrying what he deemed the inflation of silver prices, and altering the Mint gold/silver ratio to increase the value of the former metal.[21] In this James was in some sense reverting to a quasi-alchemical concept of gold as a touchstone of value – even as he himself undermined that concept and altered that value. His proclamation took pains to reinforce this essentialist ideal; his aim, as outlined in a subsequent proclamation, was to create a large reserve of gold and retain it within his realm: 'an immovable and perpetuall stocke, which should never goe forth againe'.[22] The practical outcome of James' edict was that the main output from the Mint became gold coins, an approach that ran completely counter to the requirements of a circulating and functioning monetary system and compounded the national cashflow crisis.

Throughout James' reign the Elizabethan statutes persisted as the chief means of policing that crisis and its consequences. Elizabeth had positioned her own reforms as a 'victory and conquest of this hideous monster of the base moneys', and they were described by Holinshed as an achievement of almost godly moment.[23] She had, he said, realised 'a certaine perfection, purenesse and soundnesse, as here in hir new stamps and coines of all sorts; so also in God's religion'.[24] The collapsing of economic and spiritual here appeared to be reinforced by the legislation. A conviction for high treason, after all, automatically incurred a traitor's death, hanging, drawing and quartering for men and burning for women, together with confiscation of the offender's property by the state. The description of the sentence passed upon Thomas Marshall and Roger Newton, convicted of counterfeiting in 1605, makes clear the full rigour of the law:

> it was adjudged that each of them should be taken by the Sheriff of Middlesex to the Gaol of Newgate, and thence be drawn straightway to the gallows of Tiborne, and be hung on the same gallows, and be laid on the ground still living, and their entrails be taken from their bellies whilst they should still be living, and their heads be cut off, and their bodies be each divided into four parts, and the same quarters be placed where the Lord the King may be pleased to appoint.[25]

However, this equation was radically undermined by the very nature of coining as a crime. For every commentator who, like Fulbecke, saw the capital status of coining as the correct response to an offence 'seditiously attempted against the Prince or Commonweale', there existed another, such as the condemned London counterfeiter Barbara Spencer, who 'would not be convinc'd that her Crime was any Sin, or the least

Cheat'.[26] While the terminology of the 1562 Act seemed to suggest that, as Edward Coke noted, a key element of the crime vested in the intention of the offender – 'that if any person *for wicked lucre or gains sake*, shall by any art, wayes, or means whatsoever, impair, diminish, falsifie, scale or lighten the kings money, &c, it is High Treason' – there seemed no case in which that intention was not assumed by the courts.[27] This could be hard to reconcile where, for example, coining was a response to a particular set of circumstances, a means of sustaining trade within a community. A problematic fissure existed between the public perception of this crime and its legal status as high treason.

Returning to *The Roaring Girl*, then, Sir Alexander's attempt to destroy Moll has genuine force. Malcolm Gaskill notes the case of 'a London man who was pilloried in Leicester Square for planting clippings in a neighbour's house to pursue a grudge'.[28] Gaskill's is a late case, but as *The Roaring Girl* demonstrates, the compelling nature of physical evidence in coining cases was fully understood much earlier. The prospect of undeserved and disproportionate punishment is here explicitly, and significantly, associated with a corrupt form of law, in Sir Alexander's status as a 'worshipful bencher' (2.233). His expressed intent to 'find a law to hang [Moll] up' suggests a comment on a legal system that may have dislocated crime and punishment, word and meaning. Moreover the physical objects in the case are significant: 'angels' provided a rich source of punning possibility for early modern drama, almost always freighted with a moral resonance, and the image deployed by Trapdoor in the play's final scene is a particularly poignant rendering of spiritual lack: 'Four hollow-hearted angels he then gave you/By which he meant to trap you' (11.243–4).[29] In fact, when Moll discovers Sir Alexander's campaign against her, her response hints at another potential pun on counterfeits:

> SIR ALEXANDER: Thou art a mad girl, and yet I cannot now
>   Condemn thee.
> MOLL: Condemn me? Troth and you should, sir,
>   I'd make you seek out one to hang in my room,
>   I'd give you the slip at gallows, and cozen the people.   (11.211–14)

A 'slip' was a common term for a counterfeit coin.[30] In this reading, Moll will pass false coin at Tyburn and thus 'cozen' those who condemn her out of their desired justice, and the 'people' out of their anticipated spectacle.

Unlike other treasonable crimes of the period, the severity of punishment decreed for coining seemed to have little moral force behind it. Crucially, in a post-Reformation society where moral authority was inextricably linked to the word of God, it was difficult to position coining as a grievous sin. This problem is articulated by Gaskill:

> [U]nlike other horror crimes for which European states reserved their highest condemnation, coining offended no principal tenet of Christian morality, nor were there any immediately obvious biblical justifications for its proscription – particularly for its definition as an act of treason . . . In general, the best the authorities could do was solemnly declare the sacred status of the coin and leave it at that.[31]

In fact, the apparent futility of their task did not prevent those 'authorities', state, legal and spiritual, from attempting to construct a narrative of treason around coining – and, crucially, they would seek to fashion that discourse in precisely the moral terms that coining appeared to refute.

'The *Heads* of Princes': Defining Treason

Fundamentally, the exercise of establishing a rhetoric against coining was all about trying to close the gap between sign and meaning. This was a familiar project, as Stephen Mead indicates:

> Money came to resemble language and to become more and more a product of language. One need only look at the royal proclamations that made England's a metal-fiat currency to see the self-consciousness with which Tudor and Stuart monarchs would 'command' money to be worth what it used to be.[32]

Mead's comment upon the increasing interconnectedness of language and coin encapsulates ideas of value and intrinsic worth, but also recalls the terminology of the law, where even the dissemination of false currency, 'uttering', is a speech act. The very use of the term 'treason' is implicated in this momentum: interestingly, in the assize records for the early part of the seventeenth century, those accused are generally indicted for 'coining', but, if found guilty, convicted of 'treason', suggesting that the offence itself underwent a kind of transmutation through the very process of trial.[33] Yet throughout the seventeenth century, official and legal discourse struggled to create a meaningful link between the crime and its punishment.

That punishment was so extreme that it seemed that the crime must be figured in similarly momentous terms. We see the resulting rhetoric against coining operating in three main areas – treason secular (dishonouring the monarch); treason economic (defrauding the public) and, to a much lesser extent, treason spiritual. Much of this rhetorical effort was concerned with the production of metaphor. What did a coin, often a poorly minted disc of adulterated precious metal, really represent; what was the 'sacred status' to which Gaskill alludes? Most obviously, for many commentators it was the physical image of the monarch – coining, it was argued, defaced or diminished the portrait of the king or queen, the defender of the faith, and this itself was treason both temporal and spiritual. This theory is summed up by William Fleetwood in his 1694 *Sermon against clipping*:

> The *Heads* of Princes are not only stamp'd for Ornament and Honour, and to declare who are and have been Governours of such a Nation, but publickly to vouch the true intrinsick worth of every Piece, and tell Men that they there receive so much Silver, and of such a fineness, and that that Image warrants it . . .[34]

In this reading, the image of the sovereign functions in much the same way as the idea of precious metal content, closing the gap between symbol and meaning, guaranteeing the value of the coin itself. As an argument, however, the notion of the sanctity of the royal image was undermined by a number of factors. The first was the poor quality of the imprint itself, what John Carey describes as the 'alertingly ramshackle state of contemporary money', with coins of irregular weight and shape, imprinted with images that might be imprecise, incomplete or off-centre.[35] The second was the fact that images of multiple monarchs might be in circulation at any one time, exacerbating the difficulties of policing and, indeed, even understanding the scope of the domestic currency. Ceri Sullivan lists twenty-six different types of coins current in England in the mid-seventeenth century:

> [T]he royal, half-royal, old noble, half old noble, angel, half angel, salute, two parts of a salute, george noble; the Henrician first crown, base crown, great sovereign, best sovereign, and sovereign; the Edwardian sovereign; the Elizabethan sovereign and crown; James' unite, double crown, Britain crown, and thistle crown; the Caroline last coin, half piece and quarter piece.[36]

It is worth noting that Sullivan's list encompasses gold coins only. Certainly, it was difficult to establish precisely which monarch was being dishonoured by the activities of coiners. The list of current coins above includes the 'salute', a French coin, which had been declared legal tender in England. The circulation of foreign coin as 'English' currency was regularly legitimised; during Mary I's marriage negotiations with Spain, for example, Spanish ducats and Portuguese cruzados were among the coins declared legal, and a royal proclamation of 1625 authorised the circulation of the quart d'ecus that had formed a part of Henrietta Maria's dowry.[37] French coins had clearly been current in England well before this, however: in Middleton's *A Chaste Maid in Cheapside* (1613), Touchwood Junior pays a waterman 'a French crown' to row his fiancée Moll Yellowhammer upriver.[38] Five years later, at the 1618 Kent Winter Assizes, Peter Mundane, a tailor, and Tristram Brudenell, a cutler, were indicted for manufacturing 'from base metal a French crown, and utter[ing] it'.[39] Where representations of multiple generations of monarch coexisted in the current coinage and where representations of foreign monarchs might be deemed 'current', it became more and more difficult to argue for the sanctity of the hammered image.

What the sanctity argument really relied upon was a more sentimental idea of 'dishonour' and betrayal. '[W]hat can be more dishonourable than to have the Image of the Prince impressed upon false and counterfeited stuff?' asked the economic commentator Rice Vaughan, while a contemporary newspaper article tried to take this even further by suggesting that coining *was* biblically proscribed, being a contravention of the fifth commandment to honour one's parents.[40] Other breaches of the Decalogue were proposed; in his *Sermon*, Fleetwood surveys historical penalties for coining and clipping and explains that:

> In Henry I. time they were Condemned to lose, some their Hands, and some their Eyes: And some (in allusion to the Word) who were found to adulterate the Kings Coin, were so punish'd as if the Laws intended to prevent Adultery itself.[41]

Here the seventh commandment is invoked, an equation which, as we will see, is all too readily adopted by early modern drama.

To construct a compelling argument for coining's capital status based upon the economic problem it presented was similarly challenging. The preamble to Elizabeth's 1575 Coin Act had rather plaintively announced that the statute sought to address new methods of clipping and washing now being used, 'to the greate Damage Losse Hurte and Deceipte as well of her Majestiee as of all her faytheful and loving Subjects'.[42] In his 1623 *Sermon Preached upon Candlemas Day*, John Donne attempted to explain and humanise this threat:

> A principall reason that makes coyning and adulterating of the money capitall in all states, is not so much because hee that coynes usurpes the Princes authority, (for every coyner is not a pretender to the Crowne), ... as because he that coins injuries the publique: and no man injuries the publique more, then he, who defrauds him, who is God's steward for the publique, the King.[43]

However, this concept of 'defrauding', along with the ideal of intrinsic value, could be negated completely by a simple recognition of bad coin as part of the general economy. The value, or meaning, of coin manifested itself only in context, after all – fundamentally, whether or not a coin was accepted as payment. If local shopkeepers, innkeepers and tradesmen would accept clipped or counterfeit coin, then a happy arrangement could be reached whereby whole communities operated on this closed-economy basis. Geographical isolation played a part in this – large coining and clipping rings were uncovered in parts of Yorkshire in the 1640s, for example, and whole households were convicted in Durham and Northumberland – but as we shall see, this dynamic was not unknown in the city.[44] The trade in false coin seems to have been recognised as a democratic crime in every sense. Whilst in the records of the Home Circuit assizes and the Middlesex sessions we find labourers and tradespeople amongst those charged with clipping and counterfeiting, alongside these are a significant number of professionals and 'gentlemen' accused.[45] The coiner Thomas Madockes was described as 'late of London, gentleman' and at the sessions of March 1616, recognisances were taken to ensure the appearance of Christopher Blunte and George Hopkins, both 'gentlemen', 'touching the bespeaking of an engine to be made for counterfeytinge of coin'.[46] Such activity could come very close to the heart of power: in December 1662, the State Papers record the investigation into one 'Blunden, paymaster to the Duke of York', detailing '700l. or 800l.' of false money sold to Blunden by a coiner turned informer.[47] Moreover, there was great anxiety about corruption within the legitimate structures of the national currency. As early as 1578, the French moneyer Mestrell, who had been brought to England to assist the Royal Mint, was convicted of involvement in counterfeiting and hanged.[48] A number of high-profile engravers in the Mint were also exposed as coiners during the early seventeenth century, and there was frequent and justified concern that official Mint dies might be illicitly transported outside its walls for the purpose of copying.[49] So confirmed was this association that in 1649, when the Commonwealth government invited Pierre Blondeau, engineer of the Parisian mint, to make recommendations for the modernising of English coin, those in the Mint who opposed his innovations attempted to have him arrested as a counterfeiter.[50]

Nonetheless, the Stuart regime continued to propound an ideology of crime, and indeed sin, around clipping and coining. Increasingly histrionic tactics were used in proclamations and sermons: the chaplain of Newgate prison, for example, proclaimed that clipping coin was direct evidence of one's denial of the Christian faith: 'what is it to Clip a thing, but to Pare it Round, and what is Pareing Round call'd in Scripture but Circumcision, and who ... dares Practice Circumcision, but one that

... is a *Jew* in his Heart?'⁵¹ In his elegy 'The Bracelet', John Donne describes the poor appearance of French coins in these same terms: 'And howsoe'er French kings most Christian be/Their crowns are circumcised most Jewishly.'⁵²

Despite Donne's exploration of the limits of spiritual metaphor, what is, perhaps remarkably, missing from the rhetoric on coining is any real attempt to position the crime as a genuine offence against the Divine. Even when the context of polemic is explicitly religious, as in Fleetwood's *Sermon*, there is an acknowledgement that offenders must be at a loss to understand the nature of their transgression: '[t]hey can be sorry for their great Misfortune, but they know not how to repent of Clipping and Coining, as Sins against God.'⁵³ Whilst, as we shall see, trial transcripts and assize records might attempt to associate coining with theologically suspect practices such as alchemy, it seems that the overall approach was to observe the terms of Matthew 22:21 and to 'Render unto Cesar the things which are Cesars', including the injury of the offence.⁵⁴

'[H]er thief-whorish eye': Coining in Early Modern Drama

When Sir Alexander instructs Trapdoor to set the bait in the first of his traps for Moll Cutpurse (the German watch), he is clear: 'Place that o'the court cupboard, let it lie/Full in the view of her thief-whorish eye' (8.16–17). In that one phrase, 'thief-whorish', he encapsulates the associations that surround Moll, but also creates a connection with false coin that, as we have seen, will play out in practical terms later in the play. For even as it provides the framework for *The Roaring Girl's* conception of its eponymous heroine, this image of the 'thief-whore' specifically recalls the rhetoric surrounding coining: the conjunction of the 'thief' who defrauds the King's coffers and the 'whore', or adulterer, who dishonours his royal image. Early modern theatre plays with these configurations to complex effect, refiguring counterfeiting as a form of family drama, with questions of lineage, chastity and dishonour looming large. Crucially, it does so in front of an audience that, we might expect, would recognise both the metaphorical associations and the real-life impact of coining offences.

At the end of Thomas Middleton's *The Revenger's Tragedy* (1607/8), the play's protagonist, Vindice, considers a form of monetary disruption that would certainly realise the worst fears of the Jacobean authorities. Punning on the existence of the gold coin called the 'noble', he intimates the possibility of social revolution: 'And if we list we could have nobles clipped/And go for less than beggars.'⁵⁵ In fact Middleton's play, set in an unnamed Italian ducal court, proposes a more complex vision of coining, its amoral schema built upon multiple images of coins and counterfeits. Throughout, it rehearses and unsettles many of the state's key messages about the offence, in particular situating coining at the intersection of two key tenets of the Decalogue: thou shalt honour thy father and mother/thou shalt not commit adultery.

'Were't not for gold and women, there would be no damnation' (II.i.257): *The Revenger's Tragedy* is structured around a long-sought, but ultimately opportunistic programme of revenge, both enabled by and expediting the collapse of the sexual and material framework that sustains the ducal family unit. It is replete with suggestive language, constructing a world of questionable sexual transactions, valuations and counterfeits, and as such its central dynamic is provided by the 'cuckolds' who are 'a-coining, apace, apace, apace' (II.ii.142–3). The tone is set in the opening scene: the Duke and Duchess process across the stage, a parade of power and lineage in which the legitimate and illegitimate offspring of the ducal line, Lussurioso and Spurio, are, it seems, equally acknowledged. The revenger, Vindice, is peculiarly situated in relation to this world: the 'base-coined pandar' (I.i.81) who exposes the sexually 'counterfeit' practices of the ducal court, yet whose assumed identity, 'Piato' (meaning 'plated'), explicitly figures him as a form of adulterated coin.

As the play opens, two specific events converge to provide the momentum towards tragedy. Both are assaults upon 'good' women – the rape of Antonio's wife, 'that virtuous lady' (I.iv.5), and the attempted seduction of Castiza by Lussurioso – and by drawing virtue into the corrupt sexual dynamic of the court, these events seem to destabilise its precarious balance. This destabilising is explicitly linked to the degradation of coin; when Vindice reveals his disguise to his mother Gratiana, it is in order to damn her conduct via a formal debasement: 'I . . . /Tried you and found you base metal' (IV.iv.30–1). The play's female characters are subject to repeated assay in these terms. Thus, when Vindice sets out to test the virtue of his sister Castiza, he asserts that 'a right good woman in these days is changed/Into white money with less labour' (II.ii.27–8), an odd image of prostitution which alludes to the debasing of plated gold coin to silver even as it seems to express a trope of purification. Such collapsing of spiritual and temporal is a repeated theme, for Castiza's mother, Gratiana, has been tempted to prostitute her daughter by 'a thousand angels . . . /Men have no power; angels must work you to't' (II.i.86–7). Michael Neill regards the play's images of degraded coin as part of a representation of adultery and its consequences as 'denying the exclusive function of the womb as patriarchal mint', a depiction that sheds light upon the argument for the sanctity of the royal image:

> [T]he coin is stamped with the king's authority as the son is stamped with the authenticating features of his father. Thus offences such as clipping, gilding, restamping and counterfeiting were capital matters not simply because they constituted a form of theft, but because they amounted to iconoclastic degradation of the royal image and a bastardizing usurpation of royal authority.[56]

This recalls us directly to the contemporary association of counterfeiting with the breach of the fifth and seventh commandments, and certainly, as the play's characters are unyoked from their patrilineal destiny, the resulting self-determination can only create anarchy. As *The Revenger's Tragedy* progresses, its overtly illegitimate son, the 'falsely sown' Spurio (I.ii.198), is joined by a litany of other 'uncertain m[e]n' (135), questioning their mothers' virtue and their own heritable worth: 'I'm in doubt/Whether I'm myself or no' (IV.iv.24–5). In this sense it is particularly interesting that Middleton has Lussurioso describe his intervention in his stepmother's adultery in capital terms, as 'treason on the lawful bed' (IV.i.23).

While the value system summarised by Neill seems to rewrite counterfeiting as simply a discourse of misogyny – 'Women are apt, you know, to take false money,' Vindice claims (I.i.104) – further analysis of the play's complex sexual economy reveals that its characters may be at once coiner and counterfeit. This is how the court works: in one sense, what Middleton has created here is a closed community operating on the basis of false coin. Spurio, bastard son of a duke whose compulsion to (procreative) adultery is figured by Vindice in terms of his 'spendthrift veins' (I.i.8), describes himself as one of his father's 'cast sins' (V.i.117). Given Spurio's position at the centre of the court, the self-pitying associations of '[out]cast' surely give way to a more apt allusion to the 'casting' of (imperfect) metal imprints. In his proposed seduction of the Duchess, Spurio seeks to perpetuate this series of illegitimate transactions, suggesting that this is the inevitable consequence of his own birth:

> Duke, on thy brow I'll draw my bastardy.
> For indeed a bastard by nature should make cuckolds,
> Because he is the son of a cuckold-maker.   (I.ii.201–3)

The Revenger's Tragedy hints that the undermining of structures of patrimony is just one facet of the civic decay within its world, however; like *The Roaring Girl*, the play explicitly associates corruption in this form with the law. The discourse of false coin invades the workings of the law in the opening trial scene, when Lussurioso describes the possibility of leniency for his brother: 'offences/Gilt o'er with mercy show like fairest women,/Good only for their beauties' (I.ii.29–30). The image conflates the adulteration of coin 'gilt o'er' with the 'purity' or otherwise of women and with the equitable application of justice, unconsciously echoing Vindice's earlier comment to Castiza, 'The law's a woman, and would she were you' (I.i.115). Indeed, a feature of the play's ducal court seems to be the arbitrariness of its approach to capital punishment, literalised when the Duchess's youngest son is executed on a turn of phrase. As Derek Dunne notes, Junior Brother's 'death is not connected to his crime, as one might expect'; later Lussurioso will sentence the Duke's Gentleman to death peremptorily and without foundation.[57] Lussurioso's cynicism extends to the valuation of all language in the public domain; later in the Act, when he rewards Hippolito for procuring Piato as his pander, he declares that 'words are but great men's blanks./Gold, though it be dumb, does utter the best thanks' (I.iii.27–8). The opposition of unstamped – and presumably corruptible – 'blanks' to the 'dumb' gold must surely itself be flawed, if we consider the play's recurrent imagery of falsely 'gilted' coin.

Middleton's tragedy develops the suggestions of treason and threat that are associated with counterfeiting. However, at heart the play returns us to considerations of coins in context, for it is only when the system of illegitimate coin is resisted by the dual forces of virtue and revenge that the closed economy no longer seems to function. And, as we have seen, in Vindice's final speech there are also suggestions that the sexual and familial treasons of the court could presage a more radical collapse: 'we could have nobles clipped' (V.iii.122). Whether or not social revolution is the logical destination of the world of *The Revenger's Tragedy*, his words return us inevitably to the play's opening imperative: 'We must coin' (I.i.141).

It is unlikely that the audience of *The Revenger's Tragedy* would have been surprised to hear these allusions to counterfeiting associated with a ducal court; as we have seen, coining transcended boundaries of social status. Perhaps most pertinently, the law itself was not immune to such accusations: in 1627, for example, the Newgate Sessions reported that: 'one Harwood, by the permission of one Mr Kareck an utter-barrister of the Middle Temple, lodged in a chamber in the Vine Court and there he built a fornace and coyned money'.[58] Similarly, in 1662 the informer Richard Oliver 'discovered' a 'mint in the Temple'.[59] In Middleton's *A Chaste Maid in Cheapside* (1613), the goldsmith Yellowhammer, whose own name alludes to a slang term for a gold coin, explicitly associates counterfeiting with the law, when he berates his wife:

Has no attorney's clerk been here o'late
And changed his half-crown piece his mother sent him,
Or rather cozened you with a gilded twopence ... ? (I.i.29–33)

To the play's audience, this insinuation would have layered irony upon irony, for workers in metals, particularly those of Yellowhammer's profession, were more usually regarded as the perpetrators than the victims of such transactions. Goldsmiths occupied an ambiguous position in relation to the trade in false coin, treading a very narrow line between legitimate and illegitimate employment of their skills. In Chapman, Jonson and Marston's *Eastward Hoe* (1605), the goldsmith's assistant Frank Quicksilver boasts that he can 'take you off twelvepence from every angel, with a kind of aqua fortis, and never deface any part of the image'.[60] Aqua fortis was the acid most commonly used in 'washing' coins to remove their precious metal content. Quicksilver demonstrates a wholly comprehensive knowledge of the illicit transformation and enhancement of specie: 'I have not liv'd amongst goldsmiths and goldmakers all this while, but I have learned something worthy of my time with 'em' (187–8). This association was nothing new; in his *Diary* for February 1602, the lawyer John Manningham notes the case of 'A certain goldsmith in Cheape [who] was indebted to my Cosen above 100£. And after executed for clipping gold.'[61] At the Middlesex sessions in 1609, Thomas Boswell, 'late of London gouldsmith' was accused of having 'traitorously and feloniously diminished certain current monys by clipping and filing them'.[62]

Although Yellowhammer seeks here to dissociate himself from the trade in false coin, such precarious legitimacy infuses *A Chaste Maid*, a play that offers a further development of the closed-economy coining model of *The Revenger's Tragedy*. Explicitly set at the heart of the money trade, the play's very title invites consideration of how value – moral, sexual and financial – might be assessed and understood. Cheapside was the traditional home of the London goldsmiths as well as being the capital's main shopping thoroughfare, a locus for civic pageantry and a key point on the route followed by criminals doing public penance in the City. However, by the early seventeenth century this had become a more ambiguous locale. Many goldsmiths had chosen to move their business premises to the newly fashionable West End, and concern was growing within the Goldsmith's Company about the decline of Cheapside, now home to less successful practitioners and such low-status enterprises as haberdashers and booksellers.[63]

Middleton's play is set at a point when Cheapside's decline is beginning to manifest. Even its title expresses a dubiety about the virtue, and thus the value of the thoroughfare. The likelihood of a chaste maid in Cheapside is, we assume, small. As Karen Newman usefully notes, there is a complex pun within the play's very title, a blurring of 'chaste' and 'chased', the latter referring not only to the convicted prostitutes whipped at the cart's tail on Cheapside, but also to metal that has been cut, embossed or engraved.[64] This 'chaste/chased' maid is Moll, Yellowhammer's daughter, and in her mother's eyes at least, her virtue renders her an imperfect form of currency. 'But 'tis a husband solders up all cracks', Maudline Yellowhammer declares, bemoaning her 'drowsy-browed' daughter's prospects (I.i.37, 13). According to her mother, Moll's chastity will never bring her, or her family, the social elevation of 'a knight's bed' (I.i.12), and the later valuation of her maidenhead at 'forty pounds' (IV.iv.50) seems to confirm this assessment of virtue's worth in Cheapside.

In fact, throughout *A Chaste Maid*, Moll is depicted as a wholly mutable form of coin. She is a goldsmith's child, who dances 'like a plumber's daughter' (I.i.21) – the allusion here is to base metal, a plumber's chief material was lead – and this is further reinforced as Maudline predicts that Moll will have 'two thousand pound in lead' as her dowry (22). Yet elsewhere her father restores her association with 'goldsmith's ware' (I.i.23), declaring that:

> I will lock up this baggage
> As carefully as my gold: she shall see
> As little sun   (III.i.40–2)

As the play closes and her story nears conclusion, however, Moll's monetary integrity deteriorates once again, when her brother comments upon her pallor: 'gold into white money was never so changed/ As is my sister's colour' (V.ii.16–17). Certainly, Moll is not too pure to practise deception in order to achieve her desires – 'You that have tricks can counterfeit' her mother exclaims (IV.iii.23) – even if her attempt at eloping with Touchwood Junior is thwarted. Like *The Revenger's Tragedy*, *A Chaste Maid* invests value in the sexual or marital 'worth' of its female characters; and like Middleton's earlier play, that worth is not anchored in any recognisable morality, but rather in a perpetuation of Cheapside's specific value system. The play's very structure – its four plots, each based on a triangle of sexual transaction or intent, and all interconnected by devices of inheritance or dowry – suggests a closed society operating via an endless round of dubious transactions. Even when an apparently foreign element is introduced, in the person of the Welsh Gentlewoman, it emerges that, as Sir Walter's cast-off mistress, she is already in circulation. The outcome of such a structure is inevitable. If the operation of the closed court of *The Revenger's Tragedy* is predicated upon the acceptance of 'false' coin alongside 'true', then in *A Chaste Maid* we find a wholly unlawful economy. For as Arthur Kinney notes, *all* the babies in *A Chaste Maid* are illegitimate: 'the putative heirs of the next generation – the Country Wench's, Mistress Allwit's, Lady Kix's – are bastards'.⁶⁵ If indeed this recalls the multiple 'false sons' of the *Revenger's Tragedy*, then it does so in a more knowing way; anxieties about paternity here dissolve into a complacent acceptance, personified *in extremis* in Allwit's active connivance at his cuckolding by Sir Walter – 'he gets me all my children and pays the nurse . . . the happiest state that ever man was born to!' (I.ii.18, 21). Of course, *A Chaste Maid* is a comedy, and thus the rampant promiscuity of Touchwood Senior, for example, is a very different matter from the lecher Duke's 'spendthrift veins' and murderous impulses.⁶⁶ Nonetheless both are actively associated with coin, the Duke in his momentum of excess – 'a-coining [cuckolds]' (II.ii.142–3) – and the impecunious Touchwood in his begetting of 'beggars' (II.i.40) and a procession of impregnated 'wenches' demanding maintenance. Moreover, this perpetuation of illegitimacy is specifically linked to the stability – or instability – of gold. For even Yellowhammer, whose very name should proclaim his value and integrity, notes, almost in passing, that 'I've kept a whore myself, and had a bastard . . . I care not who knows it' (IV.i.239–41).

The notion of perpetual exchange is comically exploited in the farcical Promoters' scene (II.ii), when the two hapless informers seek to identify and blackmail those buying or eating meat during the Lenten abstinence. Their system, by which a 'customer' may buy exemption in advance – 'he purchased the whole Lent together' (II.ii.125) – reveals their own corruption, but also the determined and cheerful subversion of church law by the people of Cheapside. The scene's characters are all pursuing 'meat', literally and sexually, and their carnality is conflated with their greed. Such temptations are in continual circulation in *A Chaste Maid*, and the Promoters' scene literalises this, as characters move across the space of the stage, bearing the illicit flesh that passes, changes hands, generates profits and is eventually transformed into – 'A child!' (II.ii.156). After their initial fury at the wench's trick, the Promoters regain their composure and settle on a plan to dispose of each of their prohibited acquisitions. The mutton will be roasted; the child sent 'to Brainford' (175).⁶⁷ As in *The Revenger's Tragedy*, the illegitimate (money, meat, children) must be kept in constant motion, but unlike the societal collapse we see in the former play, there is little in *A Chaste Maid* to challenge this process of circulation and exchange. Such perpetual movement accounts for much of our difficulty in reading the morality of the drama. This is, after all, a play in which logic can 'prove a whore an honest woman' and make her a wife (V.iv.97), and in explicitly pairing Tim Yellowhammer's marriage to Sir Walter's mistress and his sister's union with Touchwood Junior, 'two marriages with one hand/And both lucky' (V.iv.113–14), Middleton's schema seems to suggest that, in Cheapside, a 'half-crown piece' is always really a 'gilded twopence' (I.i.30–1).

The Revenger's Tragedy and *A Chaste Maid* rehearse and undermine the two main tenets of the treason argument, it seems: transforming the assault upon the monarchical image into a discourse of sexual incontinency and rewriting the concept of economic instability as its very opposite. Returning to *The Roaring Girl*, we find this framework imagined in even more practical, and personal, terms. In fact, the latter play locates its momentum of circulation firmly within its central character. 'She slips from one company to another like a fat eel between a Dutchman's fingers' (3.187–8), the perpetually mobile Moll Cutpurse is figured simultaneously as the play's counterfeit and as its true coin – troubling and indefinable in her 'masculine womanhood' (3.321), but simultaneously representative of her society's currency in her own aspiration to material goods: 'I come to buy' (3.213). Moll is one of many, 'more whores of that name than of any ten other' (4.148), yet she is also set in direct opposition to 'another Moll', the 'sweet maid' Mary Fitzallard (1.66, 74) within the play's romance plot. That plot, which substitutes Sebastian's 'counterfeit passion' (1.98) for Moll, for his love for the 'true' coin represented by Mary, seems to replicate this model, a truth reinforced by his father Sir Alexander's admission to Mary in the play's final scene – 'I see the brightness of thy worth appear' (11.198). In this context Laxton's assertion of his intent to seduce Moll is suggestive: 'I'll lay hard siege to her – money is that *aquafortis* that eats into many a maidenhead: where the walls are flesh and blood, I'll ever pierce through with a golden auger' (3.175–7). Moll is here imagined as the coin that may be adulterated and diminished: although in a complex compounding of metaphor, aqua fortis here simultaneously represents money and the debasement of that money.

Beyond all Moll's disruption of signs and norms, however, what she really seems to represent is not a transmutation, but a strange kind of integrity: 'in troth th'art a good wench' (11.230). Her 'disguises' are fundamentally just a resort to male clothing, 'sometimes/she goes in breeches' (2.223–4). Moll is not, after all, a woman whose virtue is to be eroded by either money or '*aquafortis*'. In this vein it is worth noting that the 'true' Mary, Mary Fitzallard, also resorts to disguise in her performance as the seamstress, a 'strange shape' (1.56) so effective that, for a time, it confounds even her sweetheart Sebastian. It seems that the play's two Marys may have more in common than at first glance, and that the play's proclaimed 'story of Moll' (1.115) does not refer to Moll Cutpurse alone. In fact, in both *The Roaring Girl* and the later *Chaste Maid* the apparent 'true' coin is proven as unstable and unknowable as the coin that is perceived to be false.

What can the drama of the period tell us about the discourses that attached to false coin? Undoubtedly, *The Revenger's Tragedy* participates in the rhetoric that surrounded coining, deploying the idea of dishonour associated with counterfeiting the image of the monarch, and hinting at connections between a simple economic offence and a wider anarchy. Yet the play is hardly complicit in these discourses of treason, presenting us with a court that is already dishonoured and a royal line dislocated by the 'coining' of false heirs. Further, Middleton's sly punning on 'nobles' seems to point towards an understanding of the slippery nature of word and meaning and the increasingly constructed status of the coin. If correct, this paves the way for *The Roaring Girl*'s more knowing presentation of the workings of the counterfeit economy; in which coins, false and legitimate, are deployed as weapons, and the law itself is exposed as inadequate and even corrupt. The dislocation of sign and meaning that so troubles the characters of *The Roaring Girl* turns out to be far less threatening than they assume, and the play's treatment of its two 'Molls' provides an active illustration of the way in which the value of coin manifests itself only in context: 'I see the brightness of thy worth appear' (11.98). Equally, *A Chaste Maid* delivers a picture of a self-contained and self-perpetuating monetary system that operates almost entirely via 'false' coin – illegitimate babies, illicit flesh, contented cuckolds – and normalises it as a picture of everyday life on the City of London's main thoroughfare. The play resists our attempts to read its moral universe, much as coining frustrates the efforts of those commentators who seek to impose a moral paradigm upon it.

Even as they delight in the possibilities of coining as metaphor, in their various ways, *The Revenger's Tragedy*, *A Chaste Maid* and *The Roaring Girl* all interrogate counterfeiting in an attempt to explore what sort of offence it is. They do so in terms of the rhetoric propounded by state and sermon, the 'thief-whore' paradigm, and in so doing expose the constructed nature of that discourse. In the case of *The Roaring Girl* in particular, the play's comedic momentum plays out against a more sinister backdrop, in which the consciousness of inequitable and unjustified punishment is key: 'all hangs well, and may she hang too/ That sight would please me' (8.36-7). This recalls us to the instances of capital sanction in *The Revenger's Tragedy*, where 'the Duke/Must have his pleasure' (III.iv.51–2). Moreover, by the very fact of dramatic representation, these plays humanise coining as a crime, exposing the broad complicity required to sustain it, and encouraging a recognition of that complicity via the audience's participation in a lexicon of financial puns and oblique metaphor. As such they exist in complex relation to the reality of coining as a prosecuted offence.

An 'unfixed evil': Prosecuting Counterfeits

As we have seen, much early seventeenth-century drama evinces a preoccupation with counterfeit coin as metaphor and indeed, in *The Roaring Girl*, as plot device. From Middleton's counterfeit ladies and slippery Molls to Jonson's corrupt goldsmiths, it is clear that urban society understood the penalty associated with crimes against the coin. It is also clear from these texts, however, that the experience of false coin was part of the fabric of the everyday. Although Middleton's goldsmith does not mint his own coin, he is alert to the possibility of being 'cozened' by customers who do, while Sir Alexander apparently has ready access to 'marked' angels with which to entrap Moll Cutpurse. The unremarkable nature of these instances within their respective plays suggests that a contemporary theatre audience might also have had some experience, direct or otherwise, of the consequences of the trade in false currency. In this section I will consider how the discourses around coining functioned during the process of prosecution and how this might further reflect the ambiguous status of the offence in both the popular and the legal imagination.

How were these crimes prosecuted in the courts? Where the language of counterfeiting was a part of the vocabulary of trade, then the full rhetoric of the law needed to be brought to bear in justifying it as a crime. As noted, it is often at the point of conviction that 'coining' becomes 'treason' in the language of the courts, suggesting a felt need to 'create' the offence as part of the legal process. Much of this seems bound up with the need to differentiate the activities of those on trial from the experience of the general public. As such, I would argue, coining cases occupy a peculiar place in relation to the didactic objectives of crime reporting in the period. By their nature, early modern case reports worked to achieve a functional balance between deterrence (implying some level of identification with the accused, even at a very basic heuristic level) and a more sensational 'criminalisation' (implying a distancing from those on trial, and justifying their punishment). In cases of coining and clipping this balance could be problematised by three factors. First was the gravity of the treason designation, which required a presentation of these crimes as somehow extraordinary. Secondly, as we have seen, the ubiquity and acceptance of coinage offences at every level of society necessitated further differentiation; for if everyone was implicated, who were the traitors? The final factor lay in the technical reality of these crimes. Essentially, coining was a – generally very accurate – simulacrum of a wholly legitimate process and, as such, the boundaries of legality could become blurred.[68] Despite the very real horror of the prescribed sanctions, then, achieving a clear rhetoric of wrongdoing was problematic, and strategies of exemplarity were repeatedly compromised.

Unfortunately, we have access to few detailed accounts of trials in the early 1600s, although indictments and assize calendars provide useful evidence. At the Croydon assizes in March 1619, a tailor, William Greene 'of St Olave, Southwark', was charged with using 'ammonia and other liquids' to scale ('wash') gold coin.[69] Greene's crime, conducted alone, was attempted, the indictment reads, 'for wicked Lucre and gain'. As we have seen, this latter phrase came from the terminology of the 1562 Act, and as such it fulfilled its purpose.[70] The assertion of 'wickedness' seems to figure Greene's activities as more than merely criminal, creating an association with more illicit practices. Central to this association was the notion that even legitimate production of coin was somehow intrinsically transformative and powerful, combining as it did the innate value of precious metal with the authority conferred by the monarch's imprint. Yet it is also based in historical fact: the notorious medium and alchemist Edward Kelly was convicted of coining in 1580, and, during the prosecution of the Mint worker Mestrell, the accused testified to his links with a London alchemist.[71] Ben Jonson's *The Alchemist* contains specific references to 'laund'ring' and 'barbing' gold (I.i. 114) and specifically associates these activities not only with alchemy, but with the 'statute of sorcery, *tricesmo, tertio*/Of Harry the Eight' (I.i.112–13).[72] This was a strategy with complex implications: if the practice of counterfeiting – a process that, to all intents and purposes, mimicked the production of coin by state-sanctioned mints – was to be positioned on the borders of sacrilege, where did that place legitimate coining?

As the century progresses, fuller reports become available, particularly from the criminal court at the Old Bailey. In such transcripts, we see further development of the strategies of differentiation noted above. The following report of the sessions from 1679 contains some particularly suggestive language, describing:

> the Tryals of two most notorious Coiners and Clippers of Money; . . . were found guilty of two Indictments of High-Treason apiece; and indeed, 'tis believed, they have not equals in that wicked Mistery in England . . . they had an Art to make a Nine-pence or Groat just new made, look as if it had been

Coined these hundred years ... Their Instruments likewise, mixt Mettals, and other Utensils taken in their respective Lodgings were publickly shown. They were both of a Gang, and confessed they had for some years been concerned in such practises.[73]

The discourses of sin here are multiple and allude directly to those other capital offences that Gaskill has termed 'horror crimes': the coiners are 'notorious', a term elsewhere used to describe those convicted of particularly sensational murders; their trade is a 'wicked mistery', a tainted rewriting of the term used by contemporary guilds to describe their craft. The coiners' 'Instruments' are displayed 'publickly'; all is suggestive of dark and shameful 'practises' brought to light.

What is also notable is the report's insistence on the defendants' membership of a 'Gang'. Aside from some key cases outside of London, the majority of seventeenth-century prosecutions were for groups of two or three defendants.[74] Yet the creation of a discourse of gangs had a number of uses. Most obviously it helped to inflate the threat of coining to the public, suggesting that this crime operated on a scale far beyond its own day-to-day experience of clipped and worn specie. It served to complicate any idea that coiners were simply performing a public service by increasing the number of coins in circulation. However, such rhetoric was also potentially counterproductive. Even as it sought to justify the treason sanction, it risked undermining its own deterrent value; inviting detachment by demonising the coiner to a degree that prevented the observer from drawing any parallel with his or her own activities. This is a strategy completely opposite to that of contemporary drama, where coining, literal and metaphorical, is presented as wholly inclusive – all characters are active or complicit in these crimes.

The polemic of trial proceedings was aimed not only at the reading public, but also at the jury itself, and this is one area of criminal prosecution, like theft, where we see juror agency at work. Coining trials were sometimes disrupted by jurors' refusals to convict: Gaskill cites a 1605 example of a case moved from Salisbury to London for fear of the likely 'pity' of a local jury, as well as a late seventeenth-century case where 'a jury of matrons appointed to search the female members of a counterfeiting gang ... concluded that all seven were pregnant ... and therefore worthy of reprieve'.[75] Fleetwood acknowledges the causes of such hesitancy, the 'soft pernicious tenderness' amongst jurors, whose:

> pity arises from hence, that we see men going to suffer death for a crime, by which we know of none that are undone, or greatly injured; the evil is unfixed, and undetermined, and we cannot put ourselves into their condition who are hurt by these offenders.[76]

If juries were often troubled by their requirement to convict on capital charges, at times such partiality could extend to the permanent officers of the law. The records of the Chelmsford assizes for March 1607 offer a case in point: a charge against one Stephen Asheby, a gentleman, who had been committed to Colchester gaol on suspicion of having clipped 'gold worth 2s 6d'.[77] Six days before the assizes, however, Asheby 'broke out of the gaol and escaped'. The court subsequently recorded him as 'Dead'. Later in the same proceedings, however, 'Francis Cloyse, yoman keeper of Colchester gaol' was indicted for 'felonious escape' in relation to Asheby's case, whilst a labourer, Peter Blackwell, was charged with having 'rescued' Asheby from gaol. Both charges were dropped for lack of evidence, but Cloyse was later fined £5 for 'negligent escape'. We cannot know whether Cloyse was moved to assist Asheby out of sympathy or for financial gain, but if the former he would not be alone. J. S. Cockburn notes that 'on at least one occasion a sheriff acted on his own initiative in postponing the execution of a coiner until his friends had secured a pardon, after their earlier application had been rejected by the assize judges'.[78]

Where coining convictions were secured, it was difficult to locate consistency, or logic, in the application of sanction. As treason, coining was not clergyable, and unlike, say, the prosecution of theft, where the value of the goods obtained would determine the nature of the sentence, there were apparently no technical distinctions applied. So, at the 1650 Maidstone assizes, Thomas Tuthill of Deptford was sentenced to death for coining '150 King Charles half-crowns from base metal', whilst the preceding year, John Virgoe of Sevenoaks had been condemned to the same sentence, by the same court, for the manufacture of a mere '3 halfpence'.[79] Even the particulars of such a death sentence were not consistently applied. Whilst in 1609, the goldsmith Thomas Boswell was sentenced 'to be executed as [a] traitor with all the usual incidents of such an execution', in other cases those 'incidents' might be only partially realised.[80] In 1610, for example, when John Davies and Thomas Carter were convicted of coining, their sentence was to be 'drawn [on hurdles] to the place of execution and hanged'; the grislier elements of the traitor's death were not specified. This phrasing occurs regularly in sessions records in the early seventeenth century. Essentially, this was a punishment for 'petit' rather than high treason – as Edward Coke notes, 'to be drawn and hanged till he be dead, but the forfeiture of his lands'.[81] In fact the question of the degree of punishment for coining – and thereby, implicitly the degree of treason applied to the crime – was debated throughout the century. According to Coke, the application of a partial punishment represented a misunderstanding of the law: 'antient' cases prosecuted under the original statute of 25 Edw. 3, st. 5 might have resulted in a petit treason conviction because that Act 'maketh no expression of the judgement', and so common law practice applied, but cases heard under the later statutes were clearly discussing high treason. So:

> The Abbot of Missenden [prosecuted under the 1352 Act] for counterfeiting ... of the kings money, was adjudged to be drawn and hanged, and not quartered ... But if one be attainted for diminishing of the kings money upon any of the statutes made in Queen Marie's time, or in the time of Queen Elizabeth, because it is High Treason newly made, the offender shall have judgement as in case of High Treason.[82]

'The want of observation of the said distinction hath made some to err in their judgement,' Coke notes.[83] Nonetheless the number of reduced sentences suggests that if this were merely a misinterpretation, it was widely and readily accepted by the judiciary. The question persisted and in 1674 Coke's assessment was challenged by the then Chief Justice Hale, in a King's Bench case in which:

> Three Frenchmen were indicted of Treason, in Coyning and Clipping the Kings Money ... and the Court doubted, whether Judgment for the Clipping should be Drawing, Hanging and Quartering, or Drawing and Hanging only; and having advised with all the Judges at Serjants Inn, they resolved, it should be Drawing and Hanging only ... the Opinion of Coke 3 Inst. 17. is, that a Clipper should be Drawn Hanged and Quartered. But in regard the Statute of 3 H. 5. declared Clipping and Diminishing the Kings Coyn to be within the Statute of the 25 E. 3. which mentions Coyning only; that does not stand repealed by 1 Mar. that leaves all Treasons within the Statute of the 25 E. 5. as they were before, and so 1 Eliz. against Coyning makes not a new Treason. And then, as Hale said, Coyning was esteemed as an inferiour sort of Treason, in comparison of such as concerned the Kings Person ...
> Then there was debate, whether Twisden being the antient Judge or the Chief Justice, should pronounce the Judgment.
> Twisden said, in case of Treason it belonged to the Chief Justice, tho not in Felonies; and that the Lord Foster did it in Sir Henry Vanes Case, in the 13 of this King.
> Hale, Thought the other was to do it; and therefore Twisden gave the Judgment, ut supra; and to avoid scruple, Hale pronounced it over again.[84]

The level of legal and procedural confusion demonstrated here is notable, given that the offences being considered were not uncommon, and the legislation was a hundred years old. Noting Hale's comment that coining had been considered 'an inferiour sort of treason' under Edward III, and its implications for the sentence passed upon the co-accused, it is hard to avoid the inference that that assessment had persisted. Whether we should read this trend as evidence of a tacit acceptance that the punishment of coining offences as treason was problematic per se is unclear; certainly there seems to be a sense in which courts were more comfortable with the notion of an 'inferiour' degree of that crime.

'Treason Justly Rewarded'? Coining in Popular Print

It is difficult to imagine that the severity of punishment in coining cases did not elicit some public sympathy. Tracing that potential sympathy through the archive is more complex, however. No generalised anti-treason polemic seems to survive. We do find individual instances of public support for coiners and clippers – such as the 1662 petition raised by the 'better sort' of Warwickshire attesting to the 'past deportment' of 'several persons suspected of clipping money ... beloved among their neighbours' – but was there a more general viewpoint held on the punishment of coining as treason?[85] Our strongest evidence of public opinion may, in fact, lie in the very lack of popular material surrounding these crimes. Whilst, from the late sixteenth century onwards, the meat of the print trade lay in lurid accounts of trials for murder and witchcraft, similar tales of coiners are uniformly absent. Gaskill suggests that 'public executions of coiners ... did not have the same ideological value because they were not seen as occasions when ordinary people could participate in any obvious victory over Satan'.[86] Equally, however, our consideration of coining in early modern drama might suggest that the practice was just too much a part of the scenery to arouse the type of prurient interest necessary to sustain sales of cheap print.

We must of course apply caution in making assumptions about coining pamphlets – what we have are the textual remnants of a much wider body of work, and the fact that few coining texts survive does not necessarily mean that they did not exist. However, the extant texts generally cluster around the final decades of the seventeenth century and this seems no coincidence. At that time, as England prepared for war with France, the need for good coin became a pressing one. Writing in 1694, for example, John Evelyn noted: 'many executed at London for clipping money, now done to that intolerable extent that there [is] hardly any money that [is] worth above halfe the nominal value'.[87]

Where more detailed works do appear, what we find is strange and disjointed; when coining enters popular print it does not quite conform to the expectations of that mode. The 1674 pamphlet *Treason and Murther Discovered* is an account of the 'tryal & condemnation of James Alsop the father, and William Alsop his son for treason and murder' at the Chelmsford assizes, an unusual case in which the discovery of the chief defendant's clipping activities was made as a result of the murder of his daughter, of which he was also convicted.[88] 'Written by one who was present at the tryal', the pamphlet may owe its existence to the conjunction of clipping with the 'horror crime' of murder, and as such provides a unique opportunity to witness the treatment of the two crimes – so disparate on an affective level, so closely regarded under law – in proximity. Intriguingly, the pamphlet's author pays scant attention to the details of the murder, apparently relishing instead the revelation of the accused's ongoing offence against the coin. His account of legal process in the case suggests that this was also a feature of the trial itself:

> William Alsop, alias Thomas Topham, was called to the Barr, and Two Indictments read against him; The One of Treason for Clipping of Money; The other for Murther. That of Treason to this Effect, That he the said William Alsop ... had Trayterously and Feloniously against the Peace of our Sovereign Lord the King, his Crown and Dignity, with certain Iron Instruments, Sheers, Scissers, and other Tools then and there found, Clipped Filed, and Diminished the Kings Coyn, viz. Fourty pieces of Silver ... commonly called Queen Elizabeths Shillings, and Clipped from off them silver to the value of three pence; Forty other pieces of Silver commonly called King James his Shillings, and Clipped off silver to the value of three pence ... &c.[89]

The murder indictment is all but elided in the text's impetus towards establishing economic treachery.

As it progresses, the pamphlet dwells on the investigation of the clipping offence across more than five of its seven pages. Is the text forced into this structural model by the primacy of treason in the hierarchy of early modern crime? This approach seems generically at odds with what we usually find in popular pamphlets, where the details of murders, particularly domestic murders, are relished above all.[90] In itself, the Alsops' clipping activity does not seem particularly sensational: as a text, *Treason and Murther Discovered* is barely removed from a sessions narrative, and as such it replays the process of trial: evidence is presented by the constable who discovered the crime, a goldsmith who purchased the clippings, and a former servant, who 'lived so near to the Chamber where they were supposed to Clip'. That servant testifies 'that he and his Wife often heard a Tinckling-Noise' coming from his master's room and 'that he had taken severall times Clipped m[o]ny of him for wages, and thought sometimes it looked as if it was but new done'.[91] The servant couple's suspicions are aroused precisely because they have previously encountered such illicit activity:

[H]is Wife and he had often been discoursing about the Noise they heard, and she told her husband, That when she lived in Yorkshire, she lived next to a house where she heard such Noises in the Night, and that afterwards there was a Discovery made of clipping of mony.[92]

Once again, we see the way in which clipping and coining might be a part of day-to-day experience, literally part of the background noise of everyday life.

As in the case reports considered earlier, the focus of exposition is on bringing to light the tools of the trade:

Upon this they make narrower search, and find in a Chamber where Wooll used to be laid up, in the Wooll was hid several Sheers, and a Whetstone with several furrows in it, supposed to be for the smoothing of the money after it was clipped ... and in a Window in one of the Chambers, they found Clippings and Filings, and the Impression of the Tooles, and spyed in a Crevice something glyster, upon which they took up the boards, and there found hanging in the Cobwebs several small Clippings and filings of Silver.[93]

Subha Mukherji has drawn our attention to the 'drama of discovery' that functions within providential crime texts to 'make legible the drama of divine justice which finds a mere instrument in the legal system'.[94] It would appear that *Treason and Murther Discovered* enacts this same dynamic upon the Chelmsford assizes case report. But does this layering of providentialism really fulfil its purpose here? A drama of discovery implies an audience, ready to be impressed by the revelation of evil and the operation of God's law. As we see in drama, the audience for anti-coining propaganda was chiefly composed of those for whom the idea of false or adulterated coin was generally commonplace. The murder charge is surely the real sensation of the text, yet the text itself fights that truth, attempting to contain that crime within the bounds of its 'official' treason discourse.

Perhaps the most fascinating aspect of the text lies in the detail of the punishment of its main offender. Old Alsop, convicted of both murder and clipping, is sentenced to be 'conveyed to Stratford Gaol, and to be drawn upon a Sledge from the same Gaol, to the place of Execution, *which shall be before his own house in West-Ham*; where he is to be hanged upon a Gibbet by the Neck, till his Body be dead'.[95] Again, there is no mention of the full traitor's death here – and yet clearly, by placing the gibbet outside the home of the condemned, the authorities are seeking to create an exemplary scenario. Our inference is that the deterrent possibility of execution for clipping was perceived as best served not by the full and grisly rigour of the law, but by literally 'bringing home' its consequences.

In general, authors of coining pamphlets and ballads struggle with such exemplarity. Unlike the perjury pamphlets we saw in Chapter 1, which operated to overcome the limitations of the law's ability to punish, these texts highlight an opposite but equal problem, depicting a punishment that does not seem to 'fit' its crime. Most extant late seventeenth-century coining ballads eschew individual cases in favour of a focus upon the economic implications of the coinage crisis. *England's Complaint* (1692), for example, is a litany of 'curses' issued upon 'Clippers and Coyners' by those adversely affected by their practices, whilst *The Royal Regulation* (1690s) is little more than a paean to William IV's 1696 Recoinage Act.[96] One text that does engage more directly is the 1678 ballad *The Clipper's Execution, Or, Treason Justly Rewarded*, a work based on the clipping trial of three London women and recording the Smithfield execution of one of those 'as a warning, for all others to avoid the like Dreadful Punishment'.[97] The ballad is oddly generic in tone, however; there is no first-person lament or scaffold speech, the woman at the stake is anonymous and silent, and there is little sense in which the text might function to enable us to identify with this 'wretched sinner' and her 'fall' (3). As such, *The Clipper's Execution* declines to participate in any of the affective and exemplary strategies that characterised contemporary ballads, particularly those with female protagonists.[98] While the defendants in this case are by no means innocent, their crimes are ordinary and their 'wickedness' shared by many – and we might speculate that this means that they cannot be given a voice. As it struggles to achieve exemplarity, *The Clipper's Execution* must needs close down any possibility of the same, lest in so doing it creates a space for identification that destabilises the verdict of treason.

Conclusion

The efforts of the press and the legislature alike consistently failed to provide a deterrent to the counterfeiter, it seems: as the author of a 1696 letter to John Locke noted, in a flurry of mixed metaphor, 'the forbidden fruit was of too luscious a Relish to be so easily relinquished: It was not in the Power of any Paper-spell [legislation] to stop the spreading Gangrene'.[99] Midway through his reign, Charles II authorised the introduction of mechanisation to the Mint, and milled coin became the norm in the latter part of the century. Yet, just as the Mint increased its technical sophistication, so did the coiners, several of whom developed their own machinery and, having invested so substantially in their operations, scaled them up accordingly.[100] In fact, the practices of coining and clipping were to extend forwards, not only through time, but also into new forms of currency and credit. The letter to Locke described contemporary Bank of England Bills as a 'new Species of Clip'd Money', and indeed, the Old Bailey records for 1724 indicate that one Isaak Yewel had been imprisoned for 'a Misdemeanor, in Forging, Counterfeiting, and Attempting to utter' not a half-crown or shilling, but 'a Bill of Exchange'.[101] Despite the apparent leniency afforded Yewel, the treasonable status of counterfeiting under law was not fully revoked until 1861, with the enactment of Queen Victoria's Forgery Act.[102]

Returning to the central question of this work, what conclusions can and should we draw about punishing offences against the coin in the 'neglected' years of the seventeenth century, and what do those conclusions reveal about the link between crime and consequence in that period? Unlike perjury, these are crimes that are not – except in the most oblique terms – conceived of as a sin at this time, and yet they are crimes that are punished in the most extreme manner. The efforts of the state and legislature to close the gap between crime and punishment, to impose a moral, even a biblical paradigm upon the offence, seem as painfully constructed and self-conscious as the attempts of contemporary monarchs to, in Stephen Mead's words, '"command" money to be worth what it used to be'.[103] And examining those trial records that are available, we can conclude that coining, clipping and associated offences were current and were practised, despite the penalties being known. This contradiction seems inherent in the contemporary representation of counterfeiting. Early seventeenth-century drama seems to suggest that coining is a part of the fabric of urban life, a fundamental, sometimes even a dynamic force within social and commercial economies. Drama picks up some of the rhetoric of the establishment's depiction of the offence (the motif of the thief/whore, for example), but suggests little of the moral condemnation associated with that depiction. Nor, ultimately, does it seem to display the anxiety around the disruption of face and intrinsic value that we find in the 'official' discourses of coin; or at least it transmutes that anxiety into other areas of concern. For drama, the idea of the counterfeit is a useful metaphor for a number of arguably more interesting themes – sexual incontinence, the rise of a consumer economics – but the practical reality of counterfeiting is of a crime of mass complicity, a crime in which every audience member might, consciously or unwittingly, have participated. The threat of an arbitrary and disproportionate punishment is undoubtedly present here, yet the only named 'treason' is chiefly a domestic matter, confined to the 'lawful bed'. Such a literary presentation sheds light on why the prosecution of coining as treason might have been problematised by the apparent democracy of the offence.

Turning to the process of the law, we find a further set of strategies at work, specifically targeted at differentiating those on trial, at combating the 'universality' of the offence, but inhibited in this project by that same universality. Efforts to demonise coiners via a rhetoric of dark practises and to rewrite their activities as the sinister doings of malevolent gangs exist in a complex and dysfunctional relationship with deterrence and exemplarity. Although we can perhaps discern some squeamishness amongst juries required to convict on capital charges, the main outcome of such rhetoric seems to be confusion: confusion among the judiciary as to the degree of severity applicable, and bewilderment among those condemned. It is perhaps this confusion that underlies the apparent lack of any impetus to popular protest against the severity of the penal sanctions: a lack matched, as we have seen, by the absence of any meaningful counter-discourse of pamphlet and ballad propaganda around coining at this time. Unlike the lurid tales of perjury we saw in Chapter 1, where the courts failed to convince, there was no satisfying providential narrative to fill the gap.

There were other narratives, however. In the second year of William and Mary's reign an intriguing case was heard in the Court of Common Pleas. This was a defamation suit, an 'action for words spoken':

> IN an Action for Words spoken of the *Plaintiff* in saying; *He was a Clipper and Coiner.*
>
> After *Verdict*, upon *Not guilty*, pleaded, it was moved in Arrest of *Judgment*, that the Words did not charge him with *Clipping and Coining of Money*; and *Clipping and Coining* might be apply'd to many other things.
>
> But the *Court* held the Words to be Actionable in regard of the strong Intendment.[104]

Despite the decision of the court in this case, our exploration of the punishment of early modern coining would seem to support the defendant's contention that '*Clipping and Coining* might be apply'd to many other things'. What this reference seems to reinforce, deliberately or otherwise, is coining as a uniquely participatory crime; because of the dynamic of circulation required, but also because there existed a high level of awareness of and involvement in the discourse of counterfeits. In the end, it seems, all those who discuss false coin, whether in legal comment, drama, sermon or pamphlet, are engaged in the creation of metaphor.

Notes

1. Dekker and Middleton, *The Roaring Girl*, in James Knowles (ed.), *The Roaring Girl and Other City Comedies*.
2. Middlesex Sessions Rolls: 1610, in Jeaffreson (ed.), *Middlesex county records: Volume 2*, pp. 58–70; Cockburn (ed.), *Calendar of Assize Records: Essex Indictments*, March 1610, 35/52/1, 502.
3. Cormack, *A Power to Do Justice*, p. 294.
4. Gaskill, *Crime and Mentalities*, p. 124.
5. Macfarlane, *The Justice and the Mare's Ale*; Styles, '"Our traitorous money-makers"'.
6. Dekker and Webster, *Westward Ho*, II.i.174–7, and *Northward Ho*, I.ii.81–3, in Bowers (ed.), *Dramatic Works of Thomas Dekker*.
7. It would be difficult to claim that these records are fully representative: the incidence of coining cases in seventeenth-century England was often geographically determined. Nonetheless they do represent legal proceedings contemporaneous and proximate to the plays in my study.
8. 5 Eliz. 1, c. 11.
9. See Craig, *The Mint*. Of these offences, only uttering was not capital.
10. Forman, 'Marked Angels', p. 1538.
11. See Bakewell (ed.), *Mines of Silver and Gold in the Americas*; Newman, '"Goldsmith's ware"'; and Wordie, 'Deflationary factors in the Tudor Price Rise'.
12. 25 Edw. 3, st. 5, c. 2.
13. 4 Hen. 5 st. 2, c. 5; 1 & 2 Ph. & M. c. 10.
14. Simon Wrotham notes: 'Debasement served to cheapen the manufacture of coins. It therefore enabled reductions in state spending on coinage or allowed the government to mint more money.' 'Sovereign Counterfeits: The Trial of the Pyx', p. 340.
15. Tawney and Power (eds), *Tudor Economic Documents*, vol. 2, pp. 146–7.
16. 5 Eliz. 1, c. 11.
17. Fulbecke, *A parallele or conference*, p. 3.
18. 14 Eliz. 1, c. 3; 18 Eliz. 1, c. 1; Gaskell, *Crime and Mentalities*, p. 126.
19. Muldrew, *The Economy of Obligation*, p. 100.
20. Challis, *The Tudor Coinage*, pp. 201–2.
21. 'A Proclamation for Coynes', in Larkin and Hughes (eds), *Stuart Royal Proclamations, Volume I*, pp. 99–103.
22. 'A Proclamation against Exportation of Gold and Silver', in ibid. p. 336.
23. Proclamation 'Calling in Last Base Coins by 20 July', in Hughes and Larkin (eds), *Tudor Royal Proclamations, Volume II*, pp. 169–70.
24. Holinshed, *Chronicles*, vol. 4, pp. 203–4.
25. Middlesex Sessions Rolls, July 1605, in Jeaffreson, *Middlesex county records: Volume 2*, pp. 10–15.
26. Fulbecke, *A parallele or conference*, p. 85; *Ordinary of Newgate's Account*, 5 July 1721, OBP Online (last accessed 20 June 2019) (OA17210705).
27. Coke, *Third Part of the Institutes*, p. 17 (my emphasis).
28. See Gaskill, *Crime and Mentalities*, p. 159.
29. See below discussions of *The Revenger's Tragedy* and *Eastward Hoe*.

30. Later in the seventeenth century, 'slipp' is also used to describe the metal filings of a grindstone, linking the idea of clippings and false coin: *OED Online* (last accessed 12 May 2019).
31. Gaskill, *Crime and Mentalities*, pp. 127–8.
32. Mead, '"Thou art chang'd"', p. 243.
33. This is not absolutely universal: see e.g. the William Alsop case discussed below.
34. Fleetwood, *A Sermon against clipping*, p. 6.
35. Carey, 'Donne and Coins', p. 153.
36. Sullivan, *The Rhetoric of Credit*, p. 78.
37. Challis, 'Spanish Bullion', p. 383; 'A Proclamation for making currant certain French Coyne', in Larkin (ed.), *Stuart Royal Proclamations, Volume II*, pp. 54–6.
38. Middleton, *A Chaste Maid in Cheapside*, IV.iii.19, 21.
39. Cockburn (ed.), *Calendar of Assize Records: Kent Indictments*, 16 March 1618, 35/60/7, p. 782.
40. Vaughan, *A Discourse of Coin and Coinage*, p. 45; *Athenian Mercury*, 1 July 1693, p. 2.
41. Fleetwood, *A Sermon against clipping*, p. 24.
42. 18 Eliz. 1, c. 1, Preamble.
43. Donne, *Sermon Preached upon Candlemas Day, 1623*, p. 313.
44. See Gaskill, *Crime and Mentalities*, p. 139.
45. Tailors were particularly numerous among the accused, presumably due to ready access to useful equipment. See e.g. William Bridden, tailor, who 'clipped with shears 4 King James shillings'; Cockburn (ed.), *Calendar of Assize Records: Sussex Indictments*, 23 February 1618, 35/60/5, 455.
46. Middlesex Sessions Rolls: 1610 and 1616, in Jeaffreson, *Middlesex county records: Volume 2*, pp. 58–70, pp. 119–26.
47. *Calendar of State Papers Domestic* [hereafter 'CSPD']: *Charles II, 1661–62*, p. 581.
48. Milligan, 'Counterfeiters and Coin-clippers', p. 102.
49. See the case of 'Mr Swallow', disgraced clerk of the irons, in *CSPD: Charles II, 1660–1*, p. 10.
50. See Feavearyear, *The Pound Sterling*, p. 94.
51. *Laconics*, p. 109.
52. Donne, 'The Bracelet', ll. 27–8.
53. Fleetwood, *A Sermon against clipping*, p. 25.
54. Parker, *The Holy Byble*, Matthew 22:21.
55. Middleton, *The Revenger's Tragedy*, V.iii.122–3.
56. Neill, 'Bastardy, Counterfeiting and Misogyny', pp. 399, 405.
57. Dunne, *Shakespeare, Revenge Tragedy and Early Modern Law*, p. 143.
58. Baker, 'Criminal Justice at Newgate', p. 316.
59. *CSPD: Charles II, 1661–62*, p. 580.
60. Chapman, Jonson and Marston, *Eastward Hoe*, IV.i.205–7.
61. Manningham, *The Diary of John Manningham*, p. 15.
62. Middlesex Sessions Rolls, November 1609: Jeaffreson, *Middlesex county records: Volume 2*, pp. 47–58.
63. Griffiths, 'Politics made visible', p. 179.
64. Newman, '"Goldsmith's ware"', p. 98. The *Oxford English Dictionary*

records this usage from the fifteenth century onwards: *OED Online* <http://www.oed.com>(last accessed 12 May 2019).
65. Arthur Kinney (ed.), *Renaissance Drama*, p. 593.
66. Middleton, *The Revenger's Tragedy*, I.i.8.
67. Brentford, where children were often sent out to nurse.
68. Styles notes that the coiners of the Yorkshire 'yellow trade' felt that their labour was 'honourable' because they made new coin wholly from gold clippings without adulteration: Styles, '"Our traitorous money-makers"', p. 211.
69. Cockburn (ed.), *Calendar of Assize Records: Surrey Indictments*, 3 March 1619, 35/61/6.
70. See n. 17 above.
71. Milligan, 'Counterfeiters and Coin-clippers', pp. 101–2.
72. Jonson, *The Alchemist*, I.i.111–14.
73. *The narrative of the sessions, February 26, 1678/9*, p. 6.
74. See Macfarlane and Styles for examples of larger-scale coining and clipping operations in Lancashire and Yorkshire. The rhetoric of legitimacy surrounding these cases is noteworthy; chief coiners were known as 'mint masters' and, Styles notes, 'provided a commission coining service for those who clipped independently, and instruction in how to clip for the uninitiated'; Styles, '"Our traitorous money-makers"', p. 196.
75. Gaskill, *Crime and Mentalities*, pp. 154, 153.
76. Fleetwood, *A Sermon against clipping*, pp. 11, 21.
77. Cockburn (ed.), *Calendar of Assize Records: Essex*, 23 March 1607, 35/49/1.
78. Cockburn, *A History of English Assizes*, p. 130.
79. Cockburn (ed.), *Calendar of Assize Records: Kent*, 26 March 1650, 35/91/2 and 10 July 1649, 35/90/4.
80. Middlesex Sessions Rolls: 1609. Jeaffreson, *Middlesex county records: Volume 2*, pp. 47–58.
81. Coke, *Institutes*, p. 17. Coke notes that 'a woman in that case was [still] to be burnt'.
82. Ibid. p. 17.
83. Ibid.
84. Ventris, *The reports of Sir Peyton Ventris Kt.*, p. 254.
85. *CSPD: Elizabeth, 1581–90* (London: 1865), p. 391; *CSPD: Charles II, 1664–65* (London: 1863), p. 214.
86. Gaskill, *Crime and Mentalities*, p. 128.
87. Quoted in Milligan, 'Counterfeiters and Coin-clippers', p. 104.
88. *Treason and murther discovered*.
89. Ibid. p. 3.
90. See, e.g., Dolan, *Dangerous Familiars*.
91. *Treason and Murther Discovered*, p. 5.
92. Ibid. p. 6.
93. Ibid. p. 5.
94. Mukherji, *Law and Representation*, pp. 110–11.
95. *Treason and Murther Discovered*, p. 5 (my emphasis).
96. *England's Complaint* and *The Royal Regulation*.
97. *The Clipper's Execution*, preamble.

98. See Smith, 'A "goodly sample"'; Clark, *Women and Crime in the Street Literature of Early Modern England.*
99. *A Review of the Universal Remedy for all Diseases Incident to Coin,* pp. 18–19.
100. See Gaskill, *Crime and Mentalities*, p. 145.
101. *A Review of the Universal Remedy*, p. 53. January 1724, *OBP Online* (last accessed 20 June 2019) (t17240117-68).
102. 24 & 25 Vict., c. 98.
103. Mead, '"Thou art chang'd"', p. 243.
104. Ventris, *The reports of Sir Peyton Ventris Kt.*, p. 360.

Chapter 3

'The Woman's *Case* put to the Lawyers': Miscarriage of Justice and the Case of Anne Greene

Or rather Justice, with it selfe at strife
Judg'd the Wench worthy both of death and life.[1]

In 1651, Thomas Arthur, a commoner at Christ Church, Oxford, penned the above couplet in a poem for the second edition of a pamphlet discussing the celebrated Anne Greene case, then the talk of the University.

Greene, an unmarried Oxfordshire servant in her early twenties, had been condemned and hanged in the city the preceding December for the murder of her newborn child, a child fathered by the teenage grandson of her employer and subsequent prosecutor, Sir Thomas Read. Her body, having been cut down from the gallows, was transported in its coffin to the house of John Clarke, a local apothecary, whose home was the venue for regular meetings of men of science from across the University. There it was to be dissected as part of an anatomy demonstration with accompanying lecture by Dr William Petty, the University Reader in that subject. When her coffin was opened, however, Greene was seen to be breathing, and over the next few days she was nursed back to health by the very doctors who were to have anatomised her corpse.

Greene's survival was widely interpreted as a providential revelation of her innocence, 'a contrary verdict from heaven', and a petition was raised for her pardon, supported by her doctors and representatives from across the University – and funded by the donations of the 'multitudes that flocked . . . daily to see her' on her sickbed.[2] A review of the facts of her case revealed that the child she had been convicted of murdering had almost certainly been miscarried or stillborn, delivered 'near the fourth month of her time . . . not above a span long'.[3]

Greene's case provoked a significant outpouring of interest, both locally in Oxford and in the capital. It was immediately reported in that week's edition of the London newssheet *Mercurius Politicus*, and apparently inspired so much interest that a 'further Accompt' appeared on 9 January of the following year, with the editorial comment: 'we hope there will come forth a more full and entire relation of her [Greene's] Tryall, Sufferings, &c., to the end that this great work of God may be as fully and truly known'.[4] Once she had fully recovered, 'being able to walk about the town', Greene, her reprieve obtained, departed from the scene of her resuscitation and returned to the country.[5] She went on to marry and have three children, dying almost a decade after the execution of her sentence.[6] Her afterlife as text, by contrast, was remarkable. Her story was widely referenced throughout the second half of the century, in James Heath's *Brief Chronicle of the Intestine War* (1676), for example, as an occurrence 'very fit to be transmitted to posterity'; in John Evelyn's diary for 1675; and in Robert Plot's *Natural History of Oxfordshire* (1677).[7] It continued to be debated well into the next, appearing in John Ward's *Lives of the Professors of Gresham College* (1740) and in multiple editions of William Derham's *Physico-Theology*, where the event is described as 'still well remembered among the seniors' at Oxford.[8] The story of a twenty-two-year-old maid from the village of Steeple Barton in Oxfordshire, 'of a middle stature . . . and an indifferent good feature', not only captured the imagination of her contemporaries, it seemed, but continued to resonate.[9]

Of the many retellings of Anne Greene's fate, this chapter focuses on three pamphlet accounts of the case, all appearing in early 1651; two of which, William Burdet's *A Wonder of Wonders* and the anonymous *A Declaration from Oxford*, were issued by the London printer John Clowes, while the third, *Newes from the Dead*, attributed to Richard Watkins, was produced by Leonard Lichfield, official printer to Oxford University.[10] *Newes from the Dead* is the most comprehensive of these works: a two-part document, it contains an account of the case, almost certainly drawn from William Petty's own unpublished notes of the matter, but also a number of dedicatory poems on the topic, written by students and fellows from colleges across Oxford, including a seventeen-year-old Christopher Wren, and, in the second edition, the future antiquary and pamphlet collector Anthony Wood.[11] *Newes from the Dead* was reprinted twice in the eighteenth century, first in *Phoenix Britannicus*, a 1732 collection, and as a separate work in 1741.[12]

While these texts fall broadly into the category described by Tessa Watt and others as 'cheap print'– a genre characterised satirically in its own time as 'waste paper' – in this chapter I will suggest that they have status as evidence, both literary and legal.[13] Following scholars including Laura Gowing, Alexandra Walsham and Subha Mukherji, all of whom have evaluated the evidentiary possibilities – and the limitations – of such artefacts, this chapter reads pamphlets for traces of legal process, as well as for evidence of their readers' interpretative strategies.[14] As David Stymeist notes of another seventeenth-century infanticide pamphlet (1609's *The Bloudy Mother*), such texts '[employ] basic forensic procedures of gathering physical evidence [and] providing witness depositions'.[15] The relationship between cheap print and what we might perceive as a contemporary academic or elite culture is more complex than it first appears. As Alexandra Walsham notes:

> The very fact that we owe the preservation of most sixteenth and seventeenth-century ephemera to noble and gentlemen bibliophiles like John Selden, Anthony Wood, Samuel Pepys and Robert Harley testifies to the existence of an avid, or at least casual, audience among the affluent and educated... Such printed wares clearly reached a heterogeneous cross-section of English society, a society upon which it may be premature to superimpose any rigid class divide and in which cultural fissures and splits ran along vertical as well as horizontal fault-lines.[16]

On a practical level, noting the dearth of detailed records of early modern trials, Alan Macfarlane has termed pamphlets 'a vital and reliable source, providing otherwise inaccessible material, and correcting the somewhat narrow impression of ... prosecutions provided by indictments'.[17] As lists of seventeenth-century indictments usually exist independently of any record of verdicts or gaol delivery, in some instances a pamphlet is our only evidence that an individual was actually convicted in a particular trial. Undoubtedly, this is a consideration in the Greene case, where no official court record survives. Finally, as we have seen in the perjury pamphlets of Chapter 1, such works can function as a supplement to the omissions or limitations of justice; in the case of Anne Greene their very generic indeterminacy provides valuable insight into the law's ability to determine the 'truth' of a particular set of facts.

The first two chapters of this study have considered the degree to which a perceived 'gap' between crime and sanction was acknowledged, challenged or represented within wider cultural discourses. The Greene case moves a step further, offering an opportunity to investigate how a specific act of wrongful punishment, and the simultaneous undoing of that act, exposes concerns about verdicts and their consequences. To that end, this chapter interrogates the image offered by Thomas Arthur, of 'Justice, with it selfe at strife' and asks why a concern about the uneasy relation between law and justice seems to underlie much of the public response to the incident. The model of participatory justice, discussed in the Introduction to this book, has particular bearing here, as do the questions it raises.[18] How far does communal participation in justice equate to communal responsibility for sanction? Unlike perjury or counterfeiting, the felony status of infanticide and its consequent capital sanction was indisputable; yet Greene's experience and the texts that surround it seem to suggest a high level of anxiety around the consequences of a guilty verdict. In order to illuminate this anxiety, this chapter examines the legislative dialogue surrounding the status of infanticide in the mid-seventeenth century, the problems of definition that compromised prosecution and the competing discourses of moral proscription and medical advance that might influence the decision of the court. It further suggests some of the ways in which a miscarriage of justice is a particularly useful tool in exposing and understanding these discourses. Finally, it considers a number of other cases that exist in unique relation to Greene's, exploring what Frances Dolan terms 'the capacity of stories to be actors' and asking how that active role functions when a providential narrative becomes something quite other.[19]

'A Harlot is delivered of an infant': the 1624 Infanticide Act

To fully understand the problematic nature of Greene's case we must consider the specific offence with which she was charged. Infanticide was a crime that underwent a peculiar process of revision in the first half of the seventeenth century. Prior to that date, the law on neonatal murder was at best unclear, and prosecution was difficult.[20] The English situation in this respect stood in stark contrast to that of continental Europe, where conviction figures for infanticide were robust, and growing year on year. In early modern Europe, of course, criminal prosecutions were governed by processes of investigation based on the inquisitorial methods of Roman and canon law.[21] Ascertaining the facts of a case was a professional function performed by judges, who adhered closely to theories of proof in which varying types of evidence were rated, and the verdict rigorously computed. The lynchpin of the English legal system, by contrast, was the jury, a panel of laymen, and English law very clearly distinguished between the judge as the arbiter of law and the jurors as finders of fact – as Francis Bacon commented, English law 'leaveth the discerning and credit of testimony wholly to the juries' consciences and understanding'.[22] This would have mattered less had jurors in infanticide cases had any kind of clarity on the rules of proof they were to follow. But prior to the 1620s, such cases were tried under English common-law rules of evidence, which required that it be proven that the child in question had been born alive. An unborn child had no identity as victim in law – as Gowing comments, such infants were 'still part of the mother; they were not, yet, separate legal subjects who could be injured'.[23] The difficulty of proving that the child had ever been alive made prosecution very difficult and this problem was self-perpetuating, for without convictions there was little case law, no precedent to inform a jury's decision. In Europe, by contrast, such prosecutions were, from 1532 at least, governed by the edicts of the Carolina Code, the Holy Roman Empire's legislative provision for criminal law. Carolina offered detailed scenario-based guidelines on the physical and medical proofs required for conviction, for example:

> [when] the baby was killed only such a short time before the milk in the breasts of the mother has not yet gone away, then she may be milked in the breasts; and when mother's milk is found in the breasts, there is in consequence a strong presumption for the use of examination.[24]

As Catherine Crawford notes, 'whereas the English standard of proof was that jurors should be persuaded in their "consciences", the European idea was that proof should be "as clear as the sun at noon"'.[25] Prosecuting infanticide in England, it seems, could be a flawed and inconclusive project, and, as we will see, this had implications both for the evolution of the offence under law and for a wider understanding of the crime.

All this began to change in the late sixteenth century: Peter C. Hoffer and N. E. H. Hull, for example, note a '225 percent jump in cases after 1576'.[26] They link this to a growing focus on the concealment of infant death as a signifier of guilt. This association was made explicit for the first time in 1584, when an edition of Anthony Fitzherbert's manual for justices, *L'Office et Auctorite de Justices de Peace*, included a new precedent:

> A Harlot is delivered of an infant, which she puts alive in an orchard, and covers with leaves; and a kite strikes him with its talons, from which the infant shortly dies, and she is arraigned for murder, and is executed.[27]

The implication was clear; the 'Harlot' of the case note had caused her child's death not merely by abandoning him, but by concealing him, presumably to avoid disgrace and possible punishment under the poor laws.[28] It was not a great leap therefore to conclude, providentially, that it was her original 'sin', the child's illegitimate conception, which had directly caused the greater crime of its murder. The precedent, and the rulings subsequently based upon it, crystallised a dual concern in the Reformed period – about women who concealed their unlawful sexual activity (particularly poor, itinerant maidservants like Anne Greene), and about the moral and economic cost of that activity. Certainly there is evidence for this: Bills dealing with the murder of newborns were brought – albeit unsuccessfully – in the Commons in 1607 and 1610, in the same period that the 1609 Poor Law was being heard, a statute in which bastardy was described as a 'great charge' to the country.[29] It seemed that the law was striving to punish a crime it had itself in part created.

Yet alongside this complex socio-economic imperative, we also witness the fulfilment of a legal need, which the direction on concealment offered. If the dictat that concealment created a strong presumption of guilt was followed logically, then it obviated to a great extent all the awkward uncertainty around proving infanticides, circumventing the necessity to codify the complex physical proofs previously required for conviction. We might speculate that concealment as a precept was in a legal sense very attractive. Sure enough, in 1624 the concealment reasoning was made explicit in statute form. The text of 21 James I, c. 27 runs thus:

> An Act to prevent the destroying and murthering of bastard children.
> WHEREAS, many lewd women that have been delivered of bastard children, to avoid their shame, and to escape punishment, do secretly bury or conceal the death of their children, and after, if the child be found dead, the said women do allege, that the said child was born dead; whereas it falleth out sometimes (although hardly it is to be proved) that the said child or children were murthered by the said women . . .
> II . . . be it enacted by the authority of this present parliament, That if any woman . . . be delivered of any issue of her body, male or female, which being born alive, should by the laws of this realm be a bastard, and that she endeavour privately either by drowning, or secret burying thereof, as that it may not come to light, whether it were born alive or not, but be concealed: in every such case the said mother so offending shall suffer death as in case of murther, except such mother can make proof by one witness at the least that the child . . . was born dead.[30]

The Act was clear; it targeted only the mothers of 'bastard children', constructing them specifically as 'lewd women', establishing an immediate position of censure. Crucially, it shifted the onus of the evidentiary problem onto the accused, who would 'suffer death' unless she could prove 'by one witness at least' that the child was born dead. Suddenly, a neat chain of assumption was made available to the jury: the unwed mother was a 'lewd' and sinful woman; she would naturally be secretive in regard to her sexual transgressions; that very secrecy both practically and psychologically codified her moral turpitude and her responsibility for her child's death. Essentially it was now a capital offence to conceal the death of an illegitimate newborn, regardless of whether the child had suffered any malicious action. That this legislative elision of extramarital sexual activity with murderous intent had been shaped by a Parliamentary Committee dominated by Puritan party leaders seems unsurprising – Francis Barrington, George Moore and William Lytton were all prominent members of the working party for the Act, and as Hoffer and Hull comment, 'Puritan participation in this committee was equalled only by their interest in Sabbath day laws.'[31]

The 1624 Act thus created a clear route for a jury's deliberation and, as a result, numbers of prosecutions grew. Gowing records 'seventy cases of neonatal infanticide tried at the Northern Circuit Assizes, between 1642 and 1680', for example, and Hoffer and Hull point out that, in Essex, 'for the 12-year span between 1610 and 1622, three unwed mothers were prosecuted for the death of their newborns, compared to 13 in the 12 years from 1625 to 1637'.[32] In their study of the Court of Great Sessions at Chester, J. R. Dickinson and J. A. Sharpe indicate that this continued in the second half of the seventeenth century, with sixty-three cases being heard between 1650 and 1699.[33] A record of a prosecution does not necessarily equate to a conviction – Garthine Walker, for example, has argued against claims of the severity of the Act, pointing out that conviction rates, although high, did not in total represent 'vast numbers of successful prosecutions' – but nonetheless it seems that rates of implementation of capital sentences were high.[34] Mark Jackson notes that:

> In the middle decades of the seventeenth century, when the 1624 statute was much used, a high proportion of women accused of murdering their newborn children were convicted and hanged. In Essex, between 1620 and 1680, over 40 per cent of accused women were hanged for the crime, a figure well in excess of both execution and conviction rates for general homicide in the same courts.[35]

Certainly, post-1624, excerpts from the Act would regularly be included in coroners' reports and in indictments of suspected infanticides; and the jury would repeatedly be reminded of the illegitimacy of the children involved, as a direction that this permitted them to deliberate the facts under the auspices of the new law.[36]

'Let not good lives with shame be sold': Contemporary Print Culture

Even to the modern reader Anne Greene's story is powerfully dramatic, with its two compelling motifs of reversal – the false conviction for infanticide and the miraculous return from death by hanging, the latter thrown into further relief by the sinister promise of the anatomist's knife. It seems an almost perfect hybrid of the moralised news reporting associated with the murder pamphlet and a providential discourse of signs and wonders. Yet it sits uneasily with either generic mode and, before we turn to the reporting of Greene's case, it may be productive to explore this disjunction with reference to contemporary print culture.

'Miraculous' tales of escape from hanging were not unknown. As Theresa Murphy and Peter Linebaugh, among others, have demonstrated, botched hangings were a relatively frequent corollary of the state execution system and their interpretation as miraculous phenomena was part of a long tradition.[37] In 1605, for example, Edward Alde of London had printed the story of John Johnston of Antwerp, erroneously convicted of robbery and hanged, but 'miraculously preserved' by God, so that after five days on the gallows he was still alive and able to plead his own cause.[38] As a miraculous feat, Greene's experience rather pales by comparison. Alde's pamphlet ends with the pardoning of Johnston and the conviction of the true offender who, having witnessed the miracle of Johnston's recovery, is moved to confess that he 'had wrongfully accused that youth of those felonies which he himselfe had committed'.[39]

Equally, seventeenth-century readers of pamphlet accounts of infanticides (or 'newborn child murder' – for, as Mark Jackson reminds us, the term used today was not current in the seventeenth century) were inured to, and indeed expected, far more lurid fare than the accounts of Greene's stillborn child could provide.[40] As Susan Staub comments, 'the figure of the murdering mother appears repeatedly in early modern dramas, broadsheets and news pamphlets' – but she is often a figure quite other than the 'poore wench' Anne Greene.[41] In 1637, for example, Henry Goodcole had published *Nature's Cruell Step-Dames, or Matchlesse Monsters of the Female Sex*, an account of the crimes of Elizabeth Barnes, who slit her child's throat under the influence of Satan, and of Anne Willis, who threw her newborn child into a vault to die.[42] In 1647, three years before the Greene case, the sensational pamphlet *Bloody Newes from Dover* told the story of Mary Champion, who decapitated her child during a dispute with her husband about the baby's baptism.[43] The simple fact of an infanticide conviction was rarely a subject for literary transformation; as Frances Dolan notes: 'pamphlets, ballads, and plays tend to ignore infanticide as the statutes defined it – as if there is not much of a story in it'.[44] Where there is a story, at first glance it appears to be a very tightly structured tale. Two extant seventeenth-century ballads offer us accounts of acts of infanticide that are in many respects very similar to Greene's alleged crime.

Both texts are first-person complaints and run on a common theme. The first is 'Martha Scambler's Repentance', published in 1614 as part of a pamphlet entitled *Deeds against nature and Monsters by kinde*.[45] Martha, described as a 'lascivious young damsell', is condemned to die at Tyburn for smothering her newborn child and concealing his body in order to preserve herself from the scandal of his illegitimacy.[46] Her lament comprises a rueful and heavily moralised examination of her former 'follies', and deploys the type of 'dehumanising animal imagery' that Randall Martin has found to be typical in early seventeenth-century infanticide texts:

> The Babe being borne and in my armes,
> I should have kept it from all harmes,
> But like a Beare or Woolfe in wood,
> I with it smothered up in blood.
> Whereat strange motions without feare,
> From hell to me presented were
> And bade me bury it in a Vault,
> For none alive did know my fault.[47]

The second work, *No Naturall Mother but a Monster*, a ballad attributed to Martin Parker, follows the story of another woman, known only as Besse, hanged in London in December 1633 'for making away her owne new borne childe'.[48] Like Martha, Besse is figured as having strayed from the true path: 'my carriage was too wild/woe is me'.[49] The consequences are inevitable; she is 'got with child' and, the father having abandoned her, she seeks a means to remedy her 'woes':

> How I my fault might hide,
> still I mus'd, still I mus'd,
> That I might not be spide,
> nor yet suspected,
> To this bad thought of mine
> The Devill did incline,
>
> ... Being where none me saw,
> Quite against natures law,
> I hid it in the straw,
> where it was smother'd.[50]

It is notable that, post-1624 Act, Besse's concealment of her newborn child is foregrounded; in fact the logic of her statement seems to suggest that concealment was the cause of her baby's death: 'I hid it in the straw/where it was smother'd.' Each woman is posited as exemplar and warning: Martha, for example, exhorts: 'Both maides and men/Both yong and old/Let not good lives with shame be sold.'[51] Similarly, the argument of each text rests firmly on the premise of the providential revelation of sin: in Martha's case via an extraordinarily persistent dog, who barks for three days and nights to alert neighbours to her crime, and for Besse an inquisitive employer who prompts her to confess. The message is clear: dark deeds will come to light. As Besse notes ruefully, God 'that sits on high/with his all-seeing eye' will reveal all.[52]

Rosalind Smith, writing on female gallows complaint, has considered the possibility of 'evidence, however limited, that these texts were read by early modern readers as contradictory, complex and open'.[53] The infanticide ballads seem to suggest a similar possibility, encoding alternative readings within their simple narratives, in particular an acknowledgement of the social and economic factors that underlie neonatal murder. As Garthine Walker comments, 'infanticide was sometimes understood by contemporaries in terms of women's responses to unpropitious circumstances'.[54] Martha is 'Poore I the poorest now on earth', whilst Besse's desperation on finding her child's father 'fled' is forcefully conveyed.[55] As we shall see later in this chapter, such subtext sheds light both on Greene's case and on the wider consideration of prosecuting infanticide. Yet the overall message is clear: these women are justly condemned and for them redemption lies only beyond the grave. Not so for Anne Greene. In the section that follows we will see the ways in which the retellings and redactions of her story reveal a far more complex and nuanced view of newborn child murder.

'Variously and falsely reported among the vulgar': *Newes from the Dead*

The three Greene pamphlets offer the reader a wide range of interpretative options for an assessment of their protagonist's situation. The unique conjunction of components in her story – the dramatic survival of the gallows and the distressing tale of an alleged child murder, of which she consistently maintained her innocence – was further complicated by a third element, which had much to do with the time and place of her conviction. 'On one dead by Law but reviv'd by Physick' is the title of one of the early poems in *Newes from the Dead*, and this is key.[56] As we will see in the next section, Greene's 'miraculous' story crystallised contemporary concerns about the legal treatment of alleged infanticides and, on one level, allowed those concerns to become part of a new, redemptive scientific discourse.

This process is manifest in *Newes from the Dead*. The pamphlet's very subtitle, 'A *True and Exact* Narrative of the *Miraculous* delivery of Anne Greene', encodes this contradiction, and the opening paragraph furthers the point:

> There happened lately in this Citty a very rare and remarkable accident, which being variously and falsely reported amongst the vulgar to the end that none may be deceived, and that so signall an act of God's mercy and providence may never be forgotten, I have here faith fully recorded it, according to the Information I have received from those that were the chiefe Instruments in bringing this great worke to perfection. (f. 1)

The assertion of empirical truth, along with claims to be dispelling 'false' and 'vulgar' reports with 'Information' from direct witnesses, is a classic feature of the wonder pamphlet or providential text. As Barbara Shapiro comments, 'by the late sixteenth century, broadside "news" was beginning to be characterised by the conventions for establishing "fact" or "matters of fact" . . . many news stories were validated by claims of eyewitness reports'.[57] Burdet's *A Wonder* offers a similar endorsement, claiming to be 'witnessed by Dr Petty'.[58] In *Newes from the Dead*, these textual devices work to move the pamphlet away from the 'wondrous' and towards the scientific, an identification which the piece itself simultaneously embraces and resists. Yet, as Walsham cautions: 'The notion of supplying raw and undigested information for its own sake was embryonic, but still ethically suspect . . . Bias was not only expected but inbuilt.'[59] As we will see, in *Newes* that bias manifests as an instinct to erase and suppress as well as to reveal.

We know only basic facts about Richard Watkins.[60] Anthony Wood identifies him with the Richard Watkins who gained his MA degree at Christ Church in 1647 and had a later career as a rector in Warwickshire and Gloucestershire.[61] *Newes* itself emphasises its author's position as 'a scholler in Oxford' (f. 1). Undoubtedly, the pamphlet is a peculiarly 'Oxford' text, published in the city, produced by the University printer, and its appended poems, written by commoners, scholars, fellows and alumni from at least eleven different colleges, further endorse this status.[62] Whether Watkins was instrumental in the commissioning of the poems appended to the work, or that effort was a flourish of the publisher's, their juxtaposition with his core account creates a generically hybrid text.

Newes begins conventionally enough, with a summary of Greene's discovery, conviction and execution. At the point at which she is observed to be still living, however, the text changes in mode. As 'Dr Petty of Brasen-nose Colledge . . . and Mr Thomas Willis of Christ-Church' enter the drama they bring with them a new tone, the text almost replicating that entrance with a generic shift. Not only does the pamphlet's language here become the discourse of the insider – 'Dr Petty ... *our* Anatomy-Professor' – but its timeframe slows to that of the eyewitness, the scientific observer. From this point the pamphlet becomes a meticulous account of a patient's treatment and recovery:

> All this while her pulse was very low ... her arm being bound up again, and now and then a little cordial water powr'd down her throat, they continued rubbing her in several places, caused ligatures to be made in her armes and legs ... she seemed about noon to be in a sweat. Her face also began somewhat to swell and to look very red on that side on which the knot of the halter had been fastened. (f. 3)

Newes is scrupulous to assign a clear timeframe to its description of Greene's recovery:

> On Sunday the 15 about 8 in the morning they ... found her much amended ... Monday the 16, they found that she had taken some rest ... Tuesday the 17 in the morning they found her pulse slow, but very unequall: her tongue not very dry not rough ... the 19 she was up, and did eat part of a chick. (ff. 5–6)

It records what Greene ate, how long she slept and the gradual healing of her throat and tongue which she had 'bitten ... in the time of her suffering' (f. 6). Undoubtedly Petty is the source for this detail.

Once Greene is proven to have made a full recovery and retreats from the scene to the 'countrey', Watkins turns to the medico-legal evidence in her case, the scientific 'proofs' for her innocence of the murder of her child, first presenting the evidence for the child having being miscarried:

> it is evident that the child was very unperfect, being not above a span in length ... the Midwife said also that it had no hair, and that she did not beleeve that ever it had life ... it is not likely that the Child was vital, the mischance happening not above 17 weeks after the time of her conception. (ff. 6–7).

He then offers a similar exposition of the reasons why Greene, as she asserted at her trial and in her gallows speech, did not know that she was pregnant, describing her menstrual patterns – 'she was not 10 weeks without the usual Courses of women' (f. 6) – and pointing to the scientific consistency of her testimony on this point.

Several times during the course of his text, Watkins invokes a motive for writing that goes beyond his initial assertion that he is countering 'false' and 'vulgar' reports. He returns repeatedly to the fact of Greene's body having been intended for the anatomist's hand, commenting upon the fact that her physicians 'missed the opportunity of improving their knowledge in the dissection of a Dead body' (f. 8). The practice of subjecting the bodies of executed criminals to public autopsy was growing in importance in the mid-seventeenth century and female bodies 'begged' for dissection offered a rare and fascinating opportunity. In her recovery Greene cheats the anatomists of their expected revelation – the 'science of seeing' described by Jonathan Sawday – but provides one still greater:

> [I]n the same Roome where her Body was to have beene dissected for the satisfaction of a few, she became a greater wonder, being reviv'd, to the satisfaction of multitudes that flocked thither daily to see her. (f. 6)[63]

Watkins seems to offer his text as a materialisation of that greater revelation; he has codified Greene's survival as an alternative anatomy lecture. Susan Staub suggests that 'Anne's body seems commodified and disciplined here', aligning the 'multitudes' of visitors paying their admission charge to see her with the observers of the anatomised corpse, yet its status in Watkins' narrative seems much more nuanced.[64] Quite apart from the fact that Greene uses the money 'earned' by her miraculous body to pay her physicians' bills and purchase her pardon, it is incorrect to assume that *Newes* silences Greene's actual voice in favour of the symbolic message of a dissected corpse. Despite her sore throat and her 'dead' tongue, Greene's voice is heard throughout *Newes*: she is reported to have 'laughed and talked merrily ... she complained of paine beneath the pit of her stomach; she complained also of a deadness in the tipp of her tongue' (ff. 4–5). Almost the first thing Petty and his associates attempt to do is to get her to communicate: 'they made tryal again: bidding her, if she understood them, to move her hand, or open her eies' (f. 4). In fact it is via Greene's comments that the progress of her recovery is measured, as she verbalises her own miracle.

At its core, then, *Newes from the Dead*'s project is to recreate the lost anatomy lecture and to pay tribute to the success of Petty, Willis and their colleagues, 'Mr Bathurst of Trinity Colledge, and Mr Clerke of Magdalen Colledge': 'they advanced their fame by restoring to the world a living [body]' (f. 8); but Watkins' account also celebrates its protagonist and – whether intentionally or not – inscribes her as such. The allusion to 'fame' is key here – for a significant element of Greene's 'fame' derives from a happy conjunction with the 'fame' of the men who oversaw her resuscitation. This was a significant moment for Oxford science – the group of medical men and natural philosophers who met regularly at Clarke's shop (and also at Wadham College under John Wilkins' wardenship) would go on to form the core membership of the Royal Society when it was founded in 1660. It was to Clarke's house that Greene's coffin was carried on 12 December 1650, and into that particular intellectual moment.

Certainly the 'wonder' of Greene's recovery proved a powerful piece of propaganda for Petty in particular, whose career following the case went from strength to strength.[65] In 1651 he became Professor of Anatomy and was elected vice-principal of Brasenose College. The following year his growing reputation secured him a coveted post in the Irish Civil Service, as physician general to the army, and this was to be the start of a highly successful administrative career.[66] The influence of Greene's case was still evident a quarter of a century later, when John Evelyn referred to Petty in his *Diary* as the 'Doctor of Physick ... growne famous as for his Learning, so for his recovering a poore wench that had been hanged for felonie'.[67]

As we have seen, *Newes from the Dead* formed a key part of the representation of Greene's recovery as a discourse of scientific advance, rather than a banal narrative of botched hanging. Indeed, in his discussion of *Newes*, Joad Raymond describes the pamphlet as a 'serious, scientific publication ... discursively antithetical to the populist, cheaper pamphlets'.[68] Yet *Newes* remains an inevitably conflicted piece, unable quite to make the leap away from the seductive possibilities of the sensation text. In enumerating the various 'proofs' of Greene's innocence, for example, Watkins cannot resist including a final suggestion, one which plunges *Newes* straight back to the level of cheap print:

> There is yet one thing more ... That her Grand Prosecutor Sir Thomas Read died within three daies after her Execution; even almost as soon as the probability of her reviving could be well confirmed to him.   (f. 7)

His partial qualification, 'but because hee was an old man and such Events are not too rashly to be commented on, I shall not make use of that observation', does little to redeem the pamphlet's descent into the discourse of signs and wonders.

Moreover, as a text, *Newes* struggles with the facts that do not fit its momentum of reversal, its version of the story. For whilst Greene is innocent of the murder of her child, she is undoubtedly guilty of the sin inherent in its conception and this is a fact that the text would rather erase. This tension is perhaps most evident in the *Newes* poems. As Marina Leslie comments: 'the poems belie an uneasiness ... with the problems inherent in linking Oxford's institutional prestige with a woman of such low class and compromised morals'.[69] Certainly, they exhibit a preoccupation with Greene's sexual status. John Watkins' verse, 'The Woman's *Case* put to the Lawyers', wherein Greene, her own advocate, requests judgment, is typical:

> Mother, or Maid, I pray you whether?
> One, or both, or am I neither?

The Mother dyed: may't not be said
That the Survivor is a Maid? (f. 6)

Whilst they relish the intellectual dilemmas raised by her situation, the poets display little moral condemnation of Greene's sexual activity. This stance seems inextricably linked to the poems' conviction of her innocence of the crime for which she was tried. Just as the earlier infanticide ballads needs must present their guilty protagonists as morally reprehensible (even whilst tentatively acknowledging the difficulty of their situation), for the majority of the Oxford poets, Greene must be innocent of all crimes. This desire for full exculpation reaches its climax in the final poem in the pamphlet, which contains an oblique suggestion that Greene's pregnancy was the result of rape (f. 22), a scenario for which there is no evidence whatsoever in any testimony, including her own.[70]

'Not consonant unto the Lawes': Prosecuting Infanticide

The opening lines of the poem submitted by Robert Mathew of New College to the second edition of *Newes* are addressed directly to Greene: 'Thou shalt not Swing again', they assert, 'come clear thy Brow/Thou hast the Benefit o' th' Clergie now;' (f. 7). What this statement foregrounds for us is that the most curious reversal in Greene's case is not her journey from death to life, but from guilt to innocence. Why, having been convicted of murder in a recognised court of law, 'there condemned by one *Mr Crook* appointed to sit as Judg in a Commission of Oyer and Terminer', and having accidentally survived an inept execution, was she not returned to the gallows forthwith?[71] As noted earlier, unsuccessful hangings were not uncommon, and their usual consequence was a second execution, as Blackstone affirms:

> If, upon judgment to be hanged by the neck till he is dead, the criminal be not thoroughly killed but revives, the sheriff must hang him again. For the former hanging was no execution of sentence.[72]

This makes the granting of Greene's initial reprieve all the more surprising. In his *History of the Worthies of England*, Thomas Fuller comments of Greene that 'Charitable people interpret hir so miraculous preservation a Compurgator of her innocence.'[73] But Greene had been condemned, her case had passed beyond compurgation. Because all the pamphlet accounts assert Greene's innocence from the outset, 'in striking contrast to most contemporary infanticide pamphlets', as Gowing points out, as readers we are caught up in the momentum of renewal and vindication that is her narrative, a momentum that tends to obscure, if not erase, the practical question of her pardon.[74] We know that Greene obtained her reprieve and later her pardon in part with the help of the University and using the money reaped from the fee charged to see her on her sickbed. But we know little about why she was granted that pardon in the face of a conviction for murder.

Only Burdet's account, *A Wonder of Wonders*, really touches upon the circumstances of Greene's pardon; he comments that her recovery:

> moved some of her enemies to wrath and indignation, insomuch, that a great man amongst the rest, moved to have her again carried to the place of execution, to be hanged up by the neck ... but some poor honest Soldiers then present, seemed to be very much discontented thereat, and declared, That there was a great hand of God on it, and having suffered the Law, it was contrary to all right and reason, that any further punishment should be inflicted upon her. (f. 6)

This opposition of 'poor honest Soldiers' to 'great' men is a neat set piece, but we sense something more behind it, a relief, an almost over-readiness to believe in Greene's innocence. Similarly, the *Newes* poems undercut their verbal play with allusions to the legal implications of the Greene case – herewith John Aylmer, Scholar of New College:

> Their Law would have some plea; were it to thee
> Who first the Malefactor Hang, then see
> Whe're t'were a just and equitable Cause
> Whether not consonant unto the Lawes. (f. 10)

Even beyond the dubious actions of Thomas Read, there seems to have been something fundamentally uncomfortable about Greene's drama as a legal case, a discomfort that impels this counter-reaction of relief. The case against Greene seems to implode almost as soon as she is perceived still to be breathing and its 'reopening' in *Newes* makes for a compelling revision of the existing verdict. *Newes* proves its hypothesis of Greene's innocence – 'that the child was abortive or stillborn, and consequently not capable of being murthered' (f. 6) – with a neat textual reconstruction of the trial, calling on witnesses, 'the Midwife said ... Physicians say ... her fellow-servants do testifie' (f. 7). The text constructs its revisionist narrative via a process of interrogation and analysis of evidence that conflates the scientific and the legal. It is unclear from Watkins' account whether the testimony he offers was actually given at Greene's trial, but the fact that all the Anne Greene texts report more or less the same evidence as to her child, that it was born 'about the fourth month ... not above a span in length', is suggestive.

The two other contemporary pamphlet accounts, Burdet's *A Wonder of Wonders* and *A Declaration from Oxford*, also serve to complicate our understanding of Greene's experience as a legal case, although in a very different way. Both pamphlets were published in January 1651, and they share a significant proportion of the same text. 'Behold God's Providence!' is the caption to the woodcut that opens each work and what follows seems, in many ways, to be a pleasingly schematic providential tract. Greene is discovered, convicted and goes to the gallows a wronged woman, pointedly 'desiring of God, that his Divine Majesty would be pleased, to show some remarkable judgement on her, for a signal and testification to the world of her innocency'.[75] There follows a scaffold speech in which she expresses her humble conviction that she will 'receive that blessed Portion, which my blessed Saviour and Redeemer Jesus Christ hath purchased for me' and that her present circumstances are merely evidence that 'God hath whipped me by his Severe Rod of correction, that he might not lose me' (*Declaration*, f. 3).

Both texts then continue with an account of Greene's apparent death and actual survival, at which point they diverge. Whilst Burdet's pamphlet gives a broadly factual account of her recovery, in *A Declaration* Greene's return to life is no mere resurrection but an apotheosis. The latter text accords her a newfound insight that seems specifically aimed at satisfying the appetites of an audience hungry for moral certainty and supernatural revelation. Greene speaks fluently of God's 'Providence', and claims to have seen 'her chief enemy dead before her (which is observable, that within some hours after, Sir Tho. Read died)' (f. 4). This is not her only vision in *A Declaration*:

> [B]eing asked what apparisions she saw during her Trance, she replyed, That being (as it were) in a Garden of Paradise, there appeared to her 4. little boys with wings, being four Angels, saying Woe unto them that decree unrighteous Decrees, and take away the right from the Judges, that the innocent may be their prey. (f. 4).

Marina Leslie has noted references to Leveller interests and causes in both *A Wonder* and *A Declaration*, identifying residual sympathies in Oxford following the 1649 Banbury mutiny and commenting that the two pamphlets 'embrace a familiar and inflammatory political rhetoric that targets both the royalist abuse of privilege and the injustice of the parliamentarian courts'.[76] Greene's positioning as a Dissenter visionary in *A Declaration* seems to appropriate the concerns around justice associated with her case in order to establish a very specific political stance. Whilst *Newes from the Dead* undoubtedly and deliberately challenges the veracity of Greene's conviction, as a text its political project is far less controversial, foregrounding as it does what Leslie describes as the 'bipartisan and cross-sectarian success' of Petty and his Oxford circle.[77] Far from reporting 'what fine visions this maid saw in the other world', *Newes* indicates that Greene 'remembered not what had happened to her even while shee was yet alive' (ff. 7–8).

As we have seen, the timely death of Sir Thomas Read, Greene's erstwhile master and her 'Grand Prosecutor', was a coincidence that even the sober Watkins could not resist commenting upon. That the author of *A Declaration* not only mentions it, but has Greene foretell it as she recounts her 'Trance', signifies the emergence of an alternate meaning for her experience. Beyond the illumination of 'God's Providence', a recurrent theme in both *A Declaration* and *A Wonder* is the culpability of the law in Greene's suffering. The association of the legal and the sinful is apparent from the opening paragraphs of the pamphlets, when Greene reveals that the father of her child is 'a Gentleman of good birth, and Kinsman to a Justice of the Peace'.[78] This progress of bad justice is followed through Greene's 'short tryal' wherein she freely declares her guilt 'in committing of the sin [of fornication]', but her innocence 'for murthering of it', through her climb to the scaffold, 'she fixt her eyes on the Executioner, saying God forgive my false accusers, as I freely forgive thee' and her scaffold speech: 'Your business hither today is to see a sad spectacle, an innocent woman to be in a moment cut off.'[79] In each text, Greene's story is offered as 'president to all Magistrates and Courts of Judicature to take a special care in denouncing of sentence, without a due and legal process, according to the Laws of the Land, by an impartial and uncorrupted Jury, either of men or women &c'.[80] (The reference to women juries is interesting, in that it implicates midwives and matrons in such problematic prosecutions.) The level of anti-judicial feeling here seems to go beyond a neat moralising conclusion.

A significant proportion of the unmarried women being prosecuted for infanticide under the 1624 Act were, like Anne Greene, maidservants, young women in societal limbo between the parental home and marriage.[81] There seems to have been a sense in which, as Laura Gowing suggests:

> [servants'] sexuality was public property and a public threat. The economic and domestic situations of servants made them the most likely to produce children who they could not support, and to become indigent themselves, and their potential or actual mobility gave rise to fears that they might disappear leaving a child.[82]

Greene was a maidservant prosecuted under the Act and in this sense her story is typical. The discussions of her charge and trial in the pamphlets indicate how clearly the logic of her conviction mirrored the logic of the statute:

> [S]he conceived and was delivered of a Man-child: which being never made known, and the Infant found dead in the house of office, caused a suspicion, that she being the mother had murthered it, and throwne it there on purpose to conceal both it and her shame together.[83]

Although medical evidence in relation to stillbirth or miscarriage was still a feature of trials under the statute, it seems that, in Greene's case at least, at trial such evidence was ignored in favour of a focus on concealment. Greene had no witnesses to the fact that her child was born dead, but her fellow servant testified to a scene that reads as almost exemplary in the context of the Act's assumptions:

> Why Anne, I hope that thou art not with Child? Alas, alas! Mary, that ever I was born to live and die in shame and scorn: I was, but now I am clear of it ... look yonder where it lies.[84]

As we have seen, the question of witnesses was codified within the text of the Act itself, for a virtuous woman would of course have had multiple witnesses to her lying-in, including a midwife who could testify in court. For the unmarried woman, witnesses were unlikely – a midwife present at the birth would have been obliged to attempt to obtain the name of the child's father and to report the couple for fornication – and this very failure to secure help of any kind during delivery was rapidly translated in the courts into a clear indicia of intent to harm the child. The importance of this point was evident in the 1664 case of Anne Davis, where Sir John Kelyng, the presiding judge, ruled that a woman in labour who knocked on a wall seeking help could not be tried under the statute.[85] The seventeenth-century author and physician Percival Willughby commented on the prescience of having a midwife present at the birth 'to avoid all future suspicions and to free some of the looser sort from the danger of the statute-law, in case that the child should be found dead', citing the case of a mother 'hanged for not having a woman by her, at her delivery'.[86]

Greene's conviction, then, was vindicated under the literal terms of the Act, yet as all the pamphlets acknowledge, in the context of the physical evidence, it was deeply unsatisfactory. The simple concealment-guilt transfer removed the necessity for rigorous examination of that evidence, and judging by the reporting of Greene's experience, observers were well aware of this potential disjunction in infanticide cases. This is apparent when we examine William Petty's own account of the event.[87] In his *Papers*, published posthumously, the affair is entitled 'History of the Magdalen (Or the Raising of Anne Greene)'; it is unclear whether 'Magdalen' is Petty's designation or that of an editor, although he does refer to Greene's 'foule sin of fornication'. What is clear is that Petty and his colleagues were convinced that an avoidable miscarriage of justice had occurred. Petty appends to his case notes a copy of Greene's petition for pardon, to which he had contributed a 'certificate' of endorsement. The certificate closes with a careful exculpation of the justices in the case:

> [T]he sentence passed upon her by the law, which wee believe, rather the desires and good intentions of her Judges to discover and punish wickedness, as also their excusable unacquaintance with the physicall part of these cases, have produced.[88]

This is politic, however the remainder of Petty's testimony makes it abundantly clear that those 'Judges' must have had 'acquaintance' with the physical evidence: he refers to the testimony of the midwife upon viewing the dead child, and the assertions of the 'other women' that 'it was little above a span long and the sex scarce distinguishable'. Such evidence was not new, it could only have been given in the immediate aftermath of Greene's arrest; Petty implies that either the judges ignored it, or that it was somehow withheld from them. The support of Petty and his colleagues for Greene's case was clearly of immense value to her, for in her petition she not only asks for pardon, but seeks redress: 'some recompense from the said Mr. Read, the occasion of this, her misery', showing an extraordinary confidence in the success of her appeal.[89]

Significantly, the transcription of Petty's certificate in the *Papers* contains a paragraph that his editor describes as 'crossed through in the original'. In this paragraph he attempts to absolve Greene of the crucial charge of concealment – 'that she did not voluntarily cast it [the child] into the house of office on vere purpose to conceale it, we are apt to believe'.[90] The editorial note continues by proposing that Petty withdrew this statement because he 'had come to the conclusion that it would not strengthen the case for Anne Greene'.[91] We can only speculate that engaging with the fraught logic of the concealment assumption was too problematic even for William Petty.

Richard Watkins' presentation of the evidence for Greene in *Newes* is thus a complete reframing of her case – a retrial in the utterly other terms of medical fact. His text suggests a simple conclusion: had Greene been tried within the framework of science, she would never have been convicted. Yet this calls attention to a key point: the status of medical evidence in this period. Although midwives might be called upon to testify as to their opinion on a child's potential for life, and juries of local matrons might examine suspected infanticides for evidence that they had given birth, there was little consistency of approach. Until the coming into force of the Medical Witnesses Act 1836 there was no provision in English law for paying for expert witness testimony, and the consequent inconvenience of testifying meant that credible medical witnesses were reluctant to attend court.[92] This factor, combined with what Catherine Crawford describes as a 'dearth of English texts on forensic medicine pre-1800', meant that those cases that were tried outside the jurisdiction of the 1624 Act (for example where the child was not illegitimate, or there was evidence that the mother had prepared for the birth, such as having provided clothes for the infant) were often inconsistent in their provision and valorisation of medical evidence.[93] Watkins' account is persuasive and technically thorough as a scientific discourse, but it is uncertain whether it would have prevailed as a legal proof.

'The Gallows her exacter balance is': Redeeming Anne Greene

Towards the end of the seventeenth century and into the early eighteenth, the Puritan association of illegitimate pregnancy with whoredom, and thus the association of concealment with guilt, began to be unpicked by legal and medical commentators. Bernard Mandeville's 1732 *Fable of the Bees*, for example, contends that 'Common whores, whom all the World knows to be such, hardly ever destroy their children ... because they have lost their Modesty to a greater degree, and the fear of Shame makes hardly any Impression,' suggesting that concealment was a natural reaction of a 'Modest' woman who had been seduced, regardless of whether there was intent to harm the child.[94] Courts increasingly reverted to trying cases under common law, and, as medical evidence for the establishment of live birth became more sophisticated, prosecution and conviction rates dropped.[95] By the time of the Act's repeal at the start of the nineteenth century, the physician Thomas Percival, for example, noted that concealment was 'the lowest degree of presumptive evidence of felonious homicide'.[96]

But Greene's case was tried in 1650, at the height of the Act's enforcement in the courts. Furthermore, May of that year had seen the passing of 'An Act for suppressing the detestable Sins of Incest, Adultery and Fornication', which introduced the death penalty for adulterous liaisons.[97] The mechanisms of the law, it seemed, were ranged against the sexual transgressor. We must be cautious, however, in drawing conclusions from this. J. S. Cockburn has claimed that, post-1624, 'the prosecution rate [for infanticide] remained peculiarly susceptible to shifts in public opinion' and Keith Wrightson notes 'the enormous symbolic significance which infanticide had acquired ... identified as an unnatural act'.[98] Yet what Greene's case indicates is that we must qualify our idea of a single, uniform 'public opinion' in this instance, and acknowledge the separation of law and practice – and indeed the possibility of Walsham's 'cultural fissures and splits' – in any study of infanticide conviction.[99] As we have seen, the grand narrative encoded in statute was condemnatory in cases such as Greene's, yet the readiness with which her innocence, once propounded, was accepted, the 'poor soldiers' who defended her reprieve, and the academics who assisted in obtaining her pardon, all suggest a different discourse on illegitimate births. We must also recognise how far changing trends in prosecution and punishment were directed by legal need – initially the requirement for a clear direction for juries, and later the perceived instability of that direction. Looking at the legal situation in 1650, we might assume a general and popular revulsion for crimes of child murder, yet Greene's case suggests that the whole question of punishing infanticide was particularly conflicted in the period.

In fact, in May 1658, another maidservant was hanged for infanticide in the city of Oxford and was revived by the doctors who were to anatomise her (who presumably were a little more alive to the possibility following Greene's case). She was not so fortunate; the local bailiffs seized her by night and hanged her once again, on a tree in what is now Gloucester Green. There were no soldiers and no academics to speak up for her. Only 'the Womn [sic]', Anthony Wood recounts, 'were exceedingly enraged at it, cut down the tree whereon she was hang'd, and gave very ill language to Henry Mallory, one of the baillives ... because he was the chief man that hang'd her'.[100] Wood cannot resist adding a providential coda to his report of this affair:

> And because that he afterwards broke, or gave up his trade thro povertie (being a cutler), they did not stick to say that God's judgments followed him for the cruelty he shew'd to the poor maid.[101]

It is in this spirit that the Anne Greene pamphlets redeem their protagonist, whilst simultaneously acknowledging why the 'suspition' of her guilt had arisen. In *A Wonder* and *A Declaration*, authorial comment goes beyond mere simple admission of the problematic nature of infanticide law. These texts demonstrate that providential narratives may encode more than a simple dynamic of righteous vindication; here harsh criticism is directed at those Greene describes as her 'false accusers' and their actions are framed specifically as malicious (f. 5). Central to this criticism is Sir Thomas Read, himself a Justice of the Peace, who presented Greene for trial and, it is implied, may have had some influence upon her conviction. Yet this perception of the conflicted nature of justice was not merely an expression of political frustration at the power of 'a Gentleman of good birth', a fact made clear both in William Petty's testimony and in the poems appended to *Newes*.[102] Those poems make repeated references to perceived deficiencies of legal process in the case: 'Whose scruples palsie-Juryes weigh amisse,/The Gallows her exacter balance is,' writes William Bell (f. 19). While Charles Capell's verse makes an overt reference to the death of Thomas Read – 'Wee'l write on her Accuser, Here he *Lies*' (f. 18) – the scorn of the *Newes* poets is directed at all aspects of Greene's prosecution. They allude directly to the elision of medical evidence by statute law: Greene is 'hang'd for her Abortive fruit' (f. 14), her 'Embryo's Birth's Abortive' (f. 12), and even, in the verse authored by Walter Pope of Wadham College, acknowledge the implication of concealment – 'Despightfull *Embryo* in secret plac't/ By Her, by thee Shee's publikely disgrac't' (f. 16). Even Thomas Arthur, who feels obliged to acknowledge Greene's illicit sexual activity, contends that '[t]he crime was heinous, but (if you know all)/T'was not soe High as to be Capitall' (f. 16).

Garthine Walker has argued that, in fact, juries in infanticide cases 'regularly acquitted women whose cases rested on concealment alone' and several of the poets seem to concur, highlighting the unfairness of the practice of denying benefit of clergy – and thus the opportunity to mitigate a capital sentence – in such cases.[103] 'Clergie looke to it, for since shee/Was rob'd the benefit of thee' writes Anthony Wood (f. 21), whilst Robert Mathew offers Greene her '*Neck-Verse*' (f. 7), the text read by those who sought to assert their right to a clergyable reprieve. This is not without its own subtext of misogyny – for Mathew it is a 'Strange Wench' who can be 'sav'd by *Booke*' (f. 7) – nonetheless it represents an acknowledgement of the problems of punishing Greene's alleged crime.

In 1651, of course, the law that the undergraduates mocked was no longer a divinely ordained jurisdiction manifested in the person of the monarch. With a new legislature only just beginning to take shape, law in interregnum Oxford was fraught with indeterminacy, and the poets pick up on this broader instability with disparaging references to a judicial system long in flux: 'What hath the Law its power lost/Since th' English tongue hath it engrost?'[104] In this context it is perhaps suggestive that at least one of the St John's poets, Francis Withins, invokes the possibility of an earlier form of trial for Greene, 'Death was thy Ordeal and Compurgatrix' (f. 15), and in his use of this particular variant of 'Compurgator', he renders this redemptive process a feminine mode.

So, whilst Watkins and Petty look to redeem Anne Greene via the scientific evidence in the case, the poets of *Newes* seem more closely aligned with the 'poor honest Soldiers' and their generalised dissatisfaction with the mechanisms of judicial process. Greene's case indicates that the fear of justice miscarried and the anxiety around the act of reaching a verdict was very real. We see this both in the efforts of Petty and others to reclaim that truth via scientific fact, and in the quality of relief that underlies the Anne Greene pamphlets. We may suggest that Greene's case plays pointedly upon this relief – enacting a fantasy of the erasure of false judgment in her survival of the gallows.

'The hanged woman miraculously saved': Stories as Actors

There was another Anne, or rather there had been another, some sixty years before, and in another country. Her story both complicates and elucidates that of her successor, Anne Greene, and responds to what Frances Dolan, following Michael Witmore, has described as 'the capacity of stories to be actors ... to reassert and perpetuate themselves', in this case as stories about the law.[105] In 1589, in Douai, then part of the Spanish Netherlands, the Widow Boscard, a minor publisher of religious texts and pro-Spanish works, brought to market a chapbook or *occasionnel* telling the story 'd'une fille nommé Anne Belthumier', a tale set in Montfort in Brittany, a town 'entre Nantes et Rennes'.[106] The *occasionnel* genre was close in essence to the pamphlets of early modern England – as Roger Chartier describes:

> [S]imilar tracts, produced in large quantities in the sixteenth and seventeenth centuries, told of natural calamities ... of abominable crimes and the capital punishment that usually ensued, and of extraordinary phenomena that transgressed the laws of nature ... directed ... at the most 'popular' readers.[107]

The title of Boscard's text, which describes itself as a 'Discours miraculeux et véritable', immediately recalls *Newes*' subtitle: 'A True and Exact narration', and Anne Belthumier's story, while not identical to that of her English counterpart, is in many respects startlingly similar. Anne, a girl 'of noble race', goes into service when her family becomes impoverished, obtaining a place as a servant at a hostelry, the Pot d'Estain, in Montfort.[108] While Anne lives there, her employer's daughter, who has 'abandoned herself to a lover', gives birth to the child of that liaison. The new mother suffocates her infant and conspires with her parents to claim that the murdered child was Anne's. Anne is promptly arrested, and 'within the hour sentenced to be executed'.[109]

In her scaffold speech, Anne Belthumier, like Anne Greene, makes a special devotion in the hope of salvation. This is to the Virgin, and to a specific manifestation of her cult – Anne commends herself 'to all the Our Ladies to which one goes on voyages of devotion, and principally to Our Lady of Liesse'. After some confusion (the rope breaks 'two or three times'), Anne is hanged and her body left to decompose on the gallows. Three days later, a passer-by notices a curious phenomenon: 'seeing her move her legs [he] suspected that she was not dead . . . he gave word of what he had seen to several of the town'. Anne is discovered to be still living: 'they cut the cord by which she was hanged and they brought her into a house to get her to regain her breath and her wits'.[110]

Following her 'resurrection' Anne Belthumier embraces a celebrity of a very different kind to Anne Greene's; while the English Anne becomes, for a short time at least, a moneymaking spectacle for the 'multitudes', her predecessor takes to the road, embarking on a very public Marian pilgrimage to visit the shrines of 'all the Our Ladies' of her scaffold speech and to give thanks for her deliverance.[111] As the *occasionnel* closes, she is heading for Paris. Meanwhile, in Montfort, the local bailiff is at work, and 'the father, the mother and the daughter who had plotted the death of their servant girl by the false report of two Midwives and of a Surgeon' are all imprisoned.[112]

The provenance of the Anne Belthumier narrative is rendered more complex by the appearance of another Anne, a year earlier in 1588. This text, *Discours d'une histoire et miracle advenu en la ville de Mont-fort cinq lieues près Rennes en Bretagne*, was issued by a small printing house in Rennes.[113] The Rennes *occasionnel* relates the story of 'Damoiselle Anne des Grez', who is falsely accused of infanticide, hanged and revived after three days, at the apparent intervention of Our Lady of Liesse. The Rennes text is a peculiar mixture – it combines all the factual precision of an official account with the narrative structure and motifs of a fairy tale. It offers an exact date for the miraculous occurrence, the '22nd day of June 1588 past', together with a full exposition of Anne's antecedents, 'daughter of the late Guillaume des Gres, Esquire' and some detail about the structures of local bureaucracy – Anne is tried by 'the Bailiff of St Main, who was taken in Gonaisy in the absence of the judge of the said Montfort'.[114] Yet the story it tells is notably heightened. Anne's gentility is emphasised; in this rendering she is a lady's companion rather than a serving maid. Her scaffold speech seems to foretell her fate: 'She prayed her confessor that if God permitted in three times twenty-four hours the truth of the act be known, it was her pleasure that he go for her to Our Lady of Liesse.' Finally, the full depravity of the true infanticide, the innkeeper's daughter, emerges at the close of the text – '[she] confessed that this was the sixth infant that she had had, all done away with'.[115]

The specifics of the Rennes pamphlet, its local setting and pre-dating of the Douai text, seem to suggest that these accounts relate the details of an actual incident. The differences between the two *occasionnels* – Anne des Grez becomes Anne Belthumier, the Pot d'Estain (Pewter Pot) becomes the Plat d'Estain (Pewter Platter) – seem no more than might be expected to occur in geographically disparate editions. Both texts are presented within the framework of a Catholic universe, and the Douai account foregrounds its own religious project: 'this miracle will also serve as instruction to the followers of the new Religion, to demonstrate and prove to them how much a Christian profits from imploring the Saints and the Virgin Mary at his death'.[116] Perhaps most significantly for the purposes of this study, both texts, the Douai piece in particular, are also overtly polemical in a secular context, offering explicit criticism of the legal proceedings in the case:

> this miracle can serve as an example and a mirror to the administrators of Justice; to make it clear to them that they must take care not to condemn a criminal to death lightly when someone comes before them [and] ... to examine the witnesses closely so that they judge no one on trust.[117]

The words here recall Burdet's later condemnation of Anne Greene's judge and jury, with its imputation of corruption.[118] It is notable, however, that, in the Douai/Rennes case, the vice seems to lie primarily with the medical witnesses. Concealment was also a precept in the European prosecution of infanticide, having been formally declared so by a 1556 edict of Henri II, which announced 'the pain of death against young women who, having concealed their pregnancy and their childbirth, let their infants perish without receiving Baptism'.[119] However, as we have seen, European justice required a much more rigorous observance of medico-legal proofs and here it is the 'Surgeon and two Midwives' (in the Rennes case) who for twenty-five and ten *écus* respectively 'impute the crime to the said Demoiselle'.[120] The Rennes text also includes a surprising set piece, which occurs when the judge who condemned Anne is told of her survival:

> The said Judge began to laugh and joke at these words, and ... said these words: 'It is just as true that she is still alive as it is that I am galloping across these viands on the table.' And suddenly the said Judge began to gallop across the said table most horribly.[121]

Chartier traces a possible source for this scene to the miracles of St James, 'in which a judge, about to sit down to table, declares that he will only believe in the survival of the young pilgrim unjustly hanged if the cock and hen he is about to consume are resuscitated – which then happens'.[122] In fact, it seems that each element of the Rennes/Douai pamphlets can be unpicked into such constituent devices. Chartier locates the miracle of the Virgin saving a hanged man in Jacobus de Voragine's *Legenda Aurea* (1260), wherein a thief who has 'a great devotion to the Virgin Mary' survives the gallows because the Virgin quite literally holds him aloft for three days.[123] Similar stories appear throughout medieval hagiographic literature. What do such precedent texts tell us about the truth or otherwise of the Belthumier/des Grez narrative? Certainly, the Douai pamphlet seems self-consciously aware of its intertextuality. It appends an account of a further miracle to its main text, an almost direct parallel of the Anne Belthumier case, the story of a young man falsely accused of theft, who is saved from hanging by calling on St James. The secondary Douai miracle recalls the story of John Johnston of Antwerp, discussed earlier in this chapter, which appeared in its English edition in 1605. While there is no concrete evidence that the des Grez/Belthumier texts were available in England, the Johnston case was, and it almost certainly belongs to the tradition established by Chartier here.

So, are the Douai/Rennes 'Anne' pamphlets merely fictional pro-Catholic propaganda tracts, in which a male thief is transmuted into an innocent female to emphasise the purity of the Virgin's influence? Chartier seems largely convinced of this, although he allows a measure of doubt: 'what the text invents, perhaps by drawing on other texts, perhaps by taking details from an actual event, is the story of an innocent woman unjustly accused of infanticide and rescued on the gallows'.[124] Yet perhaps the later Anne Greene case (of which Chartier does not specifically indicate an awareness) casts a new light upon this, confounding the generic and folkloric with the real. To dispute the existence of the Greene case seems fruitless, as it would require us to propound a vast conspiracy, involving Petty and his circle, the Oxfordshire judicial system and the editor of *Mercurius Politicus*, among others. Interestingly, this is exactly what Joad Raymond does propose in his discussion of the case – 'the [Greene] story may have been a complete fiction, devised by a proto-feminist concerned over infanticide prosecutions and set at large by a number of sympathetic and influential collaborators'.[125] The existence of Petty's case notes, Greene's petition for pardon, and Evelyn's *Diary*, at the least, would seem to refute that proposition, but it is indicative of the difficulty of discerning the truth of these texts that it is made at all. For as we have seen, Anne Greene's 'true' case is rendered in a number of different ways, each with a specific project, often in forms startlingly evocative of her 'fictional' counterpart's depiction. The episode of the gallows speech, in which each Anne commends herself to her chosen object of devotion; the striking similarity of the condemnation of judicial workings; the superstitious addition of the Judge episode to the Rennes text and the 'four Angels' vision to *A Declaration* all contribute to our perception that the real may be contained and made meaningful via familiar fictional emblems. As Dolan notes, 'printed texts worked in disturbingly remote ways', acting upon each other to create shared motifs across decades and geographical distance, and as readers we must be alive to this complex construction.[126] Early modern 'readers' of crimes and consequences certainly were: providential markers, as Lorna Hutson has noted, were treated as merely one form of evidence in a wider process of investigation and assessment.[127] Chartier asserts that 'it is in fact possible that readers went along with the realistic effects imbedded in the texts without believing that what they read was true', yet Anne Greene's story suggests that the opposite may have been equally the case.[128]

Conclusion

What then do the *occasionels* tell us about the Anne Greene case? Apart from explaining some of its more stylised textual motifs, and according it a peculiarly reversed status as the actual materialisation of a tradition that – whatever we believe about the 'truth' of the *occasionel* cases – is largely folkloric, they also usefully point up the way in which the Greene texts, and in particular *Newes*, diverge from that tradition, moving 'the hanged woman miraculously saved' into the heart of the debate about the relation between the scientific, the legal and the miraculous. This may in part be a signal of a wider fluidity of genre in the early modern period; Chartier sees the texts in his study metamorphose 'from hagiography to the *occasionel*', whilst *Newes from the Dead* takes a cheap print tale and transforms it into a medico-legal commentary.[129] The Douai/Rennes texts, whilst reinforcing our sense that prosecuting infanticide might be an endeavour peculiarly vulnerable to error and abuse, also demonstrate the technical differences between the English and European regimes. In Douai and Rennes the paradigm of the false conviction is subtly rewritten to establish a comfortable moral certainty: as befits future Marian pilgrims, these protagonists are virginal. In fact, these pamphlets maintain a core of faith in the purity of the law itself, it is merely the dishonesty of its practitioners that is in question. The reporting of Greene's case, however, goes beyond accusations of corruption to point up the assumptions of contemporary legal discourse on infanticide, the slippage between 'harlot' and 'murderer' that could lead to a false conviction – a slippage that, as we have seen, would not begin to be recognised until much later in the century. It does so by creating and then disrupting a solid providential narrative, a dynamic that works in different ways in its various print manifestations.

Newes from the Dead was to be the most enduring commentary on the Anne Greene case, and we can speculate that this longevity derives from its very complexity. 'Thy strange fate/Do's contradictions Legitimate' (f. 9), John Aylmer writes of Greene, and this description might be said to apply equally to the text itself. A cheap print work that disrupts our ideas of that genre, *Newes*' curious multivocality captures the diverse and conflicting responses provoked by the Anne Greene case, the competing discourses of science, law and sensation that surround the idea of newborn child murder in the period, and the anxiety that provokes. We see this anxiety both in the efforts of Watkins to reclaim truth via scientific fact, and in the quality of relief that subtends the celebratory mode of the poems. Ultimately, even the historical Anne Greene participated in this; when, in 1651, she received her pardon and left Oxford, she took 'away with her the Coffin wherein she lay, as a Trophey' (f. 6).

Reading the case of Anne Greene, then, mediated as it is by a discourse of print sensation, seems to shed light upon the ways in which a miscarriage of justice, and its literary representation, may offer a wider perspective on the complex implications of capital sanction in the mid-seventeenth century – the legal ambiguities that influenced felony prosecution, and the way in which those ambiguities might be understood in a wider cultural space. In part this is enabled by the very particular circumstances of Greene's experience: her accidental association with an elite, academic world leads to the creation of texts that 'act' with far more confidence than might usually be expected, and act specifically to reflect perceived deficiencies in the law. Yet, as we have seen above, this complexity is not confined to Greene's case; it is possible to detect traces – admittedly more limited – of such ambiguity even within the most stylised of popular texts. As such, then, Greene's seemingly unique story may open up possibilities for more general inquiry; her 'strange fate' becomes a means to illuminate the stories about law and justice that lie beneath the surface of a wider range of popular texts, unsettling our assumptions about the ways in which those works may have been received and understood by those who encountered them.

Notes

1. Watkins, *Newes from the dead*, Wing (2nd ed.)/W1074, f. 16. References are to the second, expanded edition; this has some duplication in page numbering which is retained. For the first edition see Wing (2nd ed.)/W1072.
2. *Mercurius Politicus*, No. 28 (12–19 December 1650), p. 468.
3. Watkins, *Newes*, f. 6.
4. *Mercurius Politicus*, No. 32 (9–16 January 1651), p. 521.
5. Watkins, *Newes*, f. 6.
6. Laura Gowing, 'Anne Greene (*c.*1628–1659)', *ODNB Online* (last accessed 12 January 2020).
7. Heath, *A Chronicle of the Late Intestine War*, p. 279; Evelyn, *The Diary of John Evelyn*, pp. 252–3; Plot, *The Natural History of Oxfordshire*, pp. 197–9; Fuller, *History of the Worthies of England*, p. 341.
8. Ward, *Lives of the Professors of Gresham College*; Derham, *Physico-Theology*, p. 159.
9. Watkins, *Newes*, f. 6. In fact, in 1997, Iain Pears took Anne Greene as the model for Sarah Blundy, the central character in his novel *An Instance of the Fingerpost*, which includes narration by a fictionalised Anthony Wood.
10. Burdet, *A Wonder of Wonders*, Wing (2nd ed.)/B5620; *A Declaration from Oxford*, Wing (CD-ROM, 1996)/D585A. Randall Martin suggests the author of *Newes from the Dead* could be Ralph Bathurst, a member of Petty and Wilkins' group, although I can find no firm substantiation of this: *Women, Murder and Equity in Early Modern England*, p. 82.
11. Petty, *The Petty Papers*, vol. 2, p. 157; Christopher Wren, 'Wonder of highest Art!', in Watkins, *Newes from the Dead*, f. 13; Anthony Wood, 'I'le stretch my Muse', in ibid. ff. 16–21.
12. Morgan, *Phoenix Britannicus*; Watkins, *Newes* (Norwich: 1741).
13. Watt, *Cheap Print and Popular Piety, 1550–1640*; Nashe, *The Works of Thomas Nashe*, vol. 1, p. 20.
14. Gowing, *Common Bodies*; Walsham, *Providence in Early Modern England*; Mukherji, *Law and Representation*.
15. Stymeist, 'Criminal Biography in Early Modern News Pamphlets', p. 148.
16. Walsham, *Providence*, pp. 37–8.
17. Macfarlane, *Witchcraft in Tudor and Stuart England*, p. 86.
18. See Hutson, *Invention of Suspicion*.
19. Dolan, *True Relations*, p. 69.
20. See Hoffer and Hull, *Murdering Mothers*; Jackson (ed.), *Infanticide*.
21. See Crawford, 'Legalizing Medicine', pp. 95–7.
22. Bacon, *The Works of Sir Francis Bacon*, vol. 1, p. 513.
23. Gowing, 'Secret Births and Infanticide', p. 108.
24. Translated in Langbein, *Prosecuting Crime in the Renaissance*, appendix B.
25. Crawford, 'Legalizing Medicine', p. 96.
26. Hoffer and Hull, *Murdering Mothers*, p. 8.
27. Anthony Fitzherbert, *L'Office et Auctorite de Justices de Peace*, ed. Richard Crompton (London: 1538), trans. in Hoffer and Hull, *Murdering*

Mothers, p. 8. The case also appears in Dalton, *The countrey justice*, STC (2nd ed.)/6206, p. 218.
28. E.g. 18 Eliz. I, c. 3, which threatened punishment to parents of illegitimate children who had to be relieved 'on the parish'.
29. 7 James I, c .4.
30. *An Act to Prevent the destroying and murthering of bastard children* (21 Jac. I, c. 27), ss. I–II.
31. Hoffer and Hull, *Murdering Mothers*, p. 22.
32. Gowing, 'Secret Births and Infanticide', p. 89; Hoffer and Hull, *Murdering Mothers*, p. 23.
33. Dickinson and Sharpe, 'Infanticide in Early Modern England', p. 38.
34. Walker, *Crime, Gender and Social Order*, p. 150.
35. Jackson, 'Suspicious Infant Deaths', p. 69.
36. Ibid. p. 71.
37. Murphy, *The Old Bailey*, p. 63; Linebaugh, *The London Hanged*.
38. *A True Relation of Go[ds] Wonderfull Mercies in Preserving one Alive*.
39. Ibid. f. 3.
40. Jackson, *New-Born Child Murder*, p .6.
41. Staub, 'Early Modern Medea', p. 333.
42. Goodcole, *Nature's Cruell Step-Dames*, STC (2nd ed.)/12012.
43. *Bloody Newes from Dover*, Wing (2nd ed.)/B3267.
44. Dolan, *Dangerous Familiars*, p. 132.
45. *Deeds against Nature and Monsters by kinde*, STC (2nd ed.)/809.
46. Ibid. sig. A2.
47. Ibid. sig. B2–B3. Martin, *Women, Murder and Equity*, p. 58.
48. Parker, *No Naturall Mother but a Monster*, pp. 425–8.
49. Ibid. p. 425.
50. Ibid. p. 426.
51. *Deeds against Nature and Monsters by kinde*, sig. B3.
52. Parker, *No Naturall Mother but a Monster*, p. 427.
53. Smith, 'A "goodly sample"', p. 187.
54. Walker, *Crime, Gender and Social Order*, p. 156.
55. *Deeds against Nature and Monsters by kinde*, sig. B2; Parker, *No Naturall Mother but a Monster*, p. 427.
56. Watkins, *Newes*, f. 14.
57. Shapiro, *A Culture of Fact*, pp. 88–9.
58. Burdet, *A Wonder of Wonders*, title page.
59. Walsham, *Providence*, p. 40.
60. See n. 10 above.
61. Handwritten annotation to Anthony Wood's copy of *Newes from the Dead* in the Bodleian Library (shelfmark Wood 515(12)). See also Foster, *Alumni Oxonienses*.
62. It is unclear whether the poems were produced as an academic exercise, or were anthologised by the author, the printer or a third party. If the identification is correct, Watkins was at Christ Church, and members of his college author three poems in the first edition and four in the second. However, New College and Queen's College are both more significantly represented, whilst most of the new poems in the second edition are the work of student commoners at St John's.

63. Sawday, *The Body Emblazoned*, p. 219.
64. Staub, '"A Wench Re-Woman'd"', p. 110.
65. See Toby Barnard, 'Sir William Petty (1623–1687)', *ODNB Online* (last accessed 12 January 2020).
66. Ibid.
67. Evelyn, *The Diary of John Evelyn*, pp. 252–3.
68. Raymond (ed.), *Making the News*, p. 171.
69. Leslie, 'Representing Anne Green', p. 102.
70. Richard Garrard's poem, which contains the line: 'Night's Queen (who once herself did suffer rape)/Pitied her Parallel'. However, in her pardon petition, Greene asserts that her pregnancy was the result of 'the often temptations of one Mr. Jeffrey Read': Petty, *Petty Papers*, vol. 2, p. 165.
71. *Mercurius Politicus*, No. 28 (12–19 December 1650), f. 469.
72. Blackstone, *Commentaries on the Laws of England*, vol. 4, p. 406.
73. Fuller, *History of the Worthies of England*, p. 341.
74. Gowing, *Common Bodies*, p. 49.
75. *A Declaration from Oxford*, f. 2.
76. Leslie, 'Representing Anne Green', p. 97.
77. Ibid. p. 96.
78. *A Declaration from Oxford*, f. 2. The *Mercurius Politicus* and *Newes* accounts reveal this to be Jeffrey Read, grandson of Sir Thomas.
79. Burdet, *A Wonder of Wonders*, f. 3.
80. *A Declaration from Oxford*, f. 4; Burdet, *A Wonder of Wonders*, f. 4.
81. See Gowing, 'Secret Births and Infanticide', p. 89, on seventeenth-century Northern Circuit cases.
82. Ibid. p. 90.
83. Watkins, *Newes*, f. 1.
84. *A Declaration from Oxford*, f. 3.
85. Kelyng, *A Report of Divers Cases*, pp. 32–3.
86. Willughby, *Observations in Midwifery*, pp. 11–12.
87. Petty, *Petty Papers*, vol. 2, pp. 157–67.
88. Ibid. p. 167.
89. Ibid. pp. 164–5.
90. Ibid. p. 166.
91. Ibid. n. 1.
92. 6 & 7 Will. 4, c. 89.
93. Crawford, 'Legalizing Medicine', p. 97.
94. Mandeville, *The Fable of the Bees*, vol. 1, pp. 74–6.
95. See Jackson, 'Suspicious Infant Deaths', pp. 74–6, on the rise of forensic medicine, including the controversial testing of the child's lungs for signs of breath having been drawn. See also Gowing, 'Secret Births and Infanticide', p. 114.
96. Percival, *Medical Ethics*, p. 81.
97. Firth and Rait (eds), *Acts and Ordinances of the Interregnum, 1642–1660*, pp. 387–9.
98. Cockburn, 'Patterns of Violence in English Society', p. 96; Keith Wrightson, 'Infanticide in European history', p. 15.
99. Walsham, *Providence*, p. 38.
100. Clark (ed.), *The Life and Times of Anthony Wood*, vol. 1, pp. 250–1.

101. Ibid. p. 251.
102. For further discussion of the *Newes* poems see Hudson, '"The nine-liv'd Sex"'.
103. Walker, *Crime, Gender and Social Order*, p. 153.
104. Watkins, *Newes*, f. 18.
105. Dolan, *True Relations*, p. 69; Witmore, *Pretty Creatures*, p. 181.
106. *Discours miraculeux et véritable advenu nouvellement*. The original is in the Douai Bibliothèque Municipale, shelfmark 1589/4, octavo, 15pp.
107. Chartier, 'The Hanged Woman Miraculously Saved', p. 59.
108. All quotations are taken from the translation in Chartier's article, pp. 63–5.
109. Chartier, 'The Hanged Woman Miraculously Saved', p. 63.
110. Ibid. p. 63.
111. Watkins, *Newes*, f. 6; Chartier, 'The Hanged Woman Miraculously Saved', p. 63.
112. Ibid. p. 63. Another pamphlet account of the Belthumier case appeared in Douai in the same year. This text, in terms of content the same as the Widow Boscard's, situates itself as a second edition of a work 'imprimée à Paris par Geoffroy du Pont'. Chartier believes that the reference to a precursor may be a device deployed 'to make the miraculous event seem more credible' (p. 60).
113. Copies are held in the Bibliothèque de l'Arsenal in Paris, shelfmark 8° J 5521/5, octavo, 12 pp, and the Bibliothèque Municipale in Lille. All quotations are taken from the translation in Chartier's article, pp. 76–7.
114. Chartier, 'The Hanged Woman Miraculously Saved', p. 76.
115. Ibid. p. 77.
116. Ibid. p. 64.
117. Ibid. p. 63.
118. Burdet, *A Wonder of Wonders*, f. 4.
119. Phan, 'Les déclarations de grossesse en France (XVIe–XVIIIe siècles) Essai institutionnel', p. 61.
120. Ibid. p. 76.
121. Ibid. p. 77.
122. Ibid. p. 81.
123. De Voragine, *The Golden Legend*, vol. 2, p. 155.
124. Chartier, 'The Hanged Woman Miraculously Saved', p. 88.
125. Raymond, *Making the News*, p. 170.
126. Dolan, *True Relations*, p. 68.
127. Hutson, *Invention of Suspicion*, p. 272.
128. Chartier, 'The Hanged Woman Miraculously Saved', p. 78.
129. Ibid. p. 73.

Chapter 4

Pardon and Oblivion: Pardon, Benefit of Clergy, *Peine Forte et Dure*

> The space between sentencing and execution was, in the late seventeenth and early eighteenth century, commonly invoked as evidence of the 'particular Clemency' of the English criminal law, affording the condemned time to 'make their Peace with God, and by their sufferings under the Hands of Men, prevent eternal Condemnation'[1]
>
> BARNARDINE: I swear I will not die today for any man's persuasion.
> *Measure for Measure* (IV.iii.57)[2]

The 'particular Clemency' of the English criminal law is threaded through its narrative history in a number of ways. As Andrea McKenzie notes above, the administrative process of criminal justice was figured as opening up a space for the condemned felon's self-reflection and repentance. Yet it also functioned to other ends: in that 'space', however brief, the possibility of another outcome might be imagined and even sometimes achieved. Pardon, reprieve, benefit of clergy: all or any of these could occupy that interval, changing the equation of crime and sanction. This chapter explores the 'space' between sentence and execution and the ways in which English law complicated the relationship between the two concepts. It examines the uses of pardon in early modern society, the influence of political forces on pardon as a mechanism and the individual's agency in negotiating with those forces. It also considers the early modern literary imagining of that space, the tension of inevitability and possibility that informs it and the moral schema attached to pardon and its abuses.

There were many routes to a pardon in the period of this study and many sanctions that were in themselves a mitigation of a capital sentence. Exile, abjuration of the realm, military service, galley service and – as we shall see in Chapter 5 – transportation to the English colonies were all known or emerging mechanisms for a reprieve from death, whilst in the early part of the period, a recourse to sanctuary was still a viable means of avoiding trial in the first place. This chapter, however, focuses on two of the chief strategies by which mercy was administered under law: the royal pardon and benefit of clergy. In closing, it returns to the start of the process to examine the problematic consequence of a refusal to participate in the system, the *peine forte et dure*. One potential route to mercy that is not addressed here is reprieve for pregnancy, or pleading the belly; this in part due to space available, in part due to the differing status of that benefit. Whilst pleading the belly is often conflated with benefit of clergy, the two were not equivalents: the former was very clearly a reprieve and not a pardon. While a successful belly plea was a benefit that might subsequently allow women to participate in the processes of pardon (a subject that requires a much more substantial study), nonetheless, as Cynthia Herrup reminds us, it 'postponed rather than voided a sentence of death', delaying it until the child was delivered and usually for a month thereafter.[3]

This chapter, like those that precede it, engages with a range of literary, popular and legal texts; however, its core focus is Shakespeare's *Measure for Measure*, first performed in 1604, at the start of James I's reign. As Fiona McNeill comments: '"Measure for Measure" suggests that there is and should always be an incontrovertible equivalence between the punishment and the crime.'[4] In fact, the play is deeply preoccupied with the subversion of that equivalence, rehearsing a range of positions on the question of sanction, and exhibiting a calibration of justice that, at times, is anything but measured. Its plot is driven by a request for mercy and, as Andrew Majeske notes, it ends 'with a host of marriages and pardons'.[5] Certainly, it offers an examination of the possibilities of state clemency in relation to the individual. How should we read the figures of legal authority in *Measure for Measure* – and how do ideas of pardon inflect those readings? Whilst considerable critical effort has been expended in exploring Shakespeare's depiction of the Duke as a figure for the newly crowned James I, recent readers have revised this positioning in a number of interesting ways. In fact, rather than offering one account of justice, I argue that the play encodes multiple narratives of lawgiving and sanction, functioning as a compendium of contemporary issues and approaches. As such, and alongside a number of other early modern plays, *Measure for Measure* works here to expose both the ambivalence surrounding pardon and the problems inherent in mercy as a practice.

A note on semantics: in this chapter the terms 'pardon' and 'clemency' are both used to denote the legal or, at times, political act of waiving, adapting or reducing the official punishment stipulated for a criminal offence. 'Mercy' is also used, perhaps more problematically, for, as

Nasser Hussain and Austin Sarat observe, the status of mercy within a structure of judgment is not a given: 'Is mercy an act or an attitude? Could it function as the term that joins forgiveness and clemency?'[6] As a term, 'forgiveness' is not widely used in what follows, although, observing the discourses of subjection and salvation that attach to the pardoning process, there could be much to be learned from further investigation into the concept of forgiveness under law.

'What muffled fellow's that?': the Idea of a Pardon

DUKE: ... What muffled fellow's that?
PROVOST: This is another prisoner that I saved,
  Who should have died when Claudio lost his head,
  As like almost to Claudio as himself.
[Unmuffles Claudio.]
DUKE *[to Isabella]*:
  If he be like your brother, for his sake
  Is he pardoned. (V.i.486–491)

Pardon was as essential to the operation of English law as sanction itself and this was particularly the case as the Tudor and Stuart states negotiated the administration of justice arising from increasingly complex statutory and common law regimes, attempting to balance rigour in prosecution with a fair and equitable implementation of punishment. 'One of the great advantages of monarchy', Blackstone comments, '[is] that there is a magistrate, who has it in his power to extend mercy, ... holding a court of equity in his own breast, to soften the rigour of the general law.'[7] Far from a simple act of generosity, however, early modern pardon was a structured transaction in which both bestower and receiver performed specified roles. As K. J. Kesselring comments:

> A pardon had no intrinsic meaning: its significance depended on its proper presentation ... At least two actors participated in every performance of pardon: the monarch and the guilty party. Both benefited, although in different and unequal ways.[8]

Such an understanding exists in ambiguous relationship to many readings of clemency. Jacques Derrida, for example, identifies the pardon as fundamentally illogical and disruptive, positioned as it is in complex theological relation to conditionality. Whilst some form of provision may nominally attach itself to a pardon (the performance of repentance, for example), forgiveness is not guaranteed: in essence, 'a pardon ... must pardon the unpardonable and without condition'.[9] Thus, a pardon, for Derrida, is at once an act of grace and also a shock. For the early modern period, the gallows or scaffold pardon seems the most resonant manifestation of this dynamic. In December 1603, when James I reprieved Ralegh, Markham, Cobham and Grey, he did so via an elaborately staged proceeding, in which each offender was brought to the scaffold, and each believed the others to have been executed, before the king's grace was revealed – 'see the mercy of your Prince, who of himself hath sent hither a countermand, and hath given you your lives!'[10] The theatricality of the king's approach was aimed as much at the attending crowds at the scaffold as at the prisoners themselves, but also at James' own Privy Council members, who had advocated for mercy, and supposed their petitions unheard. The king revealed his actions to the Council only after the event and then with appropriate flourish.[11]

The awe and spectacle inherent in such a display of royal magnanimity seems to support a narrative of pardon as fundamentally disruptive; yet this was not incompatible with its transactional qualities. Despite James' efforts to conceal the imminence of mercy, a core element of the drama inherent in the gallows pardon in this period was its possibility – the hope or anticipation of which was often shared by the condemned felon and the attendant crowd. That audience understood the often random nature of pardon, but also the part they played in shoring up that very appearance of randomness, and thus the benevolent power of the sovereign and his or her law. Appropriate performance was key, and conditionality could coexist with wonder; as Andrea McKenzie has described, this was:

> a culture of deference that nominally, at least, made mercy conditional upon the observance of certain forms. Not least of these was the ritual by which those whose sentences of death were commuted or who received full pardons were obliged to beg such pardons on their knees ... to bless both the King 'and all the honourable court'.[12]

Moreover, as the seventeenth century progressed, conditionality became an increasing feature of the pardoning process, as outcomes such as transportation foregrounded the transactional nature of pardon; no longer purely 'the mercy of your Prince', by degrees the royal clemency became a practical sentencing option. This chapter, then, acknowledges the pardon's complex functioning, located in between entitlement and benevolence, procedure and disruption.

The functions of pardon have been much debated by scholars of both legal and social history. Douglas Hay's influential Marxist reading of eighteenth-century legal practice positioned pardon as a tool of the elite, consciously manipulated to bolster social hierarchy and protect property rights – a 'selective instrument of class justice'.[13] Whilst Hay's thesis successfully articulates the flexibility of sanction that we see in the period, it has been countered and inflected by other accounts of early modern clemency. Among such is that propounded by Cynthia Herrup, who considers both enforcement and equity as functions of a participatory and communal system of governance: '[t]he law relied too heavily upon communal participation to function except where the penal structure could express both modulated degrees of popular outrage and the finality of official power.'[14] This balance between state power, local influence and individual agency is key. Subsequent commentators, including Lorna Hutson and Steve Hindle, have observed the way in which early modern law in practice negotiates this relationship, describing the structures that entailed delegation and cooperation between a many and varied cast of participants in the sessions and assize processes, from Privy Councillors through assize judges, to Justices of the Peace, constables, sheriffs, bailiffs, churchwardens and jurors.[15]

Beyond this, I would argue, lay the individual's direct engagement with the law, as accused, condemned or associate, and nowhere is this more manifest than in the encounter with pardon or reprieve. 'To sue to live, I find I seek to die,' Claudio contends (III.i.43), and the negotiation, machination and desperation we see displayed in relation to pardon, in both the literary and the legal record, simultaneously illuminate and complicate our understanding of the place of the subject under the law.

'I find an apt remission in myself': General and Special Pardons

> DUKE: How came it that the absent Duke had not either delivered him to his liberty or executed him? ...
> PROVOST: His friends still wrought reprieves for him (IV.ii.130–3)

What emerges strongly from any account of its history, is that clemency was used and expected to be used as part of the rhythm of early modern justice. It is difficult to ascertain with certainty either the numbers of executions conducted in the Tudor and Stuart periods, or the proportion of the condemned represented in those numbers. John Higgins comments that estimates 'have placed the overall number of hangings in England and Wales from 1559 to 1624 at over 24,000 men and women'.[16] J. S. Cockburn suggests that of those convicted, only approximately 10 per cent were hanged, whilst J. A. Sharpe puts this proportion at 14 per cent.[17] Overall, as J. M. Beattie has commented, while the scope of capital offences grew throughout the early modern period, the consequence of this also began to be actively managed: 'after very high levels of capital punishment in the early seventeenth century ... executions fell gradually to lower and relatively stable levels'.[18] In his *Institutes*, Edward Coke summarised the position: 'Mercy and truth preserve the King and by clemency is his Throne strengthened. And hereupon is the law of England grounded.'[19]

As Henry VIII's 'Act for recontynuying of certayne liberties and francheses' had confirmed, the power to pardon vested in the monarch alone:

> That no personne or personnes ... shall have any power or auctoritie to pardon or remitte any tresons, murders, manslaughters or any kyndes of felonnyes whatsoever they be ... but that the Kinges highnesse, ... shall have the hole and sole power and auctoritie thereof ... any other thing to the contrarie hereof notwithstanding.[20]

While that sole authority might be delegated to and at times challenged by other representatives of state, nonetheless the power to pardon was deployed as a matter of course by monarchs throughout the medieval and early modern periods, in ways that reflected both personal and political agendas.[21] Inaugural pardons were a feature of monarchical accession, especially when that accession had come via some controversy or at cost. In 1553 Mary Tudor's coronation procession included the reading of her clemency by the Lord Chancellor, a process by which she pardoned all treasons, homicides, rebellions and felonies committed prior to her investiture, excluding only a number of named individuals, notably those accused of facilitating the movement to bring Jane Grey to the throne.[22] More than a century later, Charles II issued a momentous Act of Indempnity and Oblivion at the start of his restored reign, a statute that listed every one of the regicides as exceptions to his otherwise boundless mercy.[23] His grandfather, James VI, en route through England to become James I, marked his progress with a very practical form of pardon, liberating prisoners in the towns through which he passed. Nonetheless, there were parameters to the monarch's pardoning power, as Edward Coke noted in his *Institutes*. The king or queen could only pardon matters in which he or she had 'an interest', that is, a case brought by the Crown, and was not expected to intervene in private disputes. Sanctions issued as a matter of process could be waived, such as burning in the hand in a case of manslaughter, 'for it is a collateral and exemplary punishment', but judgments that were a form of restitution to a plaintiff could not.[24] Such limitations reinforced the very personal nature of the monarch's clemency.

General pardons might be issued either by royal proclamation or via parliamentary statute, the latter form introduced under Edward III and a regular feature of the later Tudor parliaments: Elizabeth, for example, issued general pardons after almost all of her parliamentary sessions, as a marker of gratitude for taxes and subsidies granted to the Crown. The two types of pardon gradually took on each their own character, with parliamentary pardons growing, as Herrup indicates, 'wordier and narrower', documenting increasing numbers of exceptions to their clemency.[25] The process for issuing a statutory pardon was, in theory, straightforward. A draft document was prepared by the Attorney General, often based upon previous pardons, and this was approved by the monarch and sent to Parliament. Unlike Bills, draft pardons would be read only once in each House and were not expected to be debated. They were published as statutes and intended to have a wide reach; as such they were usually prefaced with a detailed preamble, setting out the rationale for the monarch's move to pardon and reassuring the more conservative reader as to the persistence of the firm rule of law. The preamble to a pardon of Henry VIII, for example, emphasised that it was not intended 'to give audacity to offenders upon hope of impunity' but to be a 'preemptory monition' to the monarch's subjects.[26]

In general, copies of pardons issued by proclamation could be purchased from Chancery for presentation in court proceedings. As J. S. Cockburn notes, 'the judge regularly, if sometimes belatedly, postponed execution of judgment until pardons could be secured', citing the case of 'John Peppure, being on the ladder and the halter about his neck' when he was 'commanded down' and permitted to request a pardon.[27] Whilst pardons were described as granted 'freely', in practice their benefits came at a price. The fee for Elizabeth I's coronation pardon, for example, was 26s 8d, making it a substantial, if presumably worthwhile, investment. Such documents were structured as pro formas:

> ... by these presents we do pardon, remit and release A.B., of C., in the county of D. gent, otherwise known (etc.), or by what other name or cognomen soever, or addition of name or names, dignity, office, or place the same A.B. is known, called, or listed, or formerly was known, called or listed:
>
> All and singular treasons, capital or otherwise ... Done or perpetrated by the same A.B. before the Feast of All Saints last past.[28]

Whilst this may suggest that access to pardons was limited to the economically advantaged 'gent.', Kesselring notes that amongst the purchasers of earlier pardons were shepherds and fishmongers. Women also bought pardons, but in much smaller numbers – of the 2,725 purchasers of the coronation pardon, less than 5 per cent were female.[29]

Pardons issued by statute did not have to be individually purchased and could merely be pleaded in court; a fee (typically of 16d throughout the period) was payable to the court clerk for recording the claim in these instances. Interestingly, in some seventeenth-century cases, an equivalent or alternative fee is mentioned. Convicted of manslaughter in 1685, John Brampston pleaded 'his Majesties Pardon on his Knees, and gave the Court Papers of Gloves as is usual in such cases'.[30] It seems that this was a regular expectation: John Kelyng, recording a 1674 Newgate Sessions case, notes that a pardoned defendant 'paid Gloves to the judges, which is the due fee for that'.[31] Evidence that the gloves fee was current earlier in the century, as well as a clue to its symbolism, comes from a 1628 pamphlet, John Clavell's *A recantation of an ill-led life*, which includes the couplet: 'Those pardon'd men, who taste their Prince's loves,/(As married to new life) do give you Gloves.'[32] Gloves were typically given as gifts to guests at weddings but they also had a more explicit association with reprieve, being symbolically presented by sheriffs to judges at what were termed 'maiden assizes' – 'when no Malefactour is put to death therein; a great Rarity'.[33]

Whilst the Tudor monarchy bolstered pardoning power as a tool of royal might, in the seventeenth century the rhythm of marking each parliamentary recess with a pardon statute was disrupted by negotiation and resistance in the House of Commons. After his early display of magnanimity, James I issued only two pardons by statute (in 1609 and 1624), whilst his son, negotiating a very specific form of regnal crisis, passed no parliamentary pardons at all.[34] In part this was related to the shifting political agenda of the period, but the parliamentary pardon's complex constitutional and procedural status, as a statute which seemed exempt from the usual processes of debate, exacerbated potential tensions. Proposed pardons in 1614 and 1621 miscarried in negotiations relating to the levels of property debt to be erased, as well as the amount of royal subsidy to be granted – the 1621 parliamentary session concluded with an incredulous Edward Coke's comment that he had 'never heard of any End of a Session, but . . . a Pardon, if Subsidy'.[35]

Despite fraught negotiations, Stuart parliaments remained fundamentally in favour of general pardon, when achievable. There was no sense in which the fundamental power to pardon was perceived as an overreach on the part of the Crown, and statute pardons in particular bolstered perception of the parliamentary process, as Lords and Commons were seen to participate in royal clemency.[36] Indeed, during the Interregnum pardons continued to be granted, initially by Parliament, later moving – along with so many monarchical prerogatives – within the Protector's remit. Of course, many MPs and their constituents would have had a financial interest in debt relief and pardons were thus perceived as a universal benefit, rather than something associated explicitly with criminality and moral turpitude. In her study of a 'mock pardon' performed as part of the Christmas revels at Gray's Inn in 1594 and recorded later in the *Gesta Grayorum* (1688), Virginia Lee Strain notes the figuring of those benefiting as 'accidental' offenders who have fallen foul of a complex statutory regime and may be released from its 'snares' by the intervention of a benign sovereign.[37] The law was implicitly critiqued by the very existence of the general pardon.

Such a positioning was fundamentally pragmatic in nature; yet it also opened up a fissure between the law and the monarch. Whilst this sovereign grace, this correction of the law's excesses, might at times be characterised as 'carrying God's stampe and marke', as Henry Finch commented, in practice it was not quite divine, not quite providential.[38] The political and even personal nature of some exceptions and inclusions were well understood. Moreover, there was a persistent – and largely valid – assumption that a general pardon was, essentially, a quid pro quo for subsidies, a reciprocal pairing of taxation and absolution. In reality, this relationship was perhaps more complex, for the issuing of a general pardon could also cost the kingdom in unlevied fines and confiscations, described as a 'great increase of treasure' in an Elizabethan preamble; nonetheless the association persisted.[39]

If the rhetoric of the general pardon positioned the individual as perpetually at risk of 'divers great Penaltyes', as an instrument of mercy the pardon could itself be dangerous. In *Measure for Measure*, Vienna has functioned in what is effectively a state of general pardon for so long that its population has forgotten the performance of deference required to sustain such a benefit. Vincentio's comment on the law, 'the strong statutes/Stand like the forfeits in a barber's shop,/As much in mock as mark' (V.i.318–21), may be doom-mongering, but the expectation that pardon would be an outcome of judicial process could lead individuals to take risks, risks that disrupted the very balance of awe and mercy that the pardons sought to preserve. This was evident in the months preceding Elizabeth's coronation, as J. Strype records: '[t]he hopes of pardon and grace, usually accompanying it, occasioned many enormities, and especially robberies, to be committed.'[40]

Further, the existence of pardon as a known outcome could have unintended consequences. In 1660, at the Gloucestershire assizes, three defendants, brothers John and Richard Perry and Joan, their mother, stood accused of the robbery and murder of John's master, William Harrison, who had vanished without trace. At their first trial the Perrys were indicted not only for the murder-robbery (a charge the judge refused to hear because no body had been found), but also for an unsolved burglary of the Harrison house that had taken place the previous year. An account of the proceedings runs thus:

> they were then tried upon the other Indictment for Robbery, to which they pleaded Not Guilty; but, some whispering behind them, they soon after pleaded Guilty, humbly begging the Benefit of his Majesty's gracious Pardon and Act of Oblivion, which was granted them.
>
> But, tho' they pleaded Guilty to this Indictment, ... yet they all, afterwards, and at their Deaths, denied that they were guilty of that Robbery.[41]

The 'Act of Free and General Pardon, Indempnity and Oblivion', Charles II's restoration pardon, had received Royal Assent on 29 August 1660 and pardoned offences committed throughout the Civil War and Interregnum. As the first Harrison robbery had taken place in 1659, it came under the auspices of the Act and no sentence was imposed. However, though they escaped punishment for the burglary, the Perrys' guilty plea was to form indubitable evidence in law that they were thieves. At a second trial they were convicted of robbery and murder and were subsequently hanged. Two years after their deaths, Harrison, their supposed victim, returned home, alive and well.

For those for whom clemency under a general statute was not an option, an individual pardon remained a possibility. As Isabella pleads for Claudio, and as Barnardine's 'friends' attempt intercession on his behalf, so many offenders and their associates sought mercy directly from the Crown. Special pardons were administratively complex, requiring numerous steps to be followed to gain access to the monarch, and costs could reflect this. As we saw in Chapter 3, Anne Greene purchased her pardon with the donations of those 'multitudes' who came to witness her resurrection; by the time a pardon had been successfully pled, Cynthia Herrup calculates, it might have cost the petitioner 'more than most people's yearly income'.[42] The administration of the system once again vested in Chancery, which issued charters of pardon to successful suitors, recording their success in the patent rolls. In the interim, the petition and any supporting testimony was sent for review to the judge who had presided over the relevant criminal proceedings and whose report on the individual was the determining factor in his or her suit.

For certain offences and in certain circumstances a special pardon represented a useful response. The law of manslaughter, for example, was evolving in the period and many homicides, accidental, negligent or committed in self-defence, were still prosecuted as murder. In such circumstances an appeal to the Crown could prove key. One such successful request was made by William Sneades in 1628. Sneades, a soldier, petitioned in respect of an event thirteen years earlier, when he had fatally wounded Edward Worthington in self-defence. 'Unadvisedly' Sneades had fled overseas and, having returned, sought pardon on the grounds of manslaughter. Sneades' plea to the Crown is totemic in its humility:

> ... hee humbly prostrates, both himself att your majesties feete, and his life to your majesties service, which if your majestie be graciously pleased to give him, he most faithfully promiseth most zealously to expose the same, to the service of your majestie and the honour of his countrie, and soe longe as the same endureth to magnifie your majesties mercye, for whose happines and longe life, hee shall daylie pray.[43]

The management of such offences via the pardon process allowed effective administration of justice while a more formal legal response was still being developed. Thus, as J. M. Beattie notes, the power to pardon 'was used ... as an ordinary and established aspect of the way the law was administered'.[44]

Carefully reinforcing royal might, such 'humble' texts as William Sneades' participated in the performance of deference that attended every element of the pardon process. Whilst in her study of French pardon petitions, Natalie Zemon Davis suggests that 'when a lawyer was approached by a supplicant about a letter of remission, he was likely to be interested in it as a story, not just a legal problem', the element of narrative is less prominent in their English equivalent.[45] Instead, these texts relied on avowals of remorse, youth, steady prospects, good service and family responsibilities to sway justice in the petitioner's favour. Assistance with drafting or the provision of testimonials from local authority figures was also valuable: Barnardine's 'friends' have effectively facilitated his reprieve for nine years when *Measure for Measure* opens. While Barnardine's 'fact' (his guilt) has previously been 'doubtful', the possibility of innocence was rarely a consideration in the formal processes of clemency. Although judges might note some weakness in testimony when recommending mercy, to explicitly acknowledge a miscarriage of justice was not politic. In the absence of legal mechanisms to overturn a guilty verdict, a pardon was really the only means of addressing this hypothetical situation. Hence, Anne Greene and her well-wishers sue for her reprieve and pardon, rather than a vacation of her conviction.

One petitioner who did protest innocence was Ellen Charlton, a 'poore distressed widdowe' from Northumberland, who made a submission to the King in 1631. Her case offers an interesting account of one family's engagement with the pardon process. Charlton, a mother of six, had previously petitioned on behalf of her two sons, who had been condemned to death for horse theft.[46] While the judge in the case had 'certified that her sons were fit for mercy by the pardon for the birth of the Prince' (presumably Charles, born in 1630), still 'they were cut off'.[47] The reasons for this are not stated, but theft of horses, often linked to gangs, was regularly exempted from general pardons. Charlton's unsuccessful petitioning had cost her dear. Having 'thorowe long suite . . . spent all her meanes', not only was she financially ruined, but found herself also 'in daunger of her life', having been subsequently convicted of harbouring 'her said 2 sonns (shee knoweing noe missbehaviour or misdemeanour by them), a capital offence'.[48] This time Charlton was to have her grant of pardon, although, notably, a tender royal clemency was the determining factor, rather than her claimed innocence – the Attorney General's comment on her petition noted that 'she is very capable of his Majesty's pardon. Even if she knew her sons' offences, he inclines far to favour a mother in such a case.'[49] Despite success, Charlton was forced to continue lobbying to keep the wheels of bureaucracy turning. Two weeks after her request was accepted, she submitted a further petition: 'Her own fitness for pardon having been certified by the Attorney General, she prays that order may be given for drawing the same up.'[50]

Petitioners did not always request complete absolution; some offered an alternative means to repay their debt to society, such as military service or exile. This was a different kind of transaction, the performance of humility replaced by practical (if future) recompense. At times, conditional pardon might be agreed quite outside of protocol. Writing of a band of 'Egyptians' arrested in Huntingdonshire in 1544, David Cressy notes:

> Two of the leaders were sentenced to be hanged, but the Gypsies surprised everyone by offering three hundred pounds to save them from the gallows. This was a huge sum of money. . . . The cash-strapped Council acknowledged 'it would be hard to attain this money otherwise'.[51]

The Duke's pardons at the end of *Measure for Measure* offer a different sort of conditionality – 'look that you love your wife . . . thou shalt marry her' (V.i.497, 518) – although at first they appear to have the sweep of a general pardon, technically they have a more complex status, located, as we shall see, somewhere between conditional pardon and direct sentencing. Indeed, at first it is unclear whether, for Angelo and Lucio at least, they are only really reprieves: 'The nuptial finished/Let him be whipped and hanged' (V.i.512–13). What *Measure for Measure* here crystallises, in fact, is the often contradictory deployment of mercy as a tool of early modern law enforcement.

'There is a devilish mercy in the judge': the Delegation of Clemency

The earliest evidence of *Measure for Measure* in performance comes from the records of the Revels, which note that 'a Play called Mesur for Mesur' was performed at Whitehall on St Stephen's Night 1604, a fact that has tied readings of the play closely to James I and his incoming Stuart regime.[52] In 1598, James' *True Law of Free Monarchies* had set out the then King of Scotland's formulation of a sovereign's absolute power in relation to legal process:

> the King is above the Law, as both the author and giver of strength thereto ... and therfore generall lawes, made publikely in Parliament, may, upon knowne respectes to the King, by his authoritie be mitigated, and suspended upon causes onely knowne to him.[53]

Indeed, if Vincentio is a representation of the newly arrived Scottish monarch, his portrayal may be read as 'ominous', as Constance Jordan notes: 'The action throughout the play establishes that the Duke is a prince-legislator and his authority is absolute; ... he does not govern by means provided by the institution of a court of law.'[54]

Yet, *Measure for Measure* is a work which, as Leah Marcus comments, 'is "double written" in a way that allows for other meanings'.[55] More than double, perhaps, for the play makes reference to a range of positions and problematics associated with the enforcement of criminal law. One of these is its analysis of the role of devolved justice in practice. In Act 2, scene 2, the Provost – perhaps the play's most upright public servant – seeks assurance from Angelo that Claudio's sentence should go ahead the following day. 'Why dost thou ask again?' demands the Deputy:

> PROVOST: Lest I might be too rash:
> Under your good correction I have seen
> When after execution, judgement hath
> Repented o'er his doom. (II.ii.10–13)

This tactical attempt to suggest that Angelo reflect upon his severity is curtly dismissed – 'Do you your office or give up your place' (15) – but through his comment Shakespeare recalls his audience to a crucial part of the role of the judge.

The judiciary's role in implementing the culture of clemency was not restricted to reporting on individual requests. There was a long history of judges using discretion to recommend individuals for mercy and this latitude was formalised in the mid-sixteenth century, when assize and sessions judges began to be encouraged to submit lists of condemned prisoners who they deemed fit recipients of pardon. In 1554 Mary I's Privy Council asked assize judges to issue blanket reprieves to convicted felons, with certain exceptions (notably those convicted of treason, murder, burglary and rape). The London courts took a similar approach and, soon afterwards, large-scale pardons were issued for those who had been reprieved. Thus, judicial recommendation began to form part of the rhythm of the assize process. The 'circuit pardon', as it came to be known, enabled the Crown and Privy Council to achieve the balance of justice and mercy in a very visible way, across a wide geography, and, moreover, to demonstrate royal clemency to candidates who might have lacked the means to access other pardons. Whilst a circuit pardon was effectively a special pardon covering a number of individuals, its more streamlined administration meant that it avoided the level of cost associated with the former; official fees were often waived, although jailors might expect to levy a charge on those benefiting. In cases of felony, by the mid-seventeenth century the special pardon was increasingly superseded by its circuit equivalent, although J. M. Beattie suggests that by the 1680s this was being reviewed, citing an instruction to justices from the Lord Keeper that noted: 'No person to be inserted that is able to bear the charge of a particular pardon.'[56]

Although the circuit pardon was intended to create a two-way dialogue between centralised government and the devolved assize structure, this delegation of justice could cause problems on occasion. General administration of the process required good communication and prompt response. In 1656, for example, in a letter from Major General Edward Whalley to Secretary Thurloe, concerns were expressed:

> about the clearing of prysons of reprived persons. Every sizes adds to the number, and fills the goales fuller, to the great charge of the countery ... Some are fit to be pardoned and set at liberty; others, as hie-way-men, breakers of houses, horse-stealers, &c. you cannot do better than to send them beyond sea.[57]

J. S. Cockburn has suggested that in many cases pardons for individual circuits might only be issued 'at intervals of between three and five years', while reprieved convicts remained in gaol, possibly resorting to special pardons in the interim.[58]

Recent readers of *Measure for Measure* have set aside the play's putative dialogue with the Stuart monarchy, focusing instead on its depiction of devolved justice and common law procedures. In a compelling reading, Virginia Lee Strain suggests that the play's structure evokes the cadence of the assize process, the twice-yearly visitation and departure of judges, a momentum of absence and presence that existed alongside the day-to-day efforts of local magistrates:

> Between these two coordinates of the Duke's departure and return, or during the invisible part of the assize system, the strengths and weaknesses of local officers are exposed and finally officially recognised in the open-air hearing that concludes the play.[59]

In between assizes, local officers were exhorted to, as William Lambarde terms it, 'conserve the Peace, both by staying them that doe any way adventure towards the breache thereof, and by punishing them that doe acually enter into the verie violation of the same'.[60] They were the representatives and conduits of state justice on a local scale – and a crucial part of this responsibility inhered in knowing when and how to apply the full rigour of the law. Their success in this venture would be assessed when the circuit judges returned. For Strain, then, the Duke's ceremonial return and summary justice marks the fulfilment of the current cycle of legal process:

> Twice have the trumpets sounded.
> The generous and gravest citizens
> Have hent the gates, and very near upon
> The Duke is entering' (IV.vi.12–14).

There are a number of questions raised by the positioning of Vincentio in the role of assize judge. The play admits of no external authority, no monarch, Privy Council or legislative body beyond the Duke. Moreover, while Vincentio's fantasy of absence and presence is certainly the rhythm of the assizes, it is also, just as Lucio describes it, 'fantastical' – there is no sense in which the Duke is expected to withdraw again at the end of Act 5. Nonetheless, a depiction of the relationship between delegated and centralised justice in practice – and crucially, its operation in relation to pardon – is clearly a part of the play's multi-stranded representation of early modern law.

Angelo, it seems, is tasked with reinstatement of Vienna's 'strict statutes and most biting laws' (I.iii.19), most specifically 'to unloose this tied-up justice' (32), which will condemn Claudio. What is less noted in the Duke's commission to his Deputy is that it offers Angelo a broader spectrum of possibility: 'Your scope is as mine own/So to enforce or qualify the laws/As to your soul seems good' (I.i.64–6). Angelo's 'scope to qualify' the impact of the law is certainly under-used in the play – as Lucio notes, he 'follows close the rigour of the statute' – but it is undeniable that mercy is within his gift. It is worth noting, of course, that Escalus is also nervous about the consequences of mercy in Vienna: 'Mercy is not itself, that oft looks so;/Pardon is still the nurse of second woe' (II.i.274–5), preferring instead to follow Lambarde's pre-emptive route, as displayed in his attempts to bind Pompey over on a bond of good behaviour: 'I advise you let me not find you before me again upon any complaint whatsoever' (II.i.235–6). Pompey, of course, will ultimately participate in yet another early modern form of reprieve, accepting the Provost's offer of a role as prison hangman, to 'redeem you from your gyves' (IV.ii.10–11).

In George Whetstone's *Promos and Cassandra*, Shakespeare's main source for *Measure for Measure*, the downfall of Promos the magistrate, the play's Angelo-equivalent, is facilitated by his corrupt deputy, Phallax, a vice-figure whose influence throughout the play is unremittingly destructive.[61] That Shakespeare removes this extreme character completely in his re-rendering of the Promos story indicates a focus on a more recognisable range of positions in his depiction of local law enforcement. And it is, of course, another officer of the court, the 'gentle provost' (IV.ii.84), who ultimately enacts the Duke's commission. A fixer and facilitator, the Provost is busy about his project of practical mitigation throughout the play: offering businesslike resolutions to Pompey's situation – 'here in this prison is a common executioner who lacks a helper' (IV.ii.9) – ensuring that the 'groaning' Juliet is 'provided for' (II.ii.17; II.iii.17) and identifying the opportunity that will unlock the Duke's capacity for mercy:

> PROVOST: Here in the prison, father,
>   There died this morning of a cruel fever
>   One Ragozine, a most notorious pirate,
>   A man of Claudio's years . . .   (IV.iii.68–70)

As Derek Dunne notes, 'The distinction between the local justice and a centrally-appointed judge is crucial, . . . each brought their own values and motivations to the proceedings.'[62] The Provost's bloodless remedy may represent a victory of equitable pragmatism, rather than sovereign clemency; as such, however, it is not too far removed from many of the accommodations of the early modern system of sanction.

'Desperately mortal': Offence and Jurisdiction

PROVOST: ... Where's Barnardine?
CLAUDIO: As fast locked up in sleep, as guiltless labour
  When it lies starkly in the traveller's bones
  He will not wake. (IV.ii.63–6)

Suspended between arrest and execution for almost a decade, accused of murder, but as yet undispatched, the presence – and more particularly, the survival – of Barnardine is *Measure for Measure*'s most puzzling feature. Barnardine does not appear in Shakespeare's sources and his function within the play seems to be obviated in IV.iii, when Ragozine's death in custody provides the grisly prop for the Duke and Provost's plan. 'A creature unprepared, unmeet for death', Barnardine exists in a state of perpetual deferral of sentence, tormenting his would-be executioners with his lack of readiness to die: 'to transport him in the mind he is/Were damnable' (IV.iii.65–7). When the play concludes, with its neat, if problematic, pairings-off of the main characters, Barnardine is the outlier, destined only to be 'advised' by the Friar. Surely, Barnardine's function must be to provide the counterpoint to the acts of clemency that litter the final scene of the play? His offence, after all, is murder, his case clearly distinguished from the strained sexual policing of Vienna, he is presented at times as little more than a caged animal: 'I hear his straw rustle' (IV.iii.34). If any of the play's many and varied offenders could be unequivocally sent to his death, it is Barnardine. His punishment would have full exemplary value, a manifestation of Vienna's 'most biting laws' (I.iii.19), unlike Angelo's attempts to execute Claudio under a resurrected statutory measure, a 'drowsy and neglected act' (I.ii.165).

The 'desperately mortal' Barnardine's pardon therefore crystallises the many ambiguities surrounding mercy in the play (IV.ii.144). In one interpretation of Act 5, Andrew Majeske, drawing on Derrida's positioning of pardon, rejects the narrative of equity that has often accompanied readings of *Measure for Measure*.[63] Majeske sees the Duke's objective as a project of extreme state re-formation, which requires the repression introduced by Angelo as proxy to be spectacularly disrupted by an act of clemency existing far beyond the bounds of equitable reason. The many pardons of the play all function to this end, but Barnardine's pardon, which owes nothing to equity, is the most effective: '[P]ublicly pardoning a convicted criminal, it seems, could in theory be every bit as potent a display of the state's power over its subjects – every bit as shocking – as the actual execution of a criminal would be.'[64]

Whilst Barnardine's pardon is undoubtedly questionable, I would contend that there are additional factors in play here. The audience of *Measure for Measure*, like the spectators at an execution, carry with them the possibility of mercy, not least because they have witnessed the Duke's 'behind the scenes' manoeuvring throughout the play. Moreover, Barnardine's fate – to be pardoned on condition of delivery into the Friar's care – is decided in the space of eight lines in Act 5, and the play then moves immediately to its major reveal: that Claudio remains living (V.i.489). His pardon may be set down as a marker, but it is not dwelt upon. Lucio's pronounced punishment and subsequent reprieve has a similar shock value, rendered more acute if the audience is keeping a tally of offence versus consequence. 'Slandering a prince' may 'deserve it' (V.i.524), but whipping, hanging and enforced marriage seems initially disproportionate, until we remember the early evidence of the Bawd, that Lucio has a child with Kate Keepdown (III.i.457) and is, in effect, guilty of the same crime as Claudio. We may also recall Lucio's assumption of Claudio's capital offence in I.ii: 'What is't, murder?' (132). In this context, Barnardine's sudden pardon may be surprising, but it is at least a clear-cut outcome, setting a stable benchmark for the chaos that is to follow.

On one level, the discussion surrounding Barnardine's case seems to suggest a close association with contemporary legal process:

PROVOST His friends still wrought reprieves for him;
   and indeed his fact, till now in the government of
   Lord Angelo, came not to an undoubtful proof.
DUKE, *as Friar* It is now apparent?
PROVOST Most manifest, and not denied by himself. (IV.ii.134–7)

Yet the reference to Barnardine's 'fact', or guilt, along with the information that such doubt has been eliminated under Angelo's jurisdiction, undermines this representation. It is unclear within the bounds of the play whether Barnardine has ever been tried for his crime; certainly, it does not seem that any such proceeding has reached a verdict 'till now'. In fact, it is only at the very moment of his pardon that Barnardine is condemned, his 'undoubtful proof' now apparently 'manifest': 'Thou'rt condemned./But, for these earthly faults, I quit them all.' (V.i.482-3). This double transformation, from innocence to guilt and back again, is both a display and a mitigation of judicial power, but it simultaneously disrupts any sense that this is a true exercise of official process. Are we witnessing here the erratic nature of pardon's application? Or its power to address problematic facts and offences?

Equally, perhaps what is being presented here is a commentary on law in transition. The bulk of what is being punished or pardoned in

Act 5 is, of course, 'fornication, adultery, and all uncleanliness', as Elbow terms it (II.i.77). In 1604 legal discussion of the regulation of sexual wrongdoing centred upon the related questions of jurisdiction and sanction. A decade earlier, Richard Cosin, writing a defence of church courts, had emphasised that 'all unlawfull companie of man and woman, not being capitall by the lawes of the *Realme* is subject to the *Jurisdiction Ecclesiasticall*'.[65] However, for those, like Angelo, who 'would make him [the offender] an example' (I.iv.68), the ecclesiastical courts' recourse to penance was regarded as excessively lenient. Writing in the year of *Measure for Measure*'s first performance, for example, the clergyman John Dod traced a progression of sexual ignominy in the strongest terms: 'fornication before marriage . . . is a secret poyson that lurkes therein, and if it be not stayd it will break out to adulterie . . . And he that commit adulterie . . . doth what he can to destroy another man's soule.' For Dod, 'the adulterer is as culpable of death as the willful murderer' and, in its pairing of Claudio and Barnardine, the play toys with this equation.[66] Such thinking was underwritten by legislative effort in the period: a number of draft statutory measures were introduced into Parliament in the early seventeenth century, including a 1601 Bill advocating the loss of lands and tenures for adulterous spouses and a 1604 Bill aimed at the 'better repressing of the detestable Crime of Adultery', which was halted at its second reading in the Lords after being found 'rather to concern some particular persons than the public good'.[67] This latter measure in particular expressed the desire for a jurisdictional shift for sexual offences, a movement that would culminate in the introduction of the short-lived Adultery Act of 1650.[68] In the early part of the century, however, there remained parliamentary reluctance to complete the transition from spiritual regulation to secular, unless there were compelling economic reasons to do so, as we have seen in the case of bastardy, for example.[69] As Joan Kent writes, '[t]here is some evidence that moral reform, in itself, was regarded by many members as insufficient ground for penal laws regulating men's conduct.'[70] So official jurisdiction over sexual offences remained with the ecclesiastical courts, although, as Keith Thomas notes, at a local level this might operate somewhat differently:

> [T]he courts held up the doctrine, rooted in the custom of London, that adultery was a breach of the peace which the officers of the law were entitled to avert. Many legal handbooks taught that constables could arrest would-be fornicators and that J.P.s might bind them over to good behaviour.[71]

Escalus' binding over of Pompey in II.i is of a piece with such custom and practice.

The relationship between pardon and jurisdiction for church court offences was equally fraught. Kesselring has noted how the treatment of such offences in statutory pardons fluctuated under Elizabeth I, and the same pattern seems evident in her successor's approach.[72] James I's first parliamentary pardon concludes with a clause which seems to distance its scope from the ecclesiastical regime: 'That neither this Acte nor any thing therin conteined, shall extend to pardon ... any offence committed or done by and against the Ecclasticall State or Government established in this Realme.'[73] There is no similar clause in his 1624 pardon, which instead explicitly excepts a list of church court offences: 'Heresie Schisme Incest Adulterie Fornicacion and Simonie, and all such Usurie.'[74] Arguably the exclusion of these offences implies the inclusion of other ecclesiastical crimes within the pardon's scope. In fact, R. H. Helmholz finds that, where they were relevant, 'legislative pardons were regularly applied in the spiritual courts, although the ecclesiastical officials were usually careful to describe them as resting on royal authority, not on mere passage through the Houses of Parliament.'[75] The church courts were careful of their own authority and even where offences were pardoned, might order that the decree of absolution be published in the offender's parish church, effectively replicating the public penance that would otherwise have resulted.[76]

In *Measure for Measure* this push-and-pull between church and common law court, sin and crime, takes place in the space between Angelo's sentencing of Claudio and the Duke's redemption of the same. Leah Marcus suggests that 'law in the play is not one single thing ... London and its environs were a crazy quilt of different legal jurisdictions.'[77] Claudio is condemned 'upon the act of fornication', Juliet described by Angelo as 'the fornicatress' (V.i.70; II.ii.25). The question of a legitimate betrothal should be key here, as Victoria Hayne notes: '[s]everal of the changes Shakespeare made to his source materials – making Claudio and Juliet clearly betrothed, adding the Angelo-Mariana relationship, adding Lucio and his involvement with Kate Keep-down – place the problems of marriage-formation at the center of the play.'[78] Betrothed couples presented in the church courts for sexual activity would usually be ordered to finalise their marriages; those accused without evidence of betrothal would be sentenced to perform penance. All three of *Measure for Measure*'s notional couples have gone through some form of betrothal rite – even Lucio 'promised her [Kate Keepdown] marriage', as the Bawd confirms (III.i.458). It may be argued therefore that, far from pardoning the couples, the Duke in fact pronounces a church court sentence upon each: 'he shall marry her' (V.i.512). If this is the case, it casts his closing words to Isabella in an interesting light.

Constance Jordan has argued that Vincentio, the 'dispenser of general pardons . . . does not of course, need to pardon himself'.[79] Yet, in fact, in his offer of marriage to Isabella, the Duke finally acknowledges that he is deserving of the same terms as those he has judged.

'Friar, advise him': Benefit of Clergy

As we have seen, in pronouncing his pardon of Barnardine, the Duke makes the prisoner's relief conditional upon his dispatch to the care of the church: 'Friar, advise him' (V.i.489). Thematically consistent with the church court sentences already announced, this removal to spiritual judgment also mimics the process of benefit of clergy, which in its original sense was the privilege of having one's case transferred from the secular courts to the ecclesiastical. Benefit of clergy was a clerical liberty which became a wider privilege and as such was fundamental to the question of the overlapping jurisdictions of church and common law. Church courts could not give capital sentences, and so a jurisdictional move, whatever the consequence, was effectively a reprieve from death. As Leona Gabel terms it:

> According to common law it [benefit of clergy] may be defined as the exemption of members of the clergy from the jurisdiction of the temporal courts in certain criminal cases . . . the privilege rested upon the principle that clergy should not be judged by laymen but only by their own judges . . . it was not an exemption at all, but something inherent in the status of clerkship.[80]

The practice seems to have originated with the separation of judicial administration post-Conquest and to have evolved in form and function over subsequent centuries.[81] The early scope of the privilege, from the thirteenth century at least, included any member of the clerical hierarchy, from 'first tonsure' (the physical rite of induction into the first stages of clergy) onwards. Initially the prerogative could be asserted at any point in a legal process; a later development was the move to a post-conviction privilege, requiring trial to be completed before benefit could be claimed. Another, in the mid-fourteenth century, was the introduction of a reading test – initially deemed just one proof of clerical status among others (including tonsure, or attestation by the local bishop), but ultimately coming to be the core requirement.[82] The court would give the prisoner a biblical text to read, in Latin, most usually the first verse of Psalm 51 ('the neck-verse') and the subsequent demonstration of literacy, if approved by a bishop's representative ('*legit*' or '*clericus*'), was deemed evidence of holy orders and eligibility for the benefit. Those who failed were pronounced '*non legit*' and their sentence preserved. Benefit of clergy gradually became 'benefit of book', as it was sometimes termed. By the fifteenth century, gaol delivery records indicated a wide range of occupations amongst those who claimed, among them 'bucher', 'couper' and 'laborer'.[83] Whilst it is true that some clerks would retain a trade alongside clerical duties, it is likely that this was also representative of growing literacy, or at least access to the neck-verse among non-clerics. Lawrence Stone's claim that, by the sixteenth century, benefit of clergy was one of the 'two powerful incentives to encourage the poor to learn to read' seems somewhat sweeping; nonetheless, for a subgroup of society a degree of literacy may have seemed like a pragmatic choice.[84]

As Stanley Grupp notes, as well as being jurisdictionally complex, clergy represented 'an encroachment upon the Crown's power of pardon'.[85] Partly in response to this, throughout the late medieval and early modern periods statutory measures were implemented to change both the conception and the consequence of a clergy plea, in an assertion of royal – and explicitly secular – control over the procedure. Whilst the Ordinary or bishop's clerk traditionally made the declaration of *legit* or *non legit*, from the fourteenth century onward the final word on the benefit rested with the judge. The former could be subject to penalties if his judgment on clerkship was deemed to be incorrect and the latter could override any such decision.[86] As Matthew Hale commented, 'in truth the king's justices were the judges both touching the competency of the clerk to be admitted, and the sufficiency or insufficiency of his performance therein'.[87]

In 1489, branding of those receiving clergy was introduced to address concerns about repeat claims: 'dyverse persones lettred hath ben the more bolde to commytte Murdre Rape Roberye Theft and all other myschevous dedes, by cause they have ben continuelly amytted to the benefice of the Clergie'.[88] As specified in the statute, the brand was to be placed on the 'brawn of the left thumbe', a letter 'M' being used to denote a murderer, and 'for eny other felony ... to be marked with a T ... er that suche persone be delivered to the Ordinary'. In Robert Yarington's play *Two Lamentable Tragedies* (1601), for example, the servant Williams, accessory to murder, pleads clergy to escape hanging: 'Williams craves his book/And so receives a brand of infamy' (V.ii.14–15).[89] It is notable that this provision was applicable to 'every persone not being within orders', a tacit acknowledgement that clergy was largely being used by those who had no claim to the religious life. In fact, legislation of Henry VIII subsequently specified that clerics who received the benefit should also be branded, an explicit confirmation that this was no longer a benefit 'of clergy' – and an inversion of the privilege itself. Whilst enforcement of the single benefit was variable, the state also began to request lists of those who had claimed clergy at each assize or sessions, these so-called 'clergy rolls' allowing a measure of cross-referencing.[90]

By the late sixteenth century, the original premise of removal to the church court for purgation or penance had also been dispensed with.[91] Hale notes: 'In ancient time the Consequent was delivery to the Ordinary, either to make Purgation or *absque Purgatione* as the case required. But by Stat. 18 El. c. 7 now only burnt in the Hand.'[92] This meant that, in general, those who pled clergy successfully were released following branding, or 'frizzing them a little in the Fist' as one commentator described it, although there was a rarely used proviso in the Act, allowing the judge to imprison offenders for up to a year, for 'further correccion' (s. 3).[93] The scope of the privilege was also being tightened. As the statute of Henry VII above reveals, there was an expectation that clergy could be viable for the most serious offences, 'Murdre Rape Roberye', many of which would have been excluded from any of the monarch's general pardons. Starting from this inequitable base, the legislative history of benefit of clergy became a narrative of de-scoping certain crimes. New limitations were disseminated via royal proclamation and statute and, as with general pardons, there were certain offences that regularly moved in and out of scope – horse theft, coining and murder being key examples – and those exemptions could be technically complex.[94] As J. A. Sharpe notes, 'a disproportionate number of those condemned for murder had killed by stabbing, which had been made non-clergyable by a statute of 1604', while during the trial of Bishop John Fisher's cook, Richard Rouse, murder by poison was briefly designated as treason to avoid Rouse being eligible for clergy.[95]

Returning to *Two Lamentable Tragedies*, after recording Williams' successful plea of clergy, the play notes that Williams' co-convicted, Rachel, is not eligible for such an outcome: 'But wretched Rachel's sex denies that grace/And therefore doth receive a doom of death' (V.ii.16–17). In the 1623/4 parliamentary session a Bill was passed 'concerning Women convicted of smale Felonies'.[96] Acknowledging that 'many Women doe suffer Death for small Causes', the Bill granted the privilege of clergy to female felons convicted of stealing money or goods worth less than ten shillings. It appears to have passed through Parliament without controversy, the Commons *Journal* records only two 'questions' being addressed before it was ingrossed; it became law in March 1624. As we saw in Chapter Three, it was a 'Strange Wench' who could be 'sav'd by Booke' and indeed, although women claiming clergy were to be branded, there is no mention made of the reading test within the text of the statute. While implementation does not seem to have been extensive, and it would be 1691 before women were granted the full benefit, the legal shift marked by this extension of the privilege was a significant one.[97] As J. A. Sharpe comments, this was 'an age when the ordination of women as priests would have been unthinkable'.[98] As a legal fiction, benefit of clergy was now entirely divorced from its original ecclesiastical premise.

When literacy was almost exclusively the province of the clergy, the neck-verse was an adequate, if not infallible, means of testing clerical status. Even in its early implementation, however, suspicions of abuse arose, with criminals allegedly and sometimes imperfectly memorising the verse to pass muster in court. The requirement of the test, '*sillibicare*', was the most basic form of literacy, requiring no understanding of the words spoken, but merely, as Stephen Greenblatt comments, 'the ability to turn the marks on the page into the appropriate sounds'.[99] As with other forms of pardon, performance was key. 'The prisoner readeth as well as he can', Thomas Smith commented in *De Republica Anglorum* (1583), '(God knoweth sometime very slenderly).'[100] Gabel cites a notorious 1366 case where a murderer claimed his clergy but, when a suspicious judge handed him the psalter, read the verse with the book upside down.[101] It emerged that he had been taught the verse while in prison by two boys who had been allowed access by the gaoler. Similarly, in the anonymous 1593/4 play *The Life and Death of Jack Straw*, the clown-rebel, Tom Miller, attempts to plead what he thinks might be a neck-verse – '*Sursum cordum, alis dictus hangum meum*' – to the Queen Mother, who he hopes will intercede on his behalf.[102] Miller is dubbed a 'starke idiot', but his pardon is pled; his attempts at legal language and church Latin reflect the level to which access to such discourses was perceived as transformative, as well as the popular assumption that many who begged for clergy based their efforts on guesswork.[103]

The role of officials in supporting clergy was also ambiguous. As noted above, gaolers were open to bribes and both they and any Ordinaries making false declarations of literacy could be punished. Andrea McKenzie finds that even in the late seventeenth century there were questions about the probity of individual Ordinaries in relation to the reading test: a mock-epitaph of Samuel Smith, Ordinary of Newgate from 1676 to 1698, included the damning couplet, 'In case he were fee'd/He'd teach one to read.'[104] From the bench, some judges displayed deep scepticism: J. H. Baker quotes a 1616 Newgate sessions case:

> One that was convict of Manslaughter praied his Clergy, and had it. But because it was in case of blood, Coventrye [the judge] tooke the booke and chose a sentence or verse himself and gave it to the Ordinary, who shewed

yt to the Prisoner and gave the booke to him to reade. And Coventry gave command to remove hym from the common place where usually they stood, and to set him apart from other the standers by, to the ende no man might prompt him, and comanded him to reade alowde – which the prisoner did, distinctly and well. And then Coventrye assigned hym another place, which he also read very well.[105]

At times, however, we see the opposite momentum at work: J. S. Cockburn cites a 1605 trial 'at Southwark assizes . . . [when] Serjeant Daniel saved a convict's life by lending him his spectacles so that he might read the "neck-verse"'[106] and Bernard Capp notes a 1638 Leicester case in which the defendant, Isabel Salter, convicted of stealing 'a blanket, dishes, porringers and a pillow', was sentenced (presumably under the 1623 Act) to be burned in the hand. In a rare confluence of clergy and belly pleas, Isabel had a 'lucky break . . . pleading pregnancy, she escaped branding and was simply pressed on the hand with a cold iron to prevent her miscarrying'.[107]

In his analysis of Middlesex sessions records, David Cressy identifies relatively high levels of clergy claimed: 32 per cent of those convicted in Elizabeth's reign; 39 per cent under James. J. S. Cockburn puts the figure at 47 per cent for the Home Circuit across the same period.[108] The availability of clergy was known and expected. In cases of bigamy, for example, a crime which became capital in 1604, the general belief was that clergy would be allowed upon conviction – as Capp comments, 'this was the standard punishment throughout the century and, in its later decades, women too were sometimes granted benefit'.[109] Yet, here again, expectations could lead to overconfidence. At the Old Bailey in 1676, for example, a 'country-fellow' was convicted of having two wives, but, the court recorded, 'seemed not much to lay that to heart, flattering himself with coming off by his Clergy'.[110] He may have felt himself on sure ground, as, of approximately twenty-seven bigamy convictions at the Old Bailey in the last three decades of the century, eighteen led to clergy and branding.[111] However, in this instance, confidence was misplaced: 'when afterwards he came to the Book, the Ordinary returned a Non legit, and he received sentence of death with the rest'.

'Dost thou use to write thy name?': Problematic Clergy

The degree to which benefit of clergy had become an expected secular legal process is evident in its presence in literary language from the late medieval period onwards. Lorna Hutson notes 'the first recorded use of the word "neck-verse"' in the morality play *Mankind* (c.1470), in which the character New Gyse advises his comrades: 'Lett us con well owr neke-verse, that we have not a cheke.'[112] Later in the play the value of such advice is made plain, as the fate of the character Mischief is described: 'Myscheff ys a convicte [i.e. imprisoned rather than hanged], for he coude [recite] hys neke-verse' (619). By 1623/4, the same imagery is being deployed as a casual insult in Thomas Drue's *The Duchess of Suffolke*, as the chaplain Sandys, escaped from the King's Bench Prison and disguised as a tiler, encounters his pursuers, Clunie and other officers. Not realising the proximity of his target, Clunie tries to attract the attention of the workman, who has mounted a ladder and is humming as he labours, crying: 'Leave singing of your neck-verse, rogue!'[113]

Dramatic renderings of clergy display a – perhaps inevitable – preoccupation with the benefit's problematic relationship with literacy and its uses. The very act of branding placed a mark of literacy upon the convicted felon and, specifically, a mark ('M' or 'T') that expected literacy from the beholder. As Tom Miller's attempts at 'eloquence' in *Jack Straw* demonstrate, the ability to perform literacy was a form of cultural currency that coexisted with literacy itself, the former regarded as a means to access the privilege of the latter. In Shakespeare's *2 Henry VI*, another drama focused on rebellion, we see the disruption of this model, as Jack Cade and his followers attack the institutions they regard as oppressors of their kind. As readers have observed, the idea of trial provides the structuring principle of *2 Henry VI;* the play features a wealth of judicial and extrajudicial process, including a trial by combat between the apprentice Peter Thumpe and his master and the 'framing' of Eleanor Cobham on charges of compassing the king's death.[114] In his representation of Cade's fifteenth-century rebellion, Shakespeare borrows also from Holinshed's account of the Peasants' Revolt in 1381; as Craig Bernthal notes, the historic 'Cade rebels presented a complaint to the crown that included a long catalog of judicial misconduct', unlike 'the John Ball rebellion of 1381, in which killing all the lawyers, burning all the law books and legal records . . . were the principal goals'.[115] The Jack Cade of *2 Henry VI* walks a line somewhere in between the two. His is an anti-legal campaign, but also, specifically, an anti-literacy crusade, and if, as Bernthal suggests, it operates by 'carnivalesque inversion' of legal practice, it does so with a very particular target.[116] Thus, the charges Cade levels against Lord Saye begin with diplomatic affairs but are quickly narrowed down to crimes against illiteracy:

> CADE: . . . Thou hast most traitorously corrupted the youth of the realm, in erecting a grammar school: . . . thou hast caused printing to be used, and contrary to the King, his crowne, and dignity, thou hast built a paper-mill . . . Thou hast appointed Justices of Peace, to call poor men before them,

about matters they were not able to answer. Moreover, thou hast put them in prison, and because they could not read, thou hast hanged them.

(IV.vii.27–41)

The final charge is at the heart of the play's representation; Cade rails against the requirement to perform social elevation to access pardon. Here, the 'benefit' of clergy is reframed, not as a privilege, but as a penalty for illiteracy, a positioning that prefigures the claims of seventeenth-century reformers who, like the the anonymous author of *The laws discovery* (1653), suggested that a capital sentence might be imposed upon a man simply 'because he cannot read'.[117] While Saye self-presents as a good judge, 'long sitting to determine poor men's causes' (81), he shall nonetheless 'die, and it be but for pleading so well for his life' (100). Embedded as he is in the discourses of the courtroom, Saye naturally follows the prescribed route to seek reprieve, but this very compliance is the cause of his downfall.

We should not be surprised to find Saye executed for successfully pleading his pardon. The earlier sham trial of Emmanuel, the Clerk of Chartam, is in effect a reversed literacy test, predicated upon his ability to read and write:

> CADE: . . . Dost thou use to write thy name? Or hast thou a mark to thyself, like an honest plain-dealing man?
> CLERK: Sir, I thank God I have been so well brought up that I can write my name.
> ALL: He hast confessed: away with him! He's a villain and a traitor.
>
> (IV.ii.93–8)

The Clerk here fails the reading test and will be hanged 'with his pen and inkhorn about his neck' (100), a sentence that conflates elements of church court shaming with secular doom. While Emmanuel's name links him with another oppressive institution, it is not its religious meaning ('God be with us') that is signalled by the rebels, but its legal use as a prefix for documents: 'they use to write that on the top of letters' (91). It is notable that the Clerk's fate is sealed by his ability to *write* his name; reading and writing were taught separately in this period and use of a mark instead of a signature did not necessarily mean an inability to read, or at least, as we have seen, to pretend to reading skills. It is not *sillibicare* that is targeted here, but a very specific type of literacy. The irony here is that in these mock-trial scenes Cade appropriates the legal structures he deplores.[118] As a judge, Cade's decision-making is as erratic as the legal fictions he attacks.

As with many of those fictions, benefit of clergy became less meaningful once reprieve for transportation began to be used regularly. It was not fully abolished until 1827, although burning in the hand was removed in 1779 and replaced with discretionary fines.[119] More suggestively, the reading test for clergy was abolished by statute in 1706, via a clause that was disarmingly honest about its efficacy: 'it hath been use to administer a Book to him [the convict] to try whether he can read as a Clerk which by Experience is found to be of no Use'.[120]

'Exquisitely severe': Refusing Justice and the *Peine Forte et Dure*

The attaching of conditions to pardons, and the dynamic of reciprocity that created, raised the complex question of whether an individual could actually refuse clemency. The rhetoric of grace and redemption that surrounded the process required a peculiar form of collaboration between each party to the pardon, a performance of magnanimity and submission which sustained vital concepts of sovereign power. A refusal to engage in such performance was therefore exceptionally problematic in the eyes of the state. Work by Simon Devereaux, Lynn MacKay and others has documented resistance to conditional pardon (largely for transportation) from a number of eighteenth-century felons.[121] MacKay, for example, discusses the case of Sarah Cowden, a young prostitute, who, in 1789, refused mercy on the grounds of her own and her co-accused's innocence. At the sessions in which Sarah was tried, no fewer than six women and nine men initially refused pardons. In such instances, the response of the court betrayed underlying panic at this rejection of the prescribed narrative: judges threatened recalcitrant convicts with immediate execution and emphasised the spiritual cost of a choice of death over life: 'you may be considered as committing murder upon yourself ... you must take the consequence'.[122] These eighteenth-century cases were further complicated by growing press coverage of the court system, subjecting the administration of justice to increased scrutiny, nonetheless they encapsulate the fragile nature of pardon as a tool of state. As MacKay asks, 'did these people act, knowing that the courts would try to avoid hanging them? Were they aware, in short, that they had leverage to resist?'[123] A rarer seventeenth-century example demonstrates just how much leverage such convicts did possess. Amid the fervour of the Popish plot trials, in April 1679, John Morgan was convicted, on his own confession, of being a Catholic priest. He was sentenced to be hanged, drawn and quartered, but reprieved. At his pardon hearing in August of that year:

> ... there were no fewer than Six and Thirty Men and Women, ... who now all did on their Knees plead his Majesties General Gracious Pardon, ... among whom was one John Morgan ... who could very hardly be brought to accept of this Pardon, or to kneel whilst it was read, alledging that he had committed no Crime, needed no Pardon, had not sued for this, &c. But as before, the Testimony of Doctor Oates and others that he was sometimes maddish, got him into the Pardon.[124]

The evidence for Morgan being 'maddish' seems largely to have inhered in his willingness to confess to being a priest, but it was gladly seized on by the court to avoid the alternative of enacting his original sentence.

When *Measure for Measure*'s Duke pronounces his sentence (itself a conditional pardon), Lucio protests vehemently, 'Marrying a punk, my Lord, is pressing to death, whipping and hanging' (V.i.522). His pun on 'pressing' does not detract from the emphasis on this first and terrible fate. In John Morgan's case and others, the authority of the court was implicitly challenged by a felon's refusal to recognise and engage with its processes. The most acute manifestation of this, of course, was not the rejection of pardon, but the refusal of a defendant to acknowledge the court's right to try him or her at all. Those who 'stood mute' when required to enter a plea of guilty or not guilty were questioning, by implication, the power of crown and legislature over the individual life. As such, their actions were met with what Thomas Smith terms 'one of the cruellest deathes that may be', the *peine forte et dure*.[125]

There is some ambiguity around the origin of the *peine*, which is likely to have derived from the thirteenth-century subjection to imprisonment 'forte et dure' of those who refused to submit to the 'new' route of trial by jury.[126] Such an experience usually involved incarceration in the most miserable of conditions, with provision of only a small amount of bread and water, often on alternate days. H. R. T. Summerson quotes the report in the *Vita Edwardi Secundi* of a 1322 case in which a prisoner who would not plead was returned to prison to 'sit on the cold bare floor, dressed only in the thinnest of shirts, and be pressed with as great a weight of iron as his wretched body shall bear'.[127] The 'iron' here and in similar reports may in fact have referred to the heavy fetters worn by prisoners; nonetheless, over time, accounts increasingly focus on the infliction of pain as a form of duress. What these accounts are also careful to specify, as Summerson notes, is the defendant's refusal of the law, '*tanquam refutans commune legem*', rejecting both its authority and its protection. This parallel with outlawry provided some salve for conscience and a defence against accusations of torture – 'if he [the prisoner] died it was nobody's fault but his own'.[128]

If the medieval prison *fort et dure* was intended as an inducement to plead, its early modern manifestation was really a form of capital penalty. In contemporary records, references to the *peine* are made interchangeable with Lucio's phrase 'pressing to death' and this 'exquisitely severe' consequence, as Blackstone describes it, became further ritualised over time:[129]

> ... he that stands Mute ... shall be put in a mean Room, and be laid Naked upon the bare Earth, but only something to cover his Privy Parts, his Head and Feet uncovered, one Arm to be drawn to one quarter of the House with a Cord, and the other Arm to another; in the same manner shall be done to his Feet, and there shall be laid upon his Body Iron and Stone, so much as he can bear and more; and shall drink of the Water next the Prison, except Running Water, with three morsels of Barley Bread, and this shall be his Diet till he Die.[130]

Those under the press might be granted the dubious boon of a sharp stone being placed under their back to hasten their death, or be allowed the assistance of spectators who added their weight to the load. The 1659 pamphlet *The Unhappy Marksman*, which recounts the pressing to death of George Strangwayes, a murderer, describes the prisoner's friends positioned 'at the corners of the press', adding:

> ... their Burthens to disburthen him of his pain, ... his dying Groans filling the uncouth Dungeon with the Voice of Terrour, but this dismall Scene soon finds a quiet Catastrophe, for in the space of eight or ten Minutes at the most, this unfettered Soul left her tortur'd Mansion.[131]

In general, courts were keen to avoid this 'dismall Scene'. Defendants refusing to plead were given three warnings of their fate, ostensibly to establish that they were in fact 'mute by malice' and not genuine mutes, but also to buy time for further persuasion tactics. Some were shown the press as a warning; the 1677 Old Bailey case of a 'fellow and his wife' is typical – 'they on view of the Press ... , submitting themselves, were admitted to Tryal'.[132] Some offenders were actually under the press when they agreed to plead: Oliver Morris, charged with housebreaking in 1688, 'was sent to be put in the Press, and after they had laid five Half hundred Weights upon him, he said he would Plead'.[133] Whilst in theory, as Andrea McKenzie notes, 'removing a prisoner from the press was represented as a favour granted at the judge's discretion', in practice, 'it would seem that a word from the sufferer could at any time call a stop to the peine'.[134]

Literary references to *peine forte et dure* are less widespread than to clergy. Where the *peine* does appear, it is largely as a metaphor for silence. In Shakespeare's *Troilus and Cressida*, for example, when

Pandarus obtains a 'chamber with a bed' for the play's central couple, he exhorts them: 'which bed, because it shall not speak of your pretty encounters, press it to death'.[135] Similarly, in *Richard II*, the Queen, on hearing that the king will be deposed, exclaims 'Oh, I am pressed to death for want of speaking!'[136] Only Lucio alludes to the severity of the penalty. For Blackstone, that very severity was the *peine*'s strength: 'by that very means it might rarely be put into execution'.[137] Yet the possibility of such a sentence was a consequence that a surprising number of indicted felons were prepared to risk. George Conklin quotes findings in the Middlesex records of '32 persons (three of whom were women) [who] died by *peine forte et dure*' between 1609 and 1616 and J. S. Cockburn finds twenty-three instances on the Home Circuit under Elizabeth and James; at the other end of the century there are at least twelve prisoners threatened with the press at the Old Bailey between 1676 and 1690, and several delivered to it.[138] Why were so many prepared to stand mute, in the face of what Coke described as 'the greatest and most severe penance and pain'?[139] The most widely held assumption about such defendants is that they sought to avoid confiscation of their property; Walter Calverley, whose murder of his children was the basis for two contemporary plays, *The Miseries of Enforced Marriage* and *A Yorkshire Tragedy* (1607/8), was said to have been seeking to escape forfeiture when pressed to death. Calverley had estates to bequeath; this does not explain the majority of early modern cases, however, wherein defendants had little or no property to protect.

For some, death on the press was a route to martyrdom. The Catholic convert Margaret Clitherow, who died in 1586 following charges of harbouring Jesuits, claimed that, '[h]aving made no offence I need no trial.'[140] Clitherow was pregnant when she died, a fact known to court officials, who had sent four women to examine her. In their account of Clitherow's life, Peter Lake and Michael Questier suggest that this was a subject of contention amongst those officials, who debated the responsibility for the death of the child she carried.[141] However, evidence elsewhere indicates that in such cases the sin was deemed to fall upon the mother; in the Newgate records, J. H. Baker finds:

> Note also by Mr. Long, Clerk of the Peace for Middlesex, ... that if a woman be to have judgment of peine fort et dure she shall not have the benefit of her belly. The reason is, because of her willfull contempt of her tryall.[142]

Beyond the realm of religious offences, others also chose the press because, like Clitherow, they felt they had committed no crime, because they sought to avoid implicating others, or because they did not recognise the authority of the court to try them. Sometimes these beliefs arose from perceptions about what constituted an appropriate penalty for their offence. George Strangwayes, for example – in a nod to the *lex talionis* – suggested he would plead only if he could meet his end by 'that manner of death by which his brother [his victim, John Fussell] fell', i.e. by gunshot. Strangwayes wished to avoid 'the ignominious Death of a publick Gibbet' and his choice of the press was intimately connected with his control over his own fate.[143]

Often, reasons for refusing to plead might be specific and technical. Baker reports a 1589 case in which Smyth and Grevyle, a servant and master, were arraigned for murder. Smyth, unusually for the period, had been tortured into a confession and when Grevyle was brought to court, he refused to plead 'unless "the said person who had made his servant Smyth approve him by torture on the rack" was tried as a felon'. Baker comments that there followed 'an inconclusive discussion as to whether Grevyle should receive the *peine forte et dure* for refusing to plead, and he was remanded to the Tower without judgment'.[144] At the other end of the scale, in the 1664 trial of Jane Jones and Thomas Wharton for burglary, Jones refused to plead to the first indictment against her, because it did not name her as Wharton's wife, which she claimed to be.[145] Unless the indictment was changed, she could not plead marital coercion as a defence. In the end, the indictment was rewritten, naming 'Jane Wharton, alias Jones, spinster'. Valerie Edwards notes that this was 'intended to induce the accused to answer the charge . . . This obviated the necessity of applying *peine forte et dure*.'[146]

Underlying all these motivations was a form of negotiation, often coming from a place of powerlessness, but also from an understanding that *peine* was rarely the preferred outcome of the court. Thus a 1676 defendant indicted for burglary:

> would not Plead till his Wife, who was accused with him might be released; The Court urg'd him in vain, and told him the Press was ready: he confidently replyed, that he was as ready for the Press: but the Court having enough to do that day, did let him alone till another.[147]

Similarly, the 'fellow and his wife' who refused to plead at the Old Bailey a decade later were described as causing the court 'much trouble' by their recalcitrance.[148] It was undoubtedly in their interest to plead, as they were ultimately acquitted for lack of evidence. For the aforementioned Oliver Morris, however, the press was a form of last stand, a final effort in controlling his own fate. When, eventually, he capitulated, '[t]he Evidence was plain upon him, and he being proved by Record to have been burn'd in the Hand before, was brought in guilty of Felony.'[149] Guilty of a crime (house-breaking) that was excluded from general pardons, and having had his clergy at least once, he had run out of options for mercy.

Measure for Measure's true refuser of the law is, of course, not Lucio but Barnardine, whose flat rejection of his fate infuriates his keepers: 'I will not consent to die today, that's certain' (IV.iii.54). The 'fact' of his guilt is 'not denied by himself' (IV.ii.137), but there is no evidence that Barnardine has ever entered a plea. His determination to spend his time 'drunk many times a day, if not many days entirely drunk' (IV.ii.148) suggests a dual intent to avoid the reality of his situation and to cause the Viennese legal system as much trouble as he can in so doing. He recognises neither the law's right to execute him, nor the prison as a place of punishment: 'give him leave to escape hence, he would not' (IV.ii.146–7). Having existed in limbo, in the space between arrest and execution, for the duration of the play, when the time comes to accept his fate, he does not speak. Commended to the Friar, but with no stage direction to indicate that he is removed from the scene, we are left with a final image of Barnardine standing mute in the face of the law.

Conclusion

Despite the apparent ambivalence as to its implementation, *peine forte et dure* would not be abolished until 1772, after which a series of statutes set forth provisions for the court to enter a 'not guilty' plea in the majority of such instances.[150] Described by Harold Skulsky as the 'most hellish fury ... of the aggrieved law itself', *peine* of course represented the inversion of the trajectory of sovereign mercy that we see so carefully managed by the Tudor and Stuart state.[151] That there was a perceived need for such a sanction at all crystallises the issues of collaboration between the individual and the legal system that underlay the whole question of justice in operation.

'Have you no countermand for Claudio yet ... ?' the Duke asks the Provost as events gather pace in *Measure for Measure* (IV.ii.90). Returning to the 'space' between sentence and execution, the Duke's question signals the expectations that filled that gap – what David Cressy has described as 'a reminder that sentencing was a stage, not an end, with multiple opportunities for alternative outcomes'.[152] Those outcomes might be revealed, dramatically or otherwise, throughout the post-sentencing process, but they required the appropriate participation of the condemned to achieve full impact. Performance was crucial: performing humility, performing literacy, performing participation – all, at times, high-risk actions for the individual, but nonetheless essential in unlocking the possibility, however unlikely, of clemency. As we have seen, performance was also expected of the state and its representatives in maintaining the semblance of the monarchical privilege, both within and outside the law, and in translating that privilege to practical ends. The pragmatic manoeuvring of *Measure for Measure*'s harried Provost is of a piece with the irritable statute negotiations of the Stuart Parliaments, the bureaucratic mercy of the circuit pardon and the judicial accommodations made to facilitate clergy and to avoid the press.

It is undoubtedly the case that the mechanisms of pardon enabled good housekeeping of the early modern state's system of sanction. Moreover, they forged connection and investment. A system that contained the idea of equity and the possibility of mercy was a system that made active participation possible, with good conscience. As Cynthia Herrup notes, '[e]arly modern punishments had simple rules (for example that the punishment for all felonies was execution) that disguised practical finesse; pardons had labyrinthine processes that obscured simple results.'[153] Nonetheless, even as it acted as a corrective to the more extreme positions of early modern sentencing, pardon also exposed, by its very operation, the lingering questions that troubled that system: questions of jurisdiction, of royal prerogative and of individual agency. We see this made clear both in the details of engagement (or otherwise) with pardon narrated in trial reports and in the 'double written' nature of *Measure for Measure*'s account of consequence, with its multiple models of law-giving and clemency.

As pardon moved closer to a model of conditionality, its transactional elements grew increasingly central, and – for a time at least – individual agency would become even more prominent, as we will see in Chapter 5. 'The miserable have no other medicine/But only hope,' contends Claudio (III.i.2–3), and the reciprocity necessary to ensure the endurance of that hope and its multiple benefits would continue to underpin the administration of criminal justice for the remainder of the century.

Notes

1. McKenzie, *Tyburn's Martyrs*, p. 255.
2. Shakespeare, *Measure for Measure*. All references are to the Arden edition (ed. A. R. Braunmuller and Robert N. Watson).
3. Herrup, *The Common Peace*, p. 143, n. 16.
4. McNeill, *Poor Women in Shakespeare*, p. 109.
5. Majeske, 'Equity's absence', p. 170.
6. Sarat and Hussain (eds), *Forgiveness, Mercy and Clemency*, p. 3.
7. Blackstone, *Commentaries on the Laws of England*, pp. 390–1.

8. Kesselring, *Mercy and Authority in the Tudor State*, p. 3.
9. Quoted in Sarat and Hussain, *Forgiveness, Mercy and Clemency*, p. 4.
10. Edwards, *The Life of Sir Walter Raleigh*, p. 454.
11. For further discussion of Ralegh's pardon, see Bernthal, 'Staging Justice'.
12. McKenzie, '"This Death Some Strong and Stout-Hearted Man Doth Choose"', p. 298.
13. Hay, 'Property, Authority and the Criminal Law', p. 48.
14. Herrup, *Common Peace*, p. 165.
15. Hutson, *Invention of Suspicion*; Hindle, *The State and Social Change*.
16. Higgins, 'Justice, Mercy and Dialectical Genre', p. 264.
17. Cockburn, *A History of English Assizes*, p. 131; Sharpe, *Crime in Seventeenth-Century England*, p. 146.
18. Beattie, 'The Royal Pardon and Criminal Procedure', p. 12.
19. Coke, *Third Part of the Institutes*, c. 105, p. 233.
20. 27 Hen. 8, c. 24, s. 1.
21. See, e.g., Kesselring, *Mercy and Authority*, and Herrup, 'Negotiating Grace', pp. 124–40.
22. Hughes and Larkin, *Tudor Royal Proclamations, Volume II*, p. 394.
23. 12 Car. 2, c. 11.
24. Coke, *Third Part of the Institutes*, c. 105, pp. 237–8.
25. Herrup, 'Negotiating Grace', p. 127.
26. 7 Hen. 8, c. 11.
27. Cockburn, *A History of English Assizes*, p. 130.
28. Hughes and Larkin, *Tudor Royal Proclamations, Volume II*, p. 104.
29. Kesselring, *Mercy and Authority*, pp. 59, 67.
30. John Brampston, 9 December 1685, *OBP Online* (last accessed 23 June 2020) (o16851209-2).
31. Kelyng, *A Report of Divers Cases*, p. 31.
32. Clavell, *A recantation of an ill-led life*, p. 8.
33. Fuller, *Mixt Contemplations in Better Times*, pp. 62–3.
34. Later, Charles would deploy pardon as a strategy of combat, issuing county-by-county pardons as the Civil War progressed: Larkin, *Stuart Royal Proclamations, Volume II*, p. xvi.
35. *House of Commons Journal, Volume 1: 1547–1629*, pp. 632–4, 31 May 1621 in *British History Online* <http://www.british-history.ac.uk/commons-jrnl/vol1/pp632-634>(last accessed 15 June 2020).
36. Herrup, 'Negotiating Grace', p. 135.
37. Strain, 'The "Snared Subject"', p. 103.
38. Finch, *Nomotechnia*, STC (2nd ed.)/10871, p. 81.
39. 8 Eliz. 1, c. 29.
40. Strype, *Annals of the Reformation*, vol. I, part I, s. III, p. 41.
41. Overbury, *A True and Perfect Account*, ff. 16–17.
42. Herrup, 'Punishing Pardon', p. 127.
43. *State Papers Domestic: Charles I*, SP 16/91, f. 45 (1628).
44. Beattie, 'The Royal Pardon', p. 11.
45. Davis, *Fiction in the Archives*, p. 18.
46. *State Papers Domestic: Charles I*, SP/16/182, f. 25b (1631).
47. *Calendar of State Papers Domestic: Charles I, 1629–31* (hereafter 'CSPD'), vol. 183, p. 488. Unfortunately, I cannot identify the text of this pardon.

48. *State Papers Domestic: Charles I*, SP/16/182, f. 25b (1631).
49. *CSPD*, vol. 182, p. 486.
50. Ibid. vol. 183, p. 488.
51. Cressy, *Gypsies*, p. 67.
52. Quoted in Braunmuller and Watson, *Measure for Measure*, p. 116. Relevant readings of the play include Dollimore, 'Transgression and Surveillance in *Measure for Measure*'; Marcus, *Puzzling Shakespeare*, p. 163.
53. James VI/I, *The True Lawe of Free Monarchies*, sig D1ᵛ. For a reading focusing on questions of kingship, see e.g. Shuger, *Political Theologies in Shakespeare's England*.
54. Jordan, 'Interpreting Statute in *Measure for Measure*', p. 102.
55. Marcus, *Puzzling Shakespeare*, p. 164.
56. Beattie, 'The Cabinet and the Management of Death', p. 221.
57. Birch (ed.), *A Collection of the State Papers of John Thurloe*, p. 538.
58. Cockburn, *Calendar of Assize Records: Home Circuit Indictments*, p. 128.
59. Strain, *Legal Reform in English Renaissance Culture*, p. 24.
60. Lambarde, *Eirenarcha*, c. XVII, p. 133.
61. Whetstone, *Promos and Cassandra* (London, 1578).
62. Dunne, *Shakespeare, Revenge Tragedy and Early Modern Law*, p. 26.
63. Majeske, 'Equity's Absence', p. 171.
64. Ibid. p. 176.
65. Cosin, *An Apologie*, vol. 1, p. 61.
66. Dod, *A treatise or exposition*, pp. 54–6.
67. *House of Lords Journal Volume 2: 1578–1614*, pp. 272–3, 4 April 1604, in *British History Online* <https://www.british-history.ac.uk/lords-jrnl/vol2/pp272-273#h3-0002>(last accessed 11 September 2020).
68. See Thomas, 'Puritans and Adultery', p. 271. Fornication was punishable by three months in gaol, then a year's security for good behaviour.
69. See Poor Laws under Elizabeth and James: 18 Eliz. 1, c. 3, 7 Jac. 1, c. 4.
70. Kent, 'Attitudes of Members of the House of Commons', p. 42.
71. Thomas, 'Puritans and Adultery', pp. 265–6.
72. Kesselring, *Mercy and Authority*, pp. 70–1.
73. 7 Jac. 1, c. 24, s. xii.
74. 21 Jac. 1, c. 35, s. x.
75. Helmholz, *Roman Canon Law in Reformation England*, pp. 161.
76. Ibid. pp. 163–4.
77. Marcus, *Puzzling Shakespeare*, p. 171.
78. Hayne, 'Performing Social Practice', p. 5.
79. Jordan, 'Interpreting Statute', p. 116.
80. Gabel, *Benefit of Clergy*, p. 7.
81. Ibid. pp. 9–11, 30–1.
82. On tonsure and its abuses, see Gabel, *Benefit of Clergy*, p. 64, and Greenblatt, 'History of Literature', p. 464; for the literacy test, see Gabel, pp. 68–9.
83. Gabel, *Benefit of Clergy*, p. 77.
84. Stone, 'The Educational Revolution', pp. 42–3.
85. Grupp, 'Some Historical Aspects of the Pardon', p. 57.
86. There are records of Ordinaries being fined for incorrect or fraudulent

pronouncements through to the seventeenth century – see e.g. 84 *English Reports* 1078.
87. Hale, *History of the Pleas of the Crown*, pp. 580–1.
88. 4 Hen. 7, c. 13.
89. Bullen (ed.), *A Collection of Old English Plays*, Vol. III.
90. See Bellamy, *Criminal Law and Society*, p. 145, and Kesselring, *Mercy and Authority*, p. 48.
91. 18 Eliz. 1, c. 7.
92. Hale, *History of the Pleas*, p. 240.
93. Nourse, *Campania Foelix*, p.230.
94. Bellamy, *Criminal Law and Society*, pp. 146–53.
95. Sharpe, *Crime in Early Modern England*, p. 69; Kesselring, 'A Draft of the 1531 "Acte for Poysoning"', pp. 894–9.
96. 21 Jac. 1, c. 6.
97. 3 & 4 Wm & Mary, c. 9.
98. Sharpe, *Crime in Early Modern England*, p. 67.
99. Greenblatt, 'History of Literature', p. 466.
100. Smith, *De Republica Anglorum*, p. 83.
101. Gabel, *Benefit of Clergy*, pp. 72–3.
102. *The life and death of Jacke Straw*, Act 3. The play is sometimes attributed to George Peele.
103. Another Clown of the same period, in Shakespeare's *Titus Andronicus*, meets his death in part through his inability to perform literacy, to 'say grace': Shakespeare, *Titus Andronicus*, IV.iii.1983–5, *The Oxford Shakespeare* (ed. Stanley Wells and Gary Taylor).
104. McKenzie, *Tyburn's Martyrs*, p. 127.
105. Baker, 'Criminal Justice at Newgate', p. 315.
106. Cockburn, 'Trial by the Book?', p. 75.
107. Capp, 'Life, Love and Litigation', p. 80.
108. Cressy, *Literacy and the Social Order*, p. 17; Cockburn, *Calendar*, p. 119.
109. Capp, 'Bigamous Marriage', p. 554.
110. Trial of Country-fellow, June 1676, *OBP Online* (last accessed 24 February 2020) (t16760628-6).
111. *OBP Online* (last accessed 19 March 2018).
112. Hutson, 'From Penitent to Suspect', p. 314; *Mankind*, ed. Kathleen A. Ashley and Gerard NeCastro, ll. 520, 619.
113. Drue, *The Duchess of Suffolke*, II.iii.15.
114. See, e.g., Hutson, 'Noises Off: Participatory Justice in *2 Henry* VI'; Knowles, 'The Farce of History'.
115. Bernthal, 'Jack Cade's Legal Carnival', p. 262.
116. Ibid. p. 264.
117. *The laws discovery*, p. 7.
118. As Hutson has demonstrated, the play further complicates its own presentation of law as privilege, notably in its depiction of the clamour of the Commons (the 'hue and cry') at Duke Humphrey's death: Hutson, 'Noises Off', pp. 156–61.
119. 19 Geo. 3, c. 74; 7 & 8 Geo. 4, c. 28.
120. 6 Anne, c. 9, s. 4.

121. Devereaux, 'Imposing the Royal Pardon'; MacKay, 'Refusing the Royal Pardon', p. 25.
122. Case of George Hyser, Sept 1789, 890 quoted in MacKay, 'Refusing the Royal Pardon', p. 25.
123. MacKay, 'Refusing the Royal Pardon', p. 35.
124. John Morgan, supplementary material August 1679, *OBP Online* (last accessed 23 June 2020) (o16790827-2).
125. Smith, *De Republica Anglorum*, p. 78.
126. *Peine* was not imposed in cases of high treason, where silence was interpreted as a 'not guilty' plea.
127. Summerson, 'Early Development of the Peine Forte et Dure', p. 116.
128. Ibid. p. 121.
129. Blackstone, *Commentaries*, vol. 4, p. 325.
130. Trial of Thomas Barlow, Oliver Morris, January 1688, *OBP Online* (last accessed 15 July 2020) (t16880113-41).
131. *The unhappy marksman*, sig. D4.
132. Trial of fellow wife, December 1677, *OBP Online* (last accessed 15 July 2020) (t16771212-8).
133. Trial of Thomas Barlow, Oliver Morris (t16880113-41).
134. McKenzie, '"This Death Some Strong and Stout-Hearted Man Doth Choose"', p. 285.
135. Shakespeare, *Troilus and Cressida*, III.ii.204–5, III.i.76, *The Oxford Shakespeare* (ed. Stanley Wells and Gary Taylor).
136. Shakespeare, *Richard II*, III.iv.73, *The Oxford Shakespeare* (ed. Stanley Wells and Gary Taylor).
137. Blackstone, *Commentaries*, vol. 4, p. 325.
138. Conklin, 'Witchcraft Trials in England', n. 30; Cockburn, *Calendar*, p. 72; Ordinary of Newgate's Account, August 1676, *OBP Online* (last accessed 15 July 2020) (OA16760830).
139. Coke, *Second Part of the Institutes*, p. 180.
140. Mush, 'The Life of Margaret Clitherow', p. 413.
141. Lake and Questier, *The Trials of Margaret Clitherow*, p. 93.
142. Baker, 'Criminal Justice at Newgate', p. 316. However, Cockburn finds a 1617 case in which a female burglar obtained release via a *peine forte* sentence and a belly plea: 'Trial by the Book', p. 75. In 1533, benefit of clergy had been removed from those who refused to plead: 25 Hen. 8, c. 3.
143. *The unhappy marksman*, p. 21.
144. Baker, 'Review', p. 340.
145. 84 *English Reports* 1071.
146. Edwards, 'The Case of the Married Spinster', p. 262.
147. Trial, January 1676, *OBP Online* (last accessed 15 July 2020) (o16760117-1).
148. Trial of fellow wife (t16771212-8).
149. Trial of Thomas Barlow, Oliver Morris (t16880113-41).
150. 12 Geo. 3, c. 20 and 7 & 8 Geo. 4, c. 28. Some initial exceptions were made, for e.g. cases of piracy, where a guilty plea was to be assumed.
151. Skulsky, 'Pain, Law and Conscience in *Measure for Measure*', p. 160.
152. Cressy, *Gypsies*, p. 79.
153. Herrup, 'Punishing Pardon', p. 129.

Chapter 5

'England's rubidg': Mary Carleton and the Early Use of Transportation

In 1671, Mary Carleton, the female adventurer, thief and polygamist, sent a letter from Port Royal in Jamaica to her 'Friends and once Fellow-Prisoners' in Newgate. In it she described her experience of life as a transported convict in surprising terms:

> At my landing, instead of a barbarous slavery accompanied with rudeness the constant Attendant thereof, I was immediately environed with a Crowd of Admirers. And no sooner was my name heard there, but it eccho'd into the remotest parts of the Island, and drew a wonderful confluence of the more vile and dissolute people to my Habitation.[1]

Carleton's 'Drolling Romantick' account is characteristic.[2] Despite humble origins as the stepdaughter of a Canterbury fiddler, she lived a picaresque life and her exploits brought her into repeated contact with the newly established Restoration legal system. She twice cheated justice with acquittals on bigamy charges, most notoriously in 1663 when she was brought to trial by the family of John Carleton, a lawyer's clerk, who had believed his new wife to be a 'German Princess', an affluent noblewoman from Cologne. Following her vindication in that case, Carleton was to resort to a more prosaic means of sustaining herself, operating within the criminal networks of Restoration London as a thief and receiver of stolen goods. In 1671 she was convicted on a charge of theft and sentenced to death, but was reprieved for transportation to Barbados. Less than a year after her arrival in the colonies she returned to England, illegally, only to be re-apprehended and hanged. Carleton's adventures generated a paper trail of astonishing comprehensiveness: Mihoko Suzuki notes that 'her exploits provided material for twenty six pamphlets', including sonnets, letters and autobiographical material.[3] Although chiefly manifest in cheap print modes, these works look ahead to newer genres, including criminal biography and novels, and anticipate the news networks of the eighteenth century.

Much critical effort has been expended upon the positioning of Carleton's 'German Princess' persona as a model of self-fashioning for the early modern Englishwoman. This is supported by the proto-feminist scheme of Carleton's own publication, *The Case of Madam Mary Carleton* (1663), which, with its attack upon 'the Laws of this Kingdom made against *Femes Covert*', works, as Janet Todd comments, as 'a plea for more female power within law'.[4] Certainly, there was contemporary interest at the time of the 'German Princess' trial: seventeen of the Carleton pamphlets were published during this period. She by no means faded from view after 1663, however. Between 1671 and 1673 a further nine texts appeared, including Francis Kirkman's biography of Carleton. In the context of this study, it is Carleton's later life that is most fascinating. Her fate, to be transported to the American colonies as an alternative to the gallows, was part of a far wider movement of judicial experimentation that crystallised legal, political and even humanitarian thinking throughout the seventeenth century, and reached its fullest expression in the years immediately following the Restoration. In its status as conditional pardon, transportation existed in a liminal position. Did it constitute a sentence or a reprieve, a punishment or a process of rehabilitation? In the preceding chapters we witnessed the struggles of the seventeenth-century legal establishment to calibrate the relationship between crime and punishment in capital cases. We also identified the discomfort of juries, judges and commentators with the legal instruments at their disposal, with the evidence upon which a capital conviction might be obtained, and with the proportionality of sanctions imposed. In the representations of Mary Carleton's experience these same themes emerge, but here we can trace an offender's own agency in this process of justice miscarried and mitigated; an agency inextricably linked to strategies of self-presentation, both legal and, crucially, literary. Carleton's transportation story, relayed in her own published texts and the accounts that attached to her exploits, raises as many questions as it does answers, and this uncertainty, I suggest, relates both to the realities of the sanction and to the nature of the texts themselves. In Chapter 3 we saw how the markers of truth within a text may be less important than the ways in which we choose to evaluate them. The texts associated with Mary Carleton magnify this difficulty; it may be anachronistic to describe her as an unreliable narrator, yet she is certainly that and more – and she moves between the legal and the literary in ways that expose the reciprocity of those modes. Reaching a 'verdict' on Carleton may be neither possible nor desirable.

Moreover, there is a further lacuna in the evidence, effected by the act of transportation itself: in the mid-seventeenth century so little was known about the experience of felons sent beyond the seas that any textual accounts effectively exist in dialogue with an absence, literal and philosophical. This problem of territory and knowledge was mirrored within the law, as the English criminal justice system gradually discovered the boundaries of its jurisdiction in respect of colonial terrain. If, as Bradin Cormack has argued, 'the law functions by keeping the source of its authority in view', then the limitations of that law's control were never more manifest than in the dispatch of a convict across the Atlantic and, most acutely, in his or her return.[5] This chapter, then, focuses on what the texts surrounding Carleton's case – its multiple reworkings and redactions – tell us about the early use of transportation as part of a system of pardon and correction marked by anxieties around consequences, and investigates why those texts seem to bear a particular relationship to emerging generic modes.

'Beyond the Seas': the Introduction of Transportation

In December 1717 a Bill was presented to Parliament 'for the further preventing Robbery, Burglary, and other Felonies; and the more effectual Transportation of Felons and unlawful Exporters of Wool'. It was passed in March of the following year. The 1718 Transportation Act, as it became known, focused concerns about rising crime levels, namely that:

> The punishments inflicted by the laws now in force against the offences of robbery, larceny and other felonious taking and stealing of money and goods, have not proved effectual to deter wicked and evil-disposed persons from being guilty of the said crimes.[6]

The Act's key measure was to allow the courts to sentence felons found guilty of offences subject to benefit of clergy to a term of seven years' transportation to America. For those pardoned from hanging for capital offences, the term was fourteen years. A formal system for the management of such transportation was to be established, centred on merchants who traded in the colonies, who would contract to arrange the physical delivery of those sentenced.

The 1718 Act is often regarded as marking the inception of the sanction of transportation within the English (and Scottish) criminal justice system, and indeed in one sense it did so, creating transportation as a direct sentencing option for the courts. Yet as numerous scholars have demonstrated, the idea and indeed the practice of transportation to America was already ingrained within British legal process, as a function of the ability to pardon those convicted of capital offences.[7] The Act itself acknowledges this, and the problems associated with that process, stating that 'many of the offenders to whom royal mercy hath been extended, upon condition of transporting themselves to the West-Indies, have often neglected to perform the said condition, but returned to their former wickedness'.[8]

As early as 1610, Governor Dale of Virginia had contacted the Colonial Office to suggest that felons should be sent out to that colony to settle the land, pointing out that the Spanish were dispatching convicts and the itinerant poor to populate their own colonies.[9] Indeed such an approach was common in continental Europe: both the Spanish and the French had used convicts in their colonising campaigns in the previous century, whilst the French practice of sentencing non-capital offenders to serve in the galleys was well established by this time.[10] Transportation had indeed been proposed for use by the English government during the sixteenth century, but only to very specific political ends, addressing problems of vagrancy and insurrection.[11] Realistically, up to this point, the principal source of English colonial labour had come from the system of indentured servitude, whereby individuals in need of employment would contract to sell their service to colonial landowners for a fixed term, in return for passage, board and lodgings and, at the end of their prescribed term, the promise of 'freedom dues' – a certain sum presented to enable them to set up for themselves in their new country.[12] In theory this was a voluntary arrangement, although in practice it was common for those deemed to be itinerant poor to be persuaded into 'transporting themselves' in return for avoiding trouble at the hands of the law. In October 1632, for example, the Corporation of London noted that some fifty vagrants had been bound as merchants' apprentices to serve in Barbados and Virginia.[13]

In 1614 James I addressed the Archbishop of Canterbury and the Privy Council with a Commission that appeared to respond directly to Governor Dale's suggestion:

> Wee ... give full power, warrant and authoritie by theis presents to you ... to reprive and stay from execucon such and soe many persons as nowe stand attaynted or convicted of or for any robberie or felonie, (wilful murder rape witchcraft or Burglarie onlie excepted) whoe for strength of bodie or other abilities shall be thought fitt to be ymploied in forraine discoveries or other services beyond the Seas.[14]

Within two days of the Commission being issued, a group of seventeen felons had been reprieved and placed into the charge of Sir Thomas Smith, then governor of the East India Company, to be conveyed into foreign service as he should decree.[15] The men were forbidden to return without a warrant being issued by the Privy Council. Clearly the King's injunction was serving a practical purpose.

James' Commission had an objective more fundamental than the stimulation of the colonial economy, however, and in order to understand this we should look at the preamble to his direction to the Archbishop:

> [W]ee finde by experience that with our people offences and offenders alsoe are increased to that number, as besides the severitie of our lawes punishing offenders in felonies to death, It is most requisite some other speedy remedie be added for ease unto our people. Wherein as in all things els tending to punishment it is our desire that Justice be tempered with mercie.[16]

As Abbot Emerson Smith notes:

> there were in this period some three hundred crimes which were designated as felonies, and that a felony, where clergy could not be pleaded, was punishable with death. The laws were strictly determinative; the judge had no alternative. He could condemn to death, or he could reprieve the felon for some good reason, but there was no third course open, and no lighter penalty which he might impose.[17]

The rhetoric of James' Commission, then, conveys this need for some sentencing measure to negotiate between the extremes of death and clergy, what John Langbein describes as 'a *via media* between the blood sanctions and the petty sanctions'.[18]

Initially this 'third way' was well received and Smith notes 'at least six' renewals of the Commission between 1617 and 1633.[19] Peter Wilson Coldham, whose work on American immigration includes the transcribing and collating of gaol records, Privy Council lists and landing certificates, records a number of typical cases:

> 1617
> 24 March. Warrant for stay of execution of persons convicted of felony so that after reprieval they may be employed in foreign discoveries or on other service overseas
> 3 April. Stephen Rogers, convicted of a killing and reprieved, orders to be sent to Virginia at the instance of Sir Thomas Smith because he is a carpenter.[20]

Whilst in the early years of transportation the majority of prisoners were sent to Virginia or Maryland, the colonies of Barbados and St Christopher were also likely destinations later in the century. In 1642 a planter in Barbados, Thomas Verney, wrote to his father in England asking him to round up one hundred men 'with the great help of bridewell and the prisons', and Carl Bridenbaugh notes that, within a few years, 'to Barbados' a person had become a verb in common usage.[21]

Indeed, by mid-century, a visitor to Barbados, Henry Whistler, somewhat caustically recorded the impact of criminal transportation upon the colony:

> This Illand is the dunghill wharone England doth cast forth its rubidg. Rodgs and hors and such like people are thos which are gennerally Broght heare.[22]

It is worth noting that, as early as 1618, prisoners themselves recognised transportation as an available alternative to capital punishment and sought to direct their own participation in this. Smith notes the case of John Throgmorton, 'illustrated by a petition from his grandmother to the council, asking for his reprieve and enclosing a certificate which she had obtained from the mayor and recorder of London. She further petitioned Sir Thomas Smith to take him to Virginia.'[23]

The dual efforts of Throgmorton's redoubtable grandmother highlight what was the fundamental stumbling block of the new regime. However desirable, the system for transportation depended first upon the intervention of the Privy Council, and then upon its ability to secure the services of merchants and entrepreneurs who would carry those reprieved from the gallows across the Atlantic. It was necessarily erratic in operation and as a result fewer than 200 felons in total were transported in the forty years following 1615.[24] An administrative breakthrough came in 1654–5, with the introduction of transportation via conditional pardon under the Great Seal.[25] This process allowed judges to pardon a convicted felon without the intervention of the Council, and to make that pardon explicitly conditional upon the individual being transported to the colonies. In a process that would become aligned with the circuit pardon, the judge would supply a list of prisoners recommended for mercy to the Secretary of State and the resulting Bill would be signed by the head of state as a formality. Beattie and Smith both identify the first instance of this as occurring at the Surrey Assizes; although Beattie dates this as 1654 and Smith as 1655, it is clearly the same event. The wording of the pardon is significant:

> If they or any of them shall refuse to bee transported being thereunto required or make any Escape or retorne into England within tenn yeares after theire said Transportacon without Lawful Licence first had then this our present Pardon to them soe refuseing escapeing or retorning to bee null and voyd.[26]

For the first time the link between pardon and transportation was made explicit and this was to constitute the basic mechanism for effecting transportation for the next sixty years. Returning from transportation before the allotted time, as Mary Carleton did, invalidated the pardon, thus presumably reinstituting the original sentence of death. It is worth noting that transportation remained a condition of pardon, rather than a direct sentence, but that it was now within the direct purview of the judiciary to impose it.

Whilst rehabilitation was never an explicit aim of the early Stuart Commissions, it formed a subtext to the whole movement of transportation to the colonies. Later in the century, Christopher Jeaffreson, a planter at St Christopher in the Caribbean, wrote to his cousin of his plans to petition for convicted felons to be sent out to boost the local population:

> If Newgate and Bridewell should spew out their spawn into these islands, it would meet with not less incouragement, for no gaolbird can be so incorrigible but there is hope for his conformity here, as well as of his preferment.[27]

Those petitioning for their lives deployed the promise of reform: in 1663, for example, a group of prisoners requested pardon, noting that they were 'unmarried and all able to do good service and steadfastly resolving through God's assistance to amend their lives for the future'.[28]

By the Restoration the emphasis on transportation as a function of state benevolence and a promulgator of personal reform was much more prominent. Although the system of conditional pardons was already in place when Charles II came to the throne, he reaffirmed the policy in a Royal Warrant of 1663. For Charles, transportation pardons were approved as a remedy 'that might become our royal clemency and be likewise an advantage to the public'.[29] The creation of a perception of merciful rule and equitable justice was of course only politic at this point: Beattie, for example, contends that 'by sixteenth century standards, capital punishment may have been imposed with a good deal of circumspection in the decades after the Restoration'.[30] Under Charles' administration, pardoning for transportation became a regular feature of circuit pardons and was at times used as a response to offences where clergy would have been the usual route.[31]

Transportation was thus positioned at the centre of a network of ideas and concerns, freighted with notions of compassion, but also linked to more practical discourses on colonialism and economic expansion. For a time, it looked as though this was a momentum towards a more extensive reform. In the same year that Charles II issued his Warrant, a Bill was introduced to the House of Commons that sought to implement transportation as a wholesale replacement for clergyable discharge itself.[32] The Bill was read twice during February 1663 and then sent for discussion by a Committee.[33] It was then heard in the House of Lords on 30 May.[34] No further progress appears to have been made with this Bill, but in March 1664 a proposed Act 'for transporting of Persons convicted of Felony within Clergy (or Petit Larceny) beyond the Seas' was read in the Lords and again referred to Committee.[35] The Bill or Bills disappear from the House *Journals* at this point, but the issue may have remained current.

Within sixty years the idea of transportation would lose much of its complexity, as the 1718 Act encoded it as one amongst a portfolio of direct sentencing options. As Beattie notes, one interesting aspect of the terms of the eighteenth-century Act was that, in cases of theft, it blurred the distinction between petty and grand larceny, making both offences potentially subject to a transportation sentence and eliminating the possibility of partial juror verdicts.[36] In Beattie's opinion this represented a wholly intentional decision to remove 'that discretion from the jury and [give] it to the judge. A prisoner convicted of any noncapital offense could now be dealt with as the bench decided.'[37] The use of transportation before the Act was therefore a strange, hybrid penalty, a measure which had yet to fulfil its real purpose and which retained some of the ambiguity that had attached to the old 'death or clergy' regime. The case of Mary Carleton, played out in the 1660s and early 1670s, offers us an intriguing picture of a period in which the use of that hybrid measure was at its height. Her career gives some insight into this post-Restoration flourishing of the 'via media' and the impact of that moment upon the fate of the habitual offender.

'I might as well have been the German Princess'

> But this thing gave me a terrible shock, for it happened just after I was married . . . It would have been enough to have ruined me to all intents and purposes with my husband, and everybody else too; I might as well have been the German Princess.[38]

Daniel Defoe's *Roxana* may allude to her incarnation as the 'German Princess', but Mary Carleton's career is regarded as inspiration for the progress of another of his heroines, 'the famous Moll Flanders, who was born in Newgate, and during a life of continu'd variety for threescore years . . . was twelve year a whore, five times a wife . . . , twelve year a thief [and] eight year a transported felon in Virginia'.[39] As Mary Jo Kietzman notes, 'Stories of [Carleton's] well-known exploits undoubtedly influenced Defoe's characterization of Moll'.[40] Carleton's story was indeed well known.[41] The *Newgate Calendar* contents page encapsulates her career neatly: 'a Kentish Adventuress who travelled the Continent, acquired several Husbands, and was executed on 22nd of January, 1673, for returning from Transportation'.[42]

Mary Carleton (née Moders) was, she claimed, born in 1642, although amongst the twenty-six pamphlet texts written about her are proposed various alternative dates, including 1634 and 1639.[43] She was a precocious child: 'confident Mall', as her biographer, Kirkman, dubs her, 'was well read in Parismus and Parismenos, Don Bellianis of Greece and ... oftentimes fancied herself to be some such princess'.[44] Mary married a Canterbury shoemaker, John (sometimes known as Thomas) Steadman, with whom she had two children, neither of whom lived for long. Eventually she made an attempt to quit her marriage by bribing a shipmaster's mate to smuggle her on board ship to Barbados. Presumably her intention, upon arrival, was to hire herself out as an indentured servant; her plan assumes a distinct irony when viewed in the light of her later career. In the end, the Barbados plot was discovered by Steadman, who 'came with an Order and fetched her ashore' and Carleton ran away to Dover instead, where she married again; this time the groom was a surgeon named Day.[45]

Carleton's progress was to be marked by a series of formative encounters with the law and this escapade prompted the first of these, when she was indicted for bigamy (a capital crime) on the grounds of the Day marriage. The case was ultimately dropped, Mary claiming that she had married in good faith, believing her former husband to be dead. She travelled to Europe, settling briefly in Cologne, where, momentarily mistaken for a German woman of a higher rank, she saw a new possibility for self-determination, an opportunity to forever banish 'that vile and impertinent falsehood, that I am of a most sordid and base extraction'.[46] Accordingly, she returned to England representing herself as Maria von Wolway, a German noblewoman fleeing an unwanted contract of marriage. She carried with her documents that suggested entitlement to a significant estate.

Landing at Gravesend and taking a 'tilt-boat' up the Thames, the newly fashioned Maria von Wolway found herself lodging at the Exchange-Tavern-against-the-Stocks in Poultry, an inn kept by a Mr King. It was there that she was to meet her landlady's brother, John Carleton.

> *Wednesday* the first of *April*, Mrs. *King* made a great Feast, where were divers persons of quality, as she said, amongst the rest, her Brother, Mr. *John Carleton* ... *Thursday* the 2d of *April*, Mr. *John Carleton* came in his Coach, with two Foot-men attending of him, calling him my *Lord*[47]

John Carleton was in fact an eighteen-year-old lawyer's clerk, sent on a fortune-hunting expedition by his family. This was to be a success, of sorts: John and Mary were married in April 1663, each believing the other to be of significant material worth. Inevitably, Mary's presumed riches failed to appear from Germany, and when the dismayed Carletons received a letter disclosing information about a potential husband in Canterbury, they acted at once to have her arrested for bigamy.

Mary's first trial offers a fascinating account of legal process and, pertinently to this study, sheds light on attitudes towards yet another capital crime in the period. Details are given in a number of the Carleton pamphlets, including the allegedly self-authored texts, *An Historicall Narrative of the German Princess* and *The Case of Madam Mary Carleton*, but the definitive account is believed to be contained in a text printed for N. Brook 'at the Angel in Cornhill', titled *The Arraignment, Tryal and Examination of Mary Moders*. Brook was to retain an involvement with Mary Carleton throughout her career, printing two further accounts of her progress in 1673; he also appears to have had connections to her self-styled biographer, Kirkman.[48] *The Arraignment* opens with a consideration of the Bill of Indictment drawn up against Carleton, a text which seeks to tether her firmly to her English roots. She was charged as 'Mary Moders late of London, Spinster, otherwise Mary Stedman, the wife of Tho. Stedman'.[49] Carol Wiener has demonstrated the way in which the construction 'Spinster' was deployed as a 'useful legal fiction', allowing the prosecution of married women, despite their *feme covert* status in law, but for a woman presenting herself as Maria von Wolway, the very phrasing of the charge constituted an assumption to be challenged.[50] Throughout her career, Carleton's approach to the law would consist in strategic associations and disconnects of her various personas, and never more publicly than at the Old Bailey Session-House in May 1663. The Carletons' case was ineptly presented: they failed to secure an appearance by Steadman, who apparently could not afford the fare to London, and their only testimony came from one John Knot, who had allegedly given Mary away at her first wedding.[51] Mary, by contrast, appeared a compelling witness in her own defence. Her speech to the court deftly summarised the flaws in the evidence against her, whilst planting the suggestion that something more sinister than outrage lay behind the Carletons' motives, 'this grounded on a letter (of their own framing) sent from Dover ... to affright me, that I might make my Estate over to them'.[52] As Janet Todd asserts, 'Mary spoke cleverly, exposing much of the belief in her aristocracy and vast wealth as self-deception by her greedy husband and his relatives.'[53] She effectively disowned the creation of the wealthy 'German Princess' – all a misunderstanding – whilst simultaneously maintaining the coherence of her Maria von Wolway identity.

What is perhaps most significant, in the context of Carleton's later encounters with the law, is the summing up offered by the judge in the case, Judge Howel. Howel refused to engage with the question of Carleton's identity – potentially the weakest element of her argument – but focused the case on the single issue of the fact, or not, of her first marriage. In so doing he highlighted two key elements, the weakness of the evidence produced for the marriage:

> The proof doth depend on one witness, that is Knot . . . All the Evidence given on that side to prove her guilty of this Indictment, depends upon his single testimony

and, most pertinently, the consequences of conviction:

> you see what the Circumstances are, it is penal, if guilty she must die; a Woman hath no Clergy, she is to die by the law, if guilty.[54]

Here the judge not only directed the jury on the facts, but foregrounded the legal problematic that rendered those facts, or the lack of them, so important. Whether or not Howel was opposed to capital punishment for bigamy – and we have no other evidence on that point – he was clearly troubled by the potential outcome of this case. It is worth noting that it was later in that same year (1663) that Charles II issued his proclamation supporting transportation as a remedy.

Howel's direction had its desired effect. After a 'short Consultation' the jury acquitted Carleton: 'and thereupon a great number of people being in and about the Court, hissed and clapped their hands'.[55] The case had caused a sensation, and public interest remained fevered throughout 1663. Its most vivid manifestations were Thomas Porter's play of the same year, *A Witty Combat* and John Holden's *The German Princess*, in which Carleton herself played the lead role in the April 1664 run. At the same time, the verdict provoked a storm of highly partisan pamphlet activity, in which the couple at the centre of the case were keen participants.[56] Mary Carleton's allegedly self-penned works are rich in detail and composed with assurance; they adopt a mode of self-assertion which supports the German Princess persona and deploy a range of textual and paratextual devices to that end. Whether or not the Old Bailey verdict had indeed endorsed her Maria von Wolway identity, Carleton continued to play with the ambiguities that surrounded her – audaciously dedicating *The Case* to Prince Rupert on the grounds of their 'common' nationality: 'Your Highness drew your first princely breath, which hath since filled the trump of fame, within the limits of that circle of the Rhine, where I was born.'[57]

Within that same dedication, however, Carleton gave the first indication of the circumscribed nature of her victory at the Old Bailey. She wrote of 'those miseries I endure, the more unsupportable because irremediable by the laws of this kingdom made against *femes covert*'.[58] For having been acquitted of bigamy effectively affirmed the validity of her marriage and her status as John Carleton's – estranged – wife. As a notoriously married woman, she could no longer engage in fortune-hunting schemes; as an estranged wife, she could derive no material support from her marital status. At the end of the trial, when she had requested return of her 'Jewels and Cloaths taken from her', the court 'acquainted her, that they were her Husbands'.[59] Whilst scholars have rightly celebrated Carleton's proto-feminist, picaresque life, it is hard to avoid the subtext of real material need underlying her bold approach, a need that was to direct the course of her subsequent career.

Under the 'eye of Justice'

'My true name is . . . well known in the records or registers at Newgate,' writes Moll Flanders, and in the years following her 1663 acquittal, Mary Carleton's career was to take a similar trajectory.[60] By the time she writes from Port Royal in 1671, Carleton has plenty of experience of Newgate and indeed offers advice to her 'fellow-collegiats' still held there:

> Do not in the least flatter yourselves with an opinion that your villainies will be connived at by the eye of Justice . . . For you cannot but be sensible that you are festered and gangrened limbs of the body politick; and therefore the experienced and grave physicians of the Commonwealth, the Judges will in time cut you off to prevent the absolute destruction of the whole Compositium . . . Some of you may be compared to ulcerated parts, or prodigious wens, and those must be absolutely cut off, . . . others to noxious and filthy humours, that must be purged away, as I myself have been, into another climate.[61]

Carleton's rapid qualification of her radical conceit of the diseased 'body politick' derives in part at least from the unique timing of her criminal career. If her acquittal on the Carleton bigamy charge came in 1663, the same year as Charles II's restatement of state support for conditional pardon, her final trial ten years later occurred at a time when, for reasons we will explore below, the penal landscape was changing once again and the 'purging' of 'noxious and filthy humours' had become a more complex endeavour. That particular timing offered Carleton an intriguing possibility of agency within the law, an agency that was located in strategies of self-presentation.

Following her acquittal, Carleton vanished from sight for some time, possibly again living on the Continent. She returned to London in 1669, styling herself as a widow, Mary Darnton. Her movement through the city from that point is matched by her movement through contemporary legal record, wherein it is possible to trace the thread of her various aliases and personas via a series of petty – and more serious – property offences. In her comprehensive study of Carleton's life, Mary Jo Kietzman terms such an approach 'serial subjectivity' and demonstrates the way in which Carleton's latter years typify the progress of criminals through the courts in this period. She notes that:

> inefficiencies in the Restoration criminal process ... enabled women like Mary Carleton to serialize themselves. Because recidivist offenders were pardoned regularly or had capital sentences mitigated, it seems possible that in some cases the court viewed self-serialization as a way for poor women to display competencies that signified potential for constructive social engagement.[62]

Kietzman suggests that Restoration justice displayed a 'high tolerance' for petty crime, informed by an understanding of the poverty that occasioned such acts, particularly in the case of female criminals for whom benefit of clergy was limited.[63] Theft of food or clothing, therefore, might be met with some degree of lenience, but when, for example, Mary Carleton was convicted of the theft of a silver tankard in 1670, she received a capital sentence. This analysis recalls us to the preoccupations of the Leveller petitioners of the 1640s and 1650s discussed in the Introduction to this book, though Kietzman locates the agency for this flexibility with 'those responsible for meting out judgments', unlike Beattie and Langbein, who identify the jury as its primary source.[64] The actions of Judge Howel in 1663 seem to support this inference, although it may be more likely that this process had multiple levers towards mercy. Further, post-1654/5, the mechanisms of the conditional pardon and its corollary of transportation were increasingly central to the ways in which *all* offenders, male and female, engaged with and manipulated the judicial system, and this is certainly true of Carleton's progress to justice.

Having settled at Enfield in Middlesex, she first appears in the court record at the January 1669/70 sessions as Maria Darnton, alias Maria Carlton, indicted for the theft of a horse from one Francis Betts.[65] Horse theft was regarded as an extremely serious offence, perceived to have links to organised, rather than opportunist, crime; it was not clergyable even for men in this period. However, it was also difficult to prosecute: many cases were dismissed on the grounds that the horse in question was grazing on common land, creating ambiguities around ownership, and it was possible to argue convincingly for mistaken identity. Perhaps unsurprisingly, then, Carleton was acquitted of this first charge.

Some months later, however, in 1670, we find Mary Carleton embroiled in a series of prosecutions which bring into focus the ways in which the penal system operated – and was understood to operate – at this time. In September 1670 she was indicted under the name Mary Kirton for the theft of the tankard previously mentioned, as well as two silver spoons.[66] This time she was convicted, sentenced to die, and then pardoned upon condition of transportation. However, in October 1670 she was convicted under the name Mary Blacke of the theft of '5 pounds worth of goods', an offence that had apparently been committed *before* the tankard theft. This peculiar chronology seems to suggest that Carleton was in flight from justice – and from her alias Mary Blacke – when she stole the tankard and was apprehended for it as Kirton. No indictment for that case survives and so we cannot say with any certainty whether Mary Blacke and Mary Kirton were identified as one and the same at trial. The fact that Mary Blacke, once convicted, was condemned to death, may imply that the court knew she was not a first offender; equally, however, the high value of the goods stolen would have precluded clergy.

At this point Carleton employed a complex and risky double strategy to ensure her survival. Immediately upon her conviction she petitioned the court for clemency, pleading the belly. A jury of matrons was charged to examine her; they confirmed her pregnancy and she was reprieved. But in the interim, presumably fearing an unfavourable result, she had also lodged a petition with the Secretary of State on a significantly different basis. As we have seen, petitioning for a conditional pardon was not uncommon. What was more unique to, and characteristic of, Carleton was the legal technicality upon which she petitioned, and the risk she took in so doing. This is summed up in the warrant ultimately issued for her reprieve:

> Oct. 17. Court at Whitehall. Warrant to Sir Wm Morton, Justice of King's Bench, and the Recorder and Sheriffs of London, to reprieve Mary Carleton, *alias* Kirton, *alias* Blacke, who has been a second time condemned to death for felony, and to cause her to be inserted in the next general transportation pardon for convicts of Newgate.[67]

Not only had Carleton made explicit in her petition the connection between her two aliases, Blacke and Kirton, she had revealed her true identity (as Carleton) to the state. Her argument was that because her later offence (committed as Kirton) had been reprieved, her conviction as Blacke was also effectively pardoned. 'We shall all choose anything rather than death', says Moll Flanders, but it was risky for Mary Blacke to reveal that she had been twice convicted, and further to admit to her identity as Mary Carleton, who could be associated with at least one previous trial (as Maria Darnton) and ultimately even with Maria von Wolway.[68] On this occasion, Carleton's bravado proved effective and her pardon was granted.

Ultimately, it would appear, Mary Carleton's conditional pardon was to prove virtually unconditional. Whilst she was remanded in Newgate to await departure, there is no record that she was transported. In this, she was not unrepresentative. The success of transportation as a policy was predicated upon an effective and – crucially – controllable system for the physical dispatch of convicts to the colonies and, prior to the 1718 Act, this was precisely what it lacked. As Beattie notes, 'from the beginning the actual machinery of transportation was in the hands of merchants trading to Virginia, Maryland and the West Indies, who looked upon the trade in convicts as they would any other commodity'.[69] The merchants' profit was gleaned from sale of the shipped convicts as indentured servants; thus the whole process was subject to supply and demand, and by the 1670s the terms of profit were gradually altering.

Hilary Beckles has traced this process in relation to Barbados, a sugar colony which experienced a boom in the late 1640s and early 1650s, and initially sought to meet its labour requirements via an influx of indentured servants and English convicts.[70] As we have seen, Thomas Verney, who operated his interests on the island, was happy to take his workers from 'the bridewell or Newgate', and indeed in 1656 the Venetian Ambassador to London reported seeing some 1,200 people collected 'from the streets' of London and shipped to Barbados.[71] However, as the mechanisms for slavery became more established, Barbadian planters began to recognise the economic advantages of an African labour pool: as Beckles notes, 'the shift from a white to a black labor regime between 1645 and 1680 was primarily a response to market forces'.[72] At the same time, in the mainland colonies, active political forces were at work. In 1670 Virginia passed an Act to prohibit the landing of the English 'jailbirds', contending that they posed 'a danger to the colony'.[73] Although in the eighteenth century similar measures would be overturned by the English Privy Council, the 1670 prohibition was not immediately challenged and in 1676 Maryland followed suit with a similar dictat.[74] The limitations of the reach of English law were being questioned and – at least initially – that legal system had no satisfactory answer to make.

Female convicts had always been less desirable transportees because they were customarily employed as indoor servants, rather than in the fields, and in the charged climate of the early 1670s they dropped ever further down the list. Physically they were generally regarded as a liability, as Christopher Jeaffreson's comments encapsulate: 'the women are forced upon us ... The risque we runn in ... mortality and other accidents is more than in all the rest.'[75] In theory, merchants were supposed to take their assigned batch of prisoners without demur, but in practice they would bribe gaolers to allow them to select the young and fit – and male. 'It seems clear that under the arrangements made at the Restoration the merchants simply left some women in jail,' Beattie asserts, and it is likely that this was Mary Carleton's fate.[76] Whether or not Carleton's non-departure was related to her alleged pregnancy, it seems probable that an awareness of the likelihood of this eventual outcome was one of the factors that influenced Carleton to petition. It was a carefully calculated gamble: as a non-transported felon it would have been relatively easy for her to bribe her way out of prison and disappear from public record, and she seems to have done so quite effectively for a period of time.

Mary Kirton and Mary Blacke vanish completely at this point, but Mary Carleton re-emerges some seven months later in July 1671, when 'Maria Lyon, wife of Walter Lyon, als Maria Lyon Spinster ... als Maria Darnton, als Maria Carleton' is indicted, with two others, including her 'husband', for the theft of goods from a shop.[77] It seems that no explicit connection was made between this Mary Carleton (alias Maria Lyon) and the Mary Carleton (alias Mary Kirton) who was believed transported, for in December 1671 Mary Carleton was once again granted a conditional pardon and ordered to be shipped to Barbados. Our evidence for Mary Carleton's actual transportation as a result of this charge obtains in a fairly diffuse selection of documents. Peter Coldham transcribes a list of nine men and three women as 'Middlesex prisoners reprieved to be transported to Barbados' in December 1671:

1671.
December. Middlesex prisoners reprieved to be transported to Barbados. John Jones, Alice Berford, Richard Benjon alias Benioge, William Thompson, *Mary Lyon alias Darton alias Carleton*, Roger Medley, Richard Whitehart, Thomas Sykes, George Moles, Henry Cockdale, Jane Pellingham, Calvin Read.[78]

However, he elsewhere records Carleton's arrival in the Americas thus:

Lyon *als* Darton, *als* Carleton, Mary. R for Barbados Dec 1671 but LC Md for *William & Mary* Mar 1672. M[79]

'LC' refers to Carleton's landing certificate; Md is the abbreviation for Maryland. This seems surprising, for although Maryland had not yet formally prohibited English convicts, the research of Abbot Emerson

Smith, among others, indicates that 'no English prisoners were sent to Maryland or Virginia between 1670 and 1718'.[80] Further, our most significant piece of evidence for Mary Carleton's transportation is the 1671 letter she purportedly sends – from Port Royal in Jamaica.

In his biography of Carleton, Francis Kirkman confuses the picture further:

> She was indicted for stealing a Silver Tankard, was found guilty and condemned to be hang'd, but had the mercy of Transportation, and was two days before Shrovetide in the year 1670 sent on board a Ship at *Gravesend* bound for *Jamaica* . . .[81]

Kirkman's source for his description of Carleton's transportation is unclear, but it is unlikely to have been the official record. His text derives much from the slightly earlier *Memoires of Mary Carleton*, which was issued anonymously but printed for the 'N. Brook' who had published *The Arraignment*. Kirkman also visited Carleton several times in Newgate and attended her final trial at the Old Bailey, and it is not unreasonable to suppose that any additional information in his text comes from courtroom and prison gossip. Kirkman's account of Carleton's time in Jamaica is entirely scripted in negatives:

> there was no thought of drawing in another Lord Carleton to marriage, no acting on the Theatre . . . Jamaica afforded her no several lodgings to cheat of tankards, nor Ale-Houses, to make Beer-Bowls and Beakers, there being none of this sort of Trade to be dealt in at this Place, she knew not what to do, she was out of her Element.[82]

Kirkman knows that Jamaica is not London, but he has no idea what else it may be. In fact, Port Royal was known to be a landing place for the privateers who roamed the Caribbean and was by this time well furnished with 'Ale-Houses' and entertainments for this transient population. Kirkman's approach reflects his ignorance of this, but also his lack of any real evidence of Carleton's dealings whilst transported. He dismisses the *Letter* as 'a piece of Romantick Wit' and seems only partially content to ascribe it to Carleton 'or the Author that writ it'.[83] Nonetheless he seems content to use it as his source.

The *Letter*, as we have seen, is the crucial artefact of and evidence for Carleton's transportation. It exists in two versions, the first published in 1671 by Peter Lillicrap, for 'Philip Brigs, in Pater Noster Row'.[84] Neither Lillicrap nor Brigs are implicated in any of the earlier 'German Princess' pamphlets, although we might posit a tenuous link to a Philip Brooksby, who published a sonnet to Carleton in 1673 and issued the *Memories of the Life of the Famous Madam Charlton* later in the same year.[85] A variant version of the *Letter* is then reproduced in full in the 1673 *Memoires*.[86]

In fact, only in the 1671 text of the *Letter* is a location given for its writer, and whilst it was published as 'News from Jamaica' and described as a 'Letter from Port Royal', this may have been a construct of the printers. Jamaica, captured from Spain in 1665, was a novelty to the English public and, as we have seen, the dissolute associations of Port Royal lent it a roguish glamour which may have been considered apt for the German Princess. If Carleton was based in Jamaica she may have arrived there in a number of circumstances, although given that she was formally reprieved for Barbados, it is unlikely that this was the original destination of her ship. There were ways to influence one's ultimate destination and it is possible that Carleton was able to buy her way out of her transported fate. Nonetheless this required hard cash and plenty of it. Defoe describes a similar process as Moll plots with the Captain of her transport ship to secure freedom for herself and her husband:

> He told me I must get somebody in the place to come and buy us as servants ... so he brought a planter to treat with him, as it were, for the purchase of these two servants, my husband and me, and there we were formally sold to him and went ashore with him. The captain went with us, and carried us to a certain house, ... we had a bowl of punch there made of rum, etc., and were very merry. After some time the planter gave us a certificate of discharge, and an acknowledgement of having served him faithfully, and we were free from him the next morning, to go whither we would.
> For this piece of service the captain demanded of us six thousand weight of tobacco ... which we immediately bought for him, and made him a present of twenty guineas besides.[87]

It seems unlikely, though not impossible, that stealing silver tankards for a living would have funded such an escape.

'Englands Slavery, or Barbados Merchandize'

The fate that Moll Flanders escapes, via bribery of the captain and the planter, is, of course, indentured servitude. Writing in 1722, four years after the Transportation Act, this would have seemed to Defoe the obvious conclusion to a sentence of transport; indeed he had himself been involved in the transport of prospective servants to Maryland as a commercial enterprise.[88] Yet the late seventeenth-century position was not so clear, and this raises some useful questions about the objectives of the conditional pardon system. For Cynthia Herrup, the formalisation of conditional pardon in 1654 represented a key step in untangling the complex legal status of mercy in seventeenth-century England: '[r]eprieves ... did not rescind the original sentence ... Conditional pardons, in contrast, seemed definitive. They exchanged a set amount of labour for freedom, putting clear limits on public supervision.'[89] Herrup suggests that this shift resolved a key constitutional issue, whereby under Magna Carta, English subjects could not be forced to leave the realm 'except by lawful judgement', that is, a direct sentence of banishment.[90] Conditional pardons were 'instruments of record', unlike the more open-ended reprieve.

In practice, though, it would seem that this ambiguity remained. The language of 'reprieve for transportation' remained in use, as we see in the documents surrounding Carleton's case, and while, by the time of Carleton's transportation, the term of a convict's exile was set at seven years for the majority of crimes, it is important not to conflate this with a prescribed term of servitude. As Smith comments:

> Although their *exile* was fixed at seven years, it does not appear that they were usually expected to remain in the status of bond servants for a time longer than that established by the custom of the country for ordinary servants ... Jamaica alone passed a law in 1681, requiring that transported felons should serve for the term of their exile.[91]

Alan Atkinson goes further, suggesting that the servitude element of the pardon may not have been legally enforceable at all: 'Under the law as it had existed before 1824, it was possible to argue that British convicts were condemned to transportation alone, and not to bondage.'[92] There was debate as to how far such felons even remained under jurisdiction of the English courts, once in colonial territories. Atkinson notes:

> the common belief that the entire process of trial and punishment should be a public one, open to the view and subject to the interests of the people. Transportation beyond the seas was consistent with this belief only if there were no prescribed punishment after transportation: on embarking (or perhaps on leaving local waters) the convict thus passed out of the reach of king, parliament and courts.[93]

This jurisdictional question itself created a more philosophical difficulty; if England sought to dispose of its 'rubidg', in the words of Henry Whistler, how far could and should the nation control the experience of punishment once a felon was transported?[94] Precisely where, in fact, did the notion of punishment reside within the process of transportation? Bradin Cormack has noted that 'the territorial threshold dividing kingdoms from one another or a kingdom from an empire cannot be understood separately from the temporal limit that divides time into past, present, and future'.[95] This paradigm of 'threshold space, threshold time' was particularly acutely felt in the earlier years of the sanction, for if the punitive element of transportation was seen to reside merely in removal from English shores, then the very fact that those transported were ultimately permitted to return seemed simultaneously to suggest a more wholesale dynamic of rehabilitation and reform.[96] By the end of the century, the narrative of the transportation experience had become normalised to some degree, and improved communication networks enabled better monitoring of offenders across spatial and jurisdictional boundaries. For the situation in the 1660s and 1670s, however, Mary Carleton's *Letter from Port Royal* can be said to construct a fantasy of this legal problematic, a world beyond the reach of English law, an anti-Newgate, where 'my pleasures are sweet and uninterrupted: My person insulted o're by none, nor chekt by any Lordly control or prohibition'.[97]

In those pardons that survive from the 1660s, whilst the condition of transportation is made explicit, servitude is not.[98] As we have seen, however, the experience of seventeenth-century transportation was shaped as much by economic as by legal imperative, and because, prior to 1718, the government would not pay a convict's passage to the Americas but relied on merchants to facilitate his or her removal, the requirement to servitude became an assumed part of the process. Nonetheless, legal ambiguities persisted once transported: it was unclear to the receiving colonies whether the treatment of such immigrants should be constructed differently from that of ordinary bonded servants. In some colonies, for example, felons who completed their term of service were entitled to the same 'freedom dues' as other servants.[99]

Even where transported servants were accorded the same rights as their non-felonious counterparts, the experience of servitude was hardly to be envied. In his 1657 study of Barbados, Richard Ligon suggested that African slaves were 'preserved with greater care than the servants': for after all, the slaves were 'subject to their masters forever' whilst the servants were bound only for a fixed period.[100] Whilst this seems highly dubious, it was certainly the case that, during their term of servitude, the indentured existed primarily in terms of the worth of their labour. Beckles's work affirms this: he finds that 'servants represented in this period the most liquid form of capital ... in plantation accounts ... indentured servants were categorized as property, like cattle, slaves and fixed assets', and notes instances of servants bequeathed in wills, for example, or being confiscated by magistrates in lieu of unpaid taxes.[101]

In 1659 the claims of English law upon the situation of servants in the colonies, and Barbados in particular, were suddenly brought into focus. On 25 March of that year, the House of Commons *Journal* records the petition of Marcellus Rivers and Oxenbridge Foyle, who had been transported to Barbados following the Salisbury rebellion of 1654.[102] Foyle and Rivers, whose petition was later published in the pamphlet *Englands Slavery or Barbados Merchandize*, requested 'redemption and reparation', or 'at least, that this Court will be pleased ... to take course to curb the unlimited power under which the Petitioners suffer'.[103] They alluded to the identification of servants as property, 'attached as horses and beasts for the debts of their masters', and made explicit the connection with slavery: 'so great a breach is made upon the free people of *England*, they having never seen the faces of those their pretended owners (Merchants that deal in slaves and souls of men)'.[104]

The petition was debated in the Commons for two days, and although it was finally rejected, concerns remained that it was 'noised abroad as if the Secretary of State could enslave, and had enslaved, the people of England at his pleasure'.[105] Already, then, the notion of transportation as a function of state or royal clemency was being subtly undermined, and this position grew in momentum even as the sanction itself increased in legitimacy. It is notable that in the years following the 1718 Act the flow of petitions from convicts requesting transportation is countered by similar texts in which petitioners seek to avoid that fate at all costs.[106] This in part stemmed from the fact that the Act had introduced transportation as a punishment for non-capital as well as capital offences, but, as we saw in Chapter 4, this was common even in capital cases – one Robert Webber, reprieved for transportation at Maidstone in 1766, was alleged to have 'made strong instances to be rather hanged, promising to make great discoveries were he permitted to die'.[107] The publication of texts such as Foyle and Rivers' petition were indubitably part of this process, as, later, were the criminal biographies of the eighteenth century. As Gwenda Morgan and Peter Rushton note, a transportation narrative, 'the American experience', was almost a prerequisite of a convict memoir in the period, and these texts universally portray 'a life of unremitting labour and harsh masters'.[108]

'My Friends and once Fellow-Prisoners': Mary Carleton's *Letter*

Mary Carleton's *Letter* displays none of these markers of the transportation experience. Carleton lives 'en Princesse ... beloved by all, dayly loaded with kindnesses ... My freedom is greater here in my confinement, than when I was among you free.'[109] On one hand it seems characteristic of Carleton to write 'en Princesse', transforming her circumstances to create a fantasy of status for her readership, and yet it seems correspondingly unlikely that, with her romantic insistence upon her gentle birth, she would have expressly aligned her Princess persona with the 'ulcerated parts [and] prodigious wens' of the Newgate multitudes.[110] Far more likely, surely, that any text written from exile would form an elaborate presentation of her innocence?

As a piece of evidence, then, the *Letter* is problematic. Kietzman inclines to its authenticity, basing her conviction partly upon stylistic similarities between the *Memoires*' version of the *Letter* and other texts written by Carleton, in particular upon its use of a particularly uncommon construction which also appears in *The Case*:

> In her letter she cites 'the eximiousness of [her] Birth and State' as an excuse for forgetting her jailbird friends, and in *The Case* she recalls being the focus of attention at a Hyde Park assembly – 'the eximiousness of [her] fortune drawing all eyes to her'.[111]

Kietzman further contends that the period of time that had elapsed since Carleton's 1663 bigamy trial would have rendered her all but forgotten in the public imagination – 'that a hack writer would have thought to have penned a letter resurrecting "the Princess" speaking from the New World seems unlikely'.[112] Whilst these are compelling arguments, I would suggest that they are not irrefutable. Certainly, the *Letter* reads like a typical Carleton act of self-assertion, and it is close in style to *The Case*. So close, in fact, that it almost seems to pick up where that text left off, erasing the intervening nine years almost completely. The *Letter* constantly returns to the parameters and preoccupations of Carleton's existence in 1663, seeming to graft them onto her current circumstances:

> When I first set sail from England I was lookt upon but strangely and despised as the base brat of a country fiddler ... You may, if you think it convenient, present my dutie to my Lord and inform him that a Princess is more acceptable in a foreign, than in her own Countrie ...[113]

It then moves to the Newgate narrative, comprising an awkward juxtaposition of Carleton's alleged advice to her peers with a fairly heavy-handed deployment of criminal cliché: 'remember me to the Old Gang, the roguish Crew of all our former acquaintance'.[114] In summary, the *Letter*, in particular the *Memoires*' version, reads like a text written by someone who knows all about *The Case*, but very little about Mary Carleton's subsequent life, in particular the likely experience of a transported felon. We should remember that the *Case* had enjoyed huge popularity, and its wide contemporary circulation would have ensured that the writing style of the German Princess was well known and potentially available to a 'hack writer' with a talent for mimicry.

Of course, all this is irrelevant if, as Kietzman proposes, Mary Carleton was 'forgotten' by 1671. Was she truly erased from public consciousness by this point? References to the Princess had been kept alive well beyond her last appearance in *A Witty Combat* in 1664. A 1667 collection of epigrams and witticisms, *Poor Robin's jests*, includes accounts of Carleton's supposed wisdom whilst in prison on her bigamy charge.[115] Intriguingly, the work, which was licensed in February 1666, was 'printed for *Francis Kirkman* and Richard Head'. As we have seen, both Kirkman and the publisher 'N. Brook' followed Carleton's career to some degree. But public awareness of Carleton by 1671 would really have depended upon the effectiveness of her serial identities, and, most importantly, upon the isolation of the German Princess persona from those identities. When petitioning for her pardon as Mary Blacke, Carleton did so in her own name, and when she was indicted for her theft with Walter Lyon, the form of the charge encompassed multiple aliases, including that of 'Maria Carleton'. It is arguably quite possible that a connection had been made between the Mary Carleton in the dock and the Mary Carleton who had once been Maria von Wolway. Such intelligence would surely have been gladly received by any opportunist publisher who remembered the popular sensation surrounding the German Princess's last encounter with the law.

What also emerges after close scrutiny of the *Letter* is a pervasive problem with dates. Even setting aside the many weeks it would have taken to transport a letter from Jamaica to London, the respective chronologies of the text and the known events of Carleton's career do not support a claim to authenticity. Maria Lyon was indicted in July 1671 and transported in February 1672. Yet Francis Kirkman has his Mary Carleton transported at Shrovetide 1670, and mentions her 'two years exile' out of England. The *Letter* is recorded as first printed in 1671, before Maria Lyon ever left England. A February 1671 date would correspond with Carleton's first transportation pardon as Mary Kirton, but not as Maria Lyon, who is the only Carleton alias for whom we have a record of likely dispatch and possible landing. This may be a mistranscription of Carleton's aliases, or a confusion of the old and new calendars around February 1671/2. And Kirkman may have doubled his error by conflating the Kirton and Lyon sentences – he describes Carleton as transported for 'stealing a Silver Tankard', which was in fact her earlier crime.[116] Nonetheless, there remain some suggestive discrepancies.

The *Letter* thus emerges as a distinctly unstable signifier in several ways: date, place of origin, authorial position and, ultimately, intention. Moreover, this instability forces us to re-examine some of our assumptions about the reality of Mary Carleton's transportation. There are multiple possibilities here, the most obvious being that the *Letter* was in fact authored by the speculative professional author whom Kietzman dismisses.[117] If this is the case, then the question of date may be irrelevant, for it is entirely possible that the author, like Kirkman after him, had assumed that Carleton had in fact been transported following her first conditional pardon, as Mary Kirton/Blacke, in later 1670 or early 1671. The *Letter* gives no details of the crime which occasioned its heroine's exile, and there is no evidence within it to suggest a specific link to the Maria Lyon case. We might conjecture then that, while Mary Carleton 'lay low' in London, having avoided banishment, a fictional account of her transportation was being circulated and sold.

If the *Letter* was indeed intended to attach to Carleton's first conditional pardon rather than her second, then it encodes two further possibilities. The first is that Mary Carleton *was* in fact transported under that first pardon. This seems unlikely, given that we find her back in court in London by July 1671, but it is not impossible, as we shall see below. The second possible explanation requires us to accept Kietzman's validation of Carleton as the author of the *Letter*, but to reposition it, not as a 'comeback', but as an insurance policy of the kind Carleton revelled in, a decoy text which established its author as safely 'confined' overseas whilst in fact she remained resident in, and criminally active among, the parishes of London. Whether this latter hypothesis is a likely one is debatable; it would, however, validate the *Letter*'s timing and account for its Carletonesque flourishes, whilst simultaneously explaining its lack of convincing reference to what should surely have been its author's central concern, her life in exile. If the *Letter* was Mary's own creation, a final manifestation of her German Princess persona, it would not have been her only foray into the genre. Back in 1663 her original impersonation of Maria von Wolway, German aristocrat, had been supported by a number of forged letters which indicated her entitlement to a significant estate, and was further bolstered by anonymous missives sent to her husband's family suggesting that she was so wealthy that she had a price on her head.[118]

Ultimately the questions posed by the *Letter* are unanswered; it remains problematically situated on that border of fiction and evidence that Frances Dolan describes as 'texts as documents *and* as literature', and perhaps this is the point.[119] After all, is only within the *Letter*'s instability that we can really locate a 'meaning' for the text. The ambiguities of Mary Carleton's *Letter* in some sense offer us a textual paradigm for the ambiguities that surrounded the process of conditional pardon in the Restoration period. Transportation is itself an unstable signifier in the seventeenth century: at a philosophical level it is impossible to establish its intended purpose, or to measure its success; on a legal and practical level it represents as a series of uncertainties – uncertainties about dispatch, uncertainties about experience, uncertainties about return. In fact, the only thing we know for certain about Carleton's transportation is that she was back in England by December 1672 at the very latest.

'The reason of her Return'

On 16 January 1673, Mary Carleton was brought from the Marshalsea prison in Southwark to face trial at the Old Bailey. She was conveyed there in a coach belonging to the governor of the Marshalsea, John Lowmans, who a month earlier had recognised the prisoner as 'his old acquaintance, the German Princess'.[120] The report of her apprehension in the *London Gazette* runs thus:

> These are to give notice, That there was lately apprehended by Mr John Lowmans, and are now in his Custody in the Marshalsea, one Mary Carleton (formerly called the German Princess) and also one William Lancaster, and Mary the wife of Robert Hodgkins ... All of them may be seen at any time of the day, at the Marshalsea.[121]

Whilst Lancaster and Hodgkins had been found in possession of goods presumed stolen, there is no mention of these in relation to Mary Carleton, although, according to Kirkman, she had been more than active in this regard since her return to London.[122] Indeed, when she reached the Sessions House, she was confronted with a lengthy exposition of her recent crimes:

> An indictment exhibited against her by a Taylor in *Chancery Lane*; for stealing a Silver Tankerd and some other pieces of Plate ... Another in *Aldersgate-street*, brought an Indictment against her likewise for stealing Plate and several other Indictments brought against her, for many Robberies and other Cheats she hath committed since she came over.[123]

The judge dismissed all these charges (for which extant indictments do exist); his interest was only in the formal reconstruction of Mary Carleton's fragmented legal identity, and in the logical conclusion of that reconstruction, her trial for returning from transportation – 'ye Judge insisted only upon the matter of her coming over, notwithstanding her Banishment, for which she is Condemned to be Hangd'.[124] According to the anonymous author of *An Exact and True Relation of the Examination, Tryal and Condemnation of the German Princess*, this process of fixing Mary Carleton's identity took only a few moments, although characteristically Carleton saw, and took, an opportunity to complicate the process:

> The Judge examined her if she were the same woman that went by the name of Mary Carlton, that was not long since Banished this Kingdom: To which she answered, she was the same person; the Judge demanded the reason of her Return: To which she answered that she had somwhat that troubled her Conscince about Treachery which she had a great desire to discover.[125]

Carleton's 'Discovery' was another seemingly fantastic tale, encompassing the dramatic themes and emphasis on personal distinction with which we associate her:

> the Tretchery she told them was thus, When she was banished, there was 25 others banished with her, and when they came out at Sea, these 25 agreed altogether with her to murther the Master and all that were in the Ship ... this she said she discovered to the Master, ... sometime after they all arrived in *Jamaica*, when they were there, she was so much in favour with the Master of the Ship and the Governour of *Jamaica*, for the Tretchery she had discovered, that she was set at liberty ... she, as she said, trusted so much to the Kings Mercy for the good she had done in saving the whole Ships Company alive, that she ventured to came over again in that very Ship that carried her.[126]

Once again, it seems impossible to establish the veracity or otherwise of this story. In some elements, such as the Jamaican location, it fits well with the *Letter*'s account of her movements, although the timings do not – a homecoming again 'in that very Ship that carried her' suggests a 1672 transportation and return, rather than a 1671 dispatch. Further, the story of the mutiny is itself dubious in detail: prisoners being transported were usually restrained in some way, and it seems unlikely such a threat could have been perceived as serious enough to warrant the level of gratitude described. Moreover, Mary Carleton knew the value of evidence at law; if she had indeed 'trusted so much to the Kings Mercy for the good she had done', she would surely have acquired testimonials to that effect in support of her return.

Our only accounts of Carleton's testimony come at second hand. Her mutiny story features in the *Exact and True Relation*, in Kirkman's text, and in the *Memoires* (wherein it is dismissed as 'a mere pretence, and absolutely fallacious').[127] Nonetheless, it does seem likely that she made this attempt; such a venture is reminiscent of her efforts to secure a pardon in 1670. As in that instance, she attempted to set up multiple lines of defence: Kirkman reports that whilst she waited in the Marshalsea for trial, she offered to make 'discoveries' to her gaolers: 'but I do not hear of any discovery she made; she promised much, but performed nothing'.[128]

Finally, Carleton fell back upon her old strategy and pled the belly, but this time the gamble was unsuccessful; she was sentenced to death, without hope of reprieve. The accounts are ambiguous on the exact conclusion of her trial: the *Exact and True Relation* indicates that she was sentenced purely on the basis of her return from transportation, the *Memoires* suggest that on the second day of her trial, the Chancery Lane indictment, which had been dismissed on 16 January, was revived, and she was found guilty.[129] If this is true it is intriguing. Return from transportation was only formally made a capital offence under the 1718 Act. Nonetheless the conditional nature of pardons for transportation created a presumption that violation of the terms of the pardon would reinstitute the original sentence of death. However, there are surprisingly few recorded cases of the enforcement of this in the period. The Old Bailey Sessions Records, for example, have only one such instance from the year of Mary Carleton's death until the coming into force of the Transportation Act, in which a female counterfeiter, Cecilie Labree, 'had broke the conditions of her pardon' and was restored to her original sentence.[130] It may be therefore that the majority of returnees only came to the attention of the authorities when they reoffended, and thus their charges were couched in terms of the new crime, rather than the old.[131] Where there is mention of a return, or a non-transportation in an indictment it does not necessarily lead to death. In a 1663 Gloucester Assizes case, for example, William Drury was sentenced to transportation for the theft of two pigs, but escaped from the barge carrying him to his ship by jumping overboard. In August of the same year, he was apprehended on a separate charge, this time of witchcraft, and, although acquitted, was held in Gloucester gaol under a writ of *habeas corpus* until he could once again be transported.[132] As we have seen manifest in Carleton's earlier career, attitudes towards recidivism were by no means as clear-cut as they seemed, and while the grounds for severity in her case were surely compelling, in the absence of clear legal precedent it may ultimately have seemed politic to her 1673 judge to admit the charge of theft, in order to reinforce his sentence.

Undoubtedly, felons were returning from transportation, even if the records of the courts did not acknowledge this explicitly prior to the 1718 statute. In the years immediately following that Act, the Old Bailey records between three and seven cases per annum.[133] Whilst it is true that by this point more criminals were being transported, their defiance of the formal categorisation of return as a capital crime surely indicated their determination to escape exile. By 1738 the editor of the *Virginia Gazette* was despairing: 'for *Transportation* does not answer the End proposed, the convicts are continually returning, and only made more desperate than before'.[134] Some of these transported felons were returning almost immediately after dispatch. Morgan and Rushton note that 'successful escapees often ran quickly after, or even immediately on, arrival in the colonies'.[135] Such a turnaround could support the possibility of Mary Carleton's first transportation, for it would have allowed her to have been transported in late 1670 and to have been back in England in the summer of 1671.

In the eighteenth century, then, despite the known sentence of death upon return, criminals would still risk the pursuit of escape to England, a risk that, as Morgan and Rushton have demonstrated, was only increased by the growing network of newspapers in seaport towns on both continents, which closely monitored the movement of criminals across the Atlantic.[136] In the seventeenth, when such documentation and monitoring was so much less ordered, it seems little wonder that Mary Carleton felt reasonably confident in seeking a passage home. Nonetheless, there does seem to be a sense in which she felt that the stakes were higher following her return. Undoubtedly, if we are to believe the pamphlet accounts, her 'Cheats' became increasingly highly wrought at this point. The *Exact and True Relation* recounts an assault upon 'Mr. *Aspinal*, one of the Kings Watchmakers' in which twenty-five watches were stolen, 'six of which were gold, and some money, in all to the value of near 700 pound'.[137] When Carleton was finally captured, however, it was as a result of someone else's crime. A thief-taker, Fisher, was searching houses in Southwark for a suspect in a robbery, including the place where Mary was then lodging:

> He knew her not, but ... seeing some Letters lye on the table, he had the Curiousity to cast his eye upon one, which was directed to one Mr *Hyde*; he takes it up ... knowing there was one of that name Prisoner in the *Marshalsea* ...[138]

Fisher communicated his suspicions about Carleton to John Lowmans, who had formerly been turnkey at Newgate. Lowmans recognised Carleton from the time of her bigamy trial:

> [U]pon some little discourse he knew her, and told her she must go along with him ... he had heard of her late practices, and believed he should do good service to the public in apprehending of her.[139]

The whole episode indicates that, despite its sprawling population, London was effectively a very small place in 1673. If John Lowmans could identify Mary Carleton as the German Princess some eight years after her last 'performance' in that role, it seems highly improbable that she had not been recognised during her progress through the courts between 1669 and her return. In this formulation, then, Mary Carleton's manipulation of identities during those years seems less a mode of agency than an activity that was obliquely permitted by the law.

Conclusion

> Here lyes one, much against her will,
> Who did lye living; and dead, lies still,
> She has more names, says the Relater,
> Than *Goldman*, or a *Nomenclator*.
> She's incleap't *Moders*, *Stedman*, nay
> *Carleton*, and *Moll et caetera*
> . . .
> Therefore look to't, lest out she steal,
> And cheat the worms of a set meal.[140]

Mary Carleton alias Moders, alias Stedman, alias Darnton, alias Kirton, alias Blacke, alias Lyon, commonly styled the German Princess, was hanged at Tyburn on 22 January 1673. She was, she claimed, only thirty-one years old. In the days between her sentence and her execution, she was exhibited to visitors in Newgate, 'come to behold that poor soul there as a wonder, when indeed she was more like a Looking-glass'.[141] Once again the centre of attention, Carleton in fact complained that 'People were so numerous, and troublesome in their visits, that they would not give her time to repent, but would have to dye with all her sins'.[142]

Nonetheless, according to the pamphlet *The Deportment and Carriage of the German Princess Immediately before her Execution* – printed for 'Nath. Brooke', who had issued *The Arraignment* in 1663 and went on to publish the *Memoires* – she played her part well.[143] The *Deportment* relates that 'she did shew the absolute symptoms of a true Penitent' at the last, 'her Ejaculations were as pious and pathetical as her former Life had been enormous and criminal'.[144] At the same time, however, her public would not let her escape her most memorable role: Kirkman has her carry a portrait of John Carleton to the gallows, whilst in the *Deportment* a member of the crowd interrupts her speech to ask her, 'have you anything to your Husband?'[145] Most appositely, perhaps, she died an avowed 'Roman Catholick', portraying an exotic otherness to the last.[146]

The fear expressed in her 'Epitaph', that Mary Carleton would 'cheat' death, was not unfounded. In December 1684, George Croom, at the Blue-Ball in Thames Street, printed a pamphlet account of the criminal progress of Jenney Voss, who had been hanged that month at Tyburn. The text was entitled *The German Princess Revived*.[147] Voss's career does indeed read like a homage to Mary Carleton's: a serial thief and trickster, she was most famously convicted of being part of a gang that had plotted to steal the Lord Chancellor's mace, for which she was transported. Returning to London, having, unlike Carleton, served her full sentence, she resumed operations almost immediately, was indicted and convicted for the theft of a silver tankard, pled the belly and was reprieved, and was finally found not to be pregnant and condemned to die.

Beyond its references to Carleton, the Voss pamphlet is notable for the way in which it demonstrates what we might term the beginnings of the 'normalisation' of the concept of transportation as early as the 1680s, a decade when that fragile system was being undermined by resistance from the colonies themselves. The idea that one might be transported, serve a sentence and return to resume life (and a criminal career) in England, perhaps anticipates the post-1718 integration of the 'American experience' into the average felon's life history.[148] From a period wherein what could be known about the experience of transportation was so limited that it remains almost impossible to establish whether Mary Carleton ever left English shores, we witness the emergence of a new discourse, in effect the inception of transportation as a fully fledged process. The experience 'Beyond Sea' is now demystified: Voss spends her time as an indentured servant engaging in 'her old Pranks, [inciting] all others that were her fellow Servants to Pilfer and Cheat what they could from their master'.[149] Some of this demystification came from the increased two-way traffic that now operated between England and the colonies, the early manifestations of what Morgan and Rushton propose as the 'Criminal Atlantic'.[150] Much of this traffic was quasi-literary in nature; criminal biographies and newsbook accounts addressed the gaps, both imaginative and legal, that had problematised transportation in its early days. Morgan and Rushton contend that 'the transatlantic circulation of news allowed English papers to follow the colonial careers of their most interesting convicts and to collect reports where they could from the colonial newspapers'.[151] Furthermore, these networks allowed an element of policing of the effectiveness of the sanction: one typical report, concerning the notorious pickpocket Jane Webb, announces her early return from transportation – 'the celebrated Jane Webb, alias Jenny Diver, who was transported last April for picking of pockets at St Paul's, is returned from her travels'.[152] It is hard to believe that had such networks existed in 1672, Mary Carleton would not have featured among those 'most interesting convicts'. It seems likely that our picture of her progress through transportation and beyond would have been far clearer.

What, then, can we conclude about the relationship between literature and criminal sanction in the case of the German Princess? It would be far too neat a claim to suggest that the rise of transportation marked a distinct cultural change in seventeenth-century society that mirrored or manifested itself in a shift in literary modes. Nonetheless, Mary Carleton's encounter with Restoration justice exposes a penal system attempting to establish an alternative to what Langbein terms 'the blood sanctions' and demonstrates the degree to which that process oscillated between the claims of expediency and reform.[153] The mechanism of conditional pardon served to expose the ambiguities inherent in existing criminal practice – ambiguities around identity and recidivism, ambivalence about appropriateness of punishment – placing them in counterpoint with a much greater uncertainty, the anxious promise of transport beyond the seas. Such a model offered opportunities for agency amongst those accused, it is clear, but would also raise the spectre of 'Barbados Merchandize', a fate arguably worse than the capital sanctions.[154]

Undeniably the dichotomy underlying conditional pardon was located in issues of identity and selfhood, and never more so than in its literary manifestations. Mary Carleton's 'memoirs' and biographies, the disingenuous *Letter*, which may be anything between a homage to celebrity and a desperately risky insurance policy, even the reports of the *London Gazette* – these all operate as differing types of evidence of the reality of transportation, evidence that must be treated with caution. Nonetheless, they all also look ahead towards a far more robust literary framework for the criminal experience, a framework that would draw structurally from the sensational reversals of crime and punishment, but that would also be driven by the complexities of individual characters, characters as unreliable and pragmatic as Mary Carleton. From criminal autobiographies to the novels of Defoe, these texts promise a new transparency of truth and revelation, but simultaneously encode their own contradiction: after all, 'it is not to be expected I should set my [true] name . . . to this work', says Moll Flanders.[155]

If we return to Holger Schott Syme's claim, quoted in the Introduction to this study, that 'the practices of the criminal law [arguably] come closer to offering a lens on the culture at large than other legal fields', then perhaps the practice of conditional pardon, particularly as manifest in the years immediately following the Restoration, is one such.[156] Crystallising issues of nationhood and empire on one hand, and exposing the fragility and the practical limitations of legal control on the other, this mechanism for reprieve also carried with it the political weight of the Interregnum debates on capital sanction. Finally, and intriguingly, it opened up the possibility of a whole new narrative of criminal experience, effectively a story from beyond the grave, a narrative that, in the case of Mary Carleton, offers us a vivid embodiment of a system struggling into a state of transformation and of the contradictions and qualifications that marked that process.

Notes

1. *Memoires of Mary Carleton*, p. 58.
2. Kirkman, *The Counterfeit Lady Unveiled*, p. 179.
3. Suzuki, 'The Case of Mary Carleton', p. 61.
4. Carleton, *The Case of Madam Mary Carleton*; Todd and Spearing (eds), *Counterfeit Ladies*, p. l.
5. Cormack, *A Power to Do Justice*, p. 7.
6. 4 Geo. I, c. 11, section I.
7. See Smith, 'Transportation of Convicts'; Beattie, *Crime and the Courts*; Langbein, 'Historical Origins of the Sanction of Imprisonment'; Coldham, *Emigrants in Chains*.
8. s. I.
9. Sainsbury (ed.), *Calendar of State Papers, Colonial 1574–1660*, p. 12.
10. John Langbein identifies an abortive 1602 attempt to establish an English galley fleet, to be manned by felons. See Langbein, 'Historical Origins of the Sanction of Imprisonment', pp. 39–43.
11. 'An Acte for Punishment of Rogues, Vagabonds, and Sturdie Beggars' (39 Eliz. I, c. 4) proposed transportation as a solution to that problem; however, it seems that this was never actually implemented. In the century following, legislation was passed by which moss troopers convicted in Cumberland or Northumberland could be transported for life to America (18 Car. I, c. 3).
12. Atkinson, 'The Free-Born Englishman Transported', p. 101.
13. Quoted in Bridenbaugh, *Vexed and Troubled Englishmen*, p. 391.
14. Grant (ed.), *Acts of the Privy Council*, pp. 23–5, 248.
15. Smith, 'Transportation of Convicts', p. 234.
16. Grant, *Acts of the Privy Council*, p. 23.
17. Smith, 'Transportation of Convicts', p. 233.
18. Langbein, 'Historical Origins of the Sanction of Imprisonment', p. 55.
19. Smith, 'Transportation of Convicts', p. 235.
20. Coldham, *The Complete Book of Emigrants*, p. 8.
21. Quoted in Bridenbaugh, *No Peace Beyond the Line*.
22. Whistler, *Voyage to the West Indies*, f. 9.
23. Smith, 'Transportation of Convicts', p. 235.
24. Ibid. p. 236.
25. Beattie, *Crime and the Courts*, p. 472.
26. Ibid. p. 472; Smith, 'Transportation of Convicts', p. 237.
27. Jeaffreson (ed.), *A Young Squire*, vol. 1, p. 225. See also Beckles, *White Servitude and Black Slavery*.

28. *State Papers Domestic: Charles I* (London: National Archives): 29/89, f. 61.
29. Quoted in Beattie, *Crime and the Courts*, p. 473.
30. Beattie, *Policing and Punishment*, p. 300. See also Sharpe, *Crime in Seventeenth-Century England*, pp. 141–2.
31. Herrup, 'Punishing Pardon', p. 132.
32. *Bill for Transporting of Felons and Rogues into Foreign Plantations*, 20 February 1663: *House of Commons Journal 1660–1667*, vol. 8 (London: 1802), <http://www.british-history.ac.uk>(last accessed 24 November 2019), p. 438.
33. Ibid. p. 443.
34. *House of Lords Journal 1660–1666*, vol. 11 (London: 1767–1830), <http://www.british-history.ac.uk>(last accessed 24 November 2019), p. 550.
35. Ibid. pp. 587–91.
36. Beattie, *Crime and the Courts*, p. 506.
37. Ibid. p. 506.
38. Defoe, *Roxana*, p. 271.
39. Defoe, *Moll Flanders*, title page.
40. Kietzman, 'Defoe Masters the Serial Subject', p. 678.
41. Mary Carleton deployed a bewildering array of aliases and given names throughout her life; in this account, I refer to her as 'Carleton'.
42. Rayner and Crook (eds), *The Complete Newgate Calendar*, title page.
43. Carleton's birth date is variously recorded as 1634, 1635, 1639 and 1642. See Janet Todd's account, *ODNB Online* <http://www.oxforddnb.com>(last accessed 18 February 2020).
44. Kirkman, *The Counterfeit Lady Unveiled*, p. 15. Kirkman's 'biography' is comprehensive but of dubious accuracy.
45. See *The Arraignment, Tryal and Examination of Mary Moders*, Sarah Williams' testimony, p. 9.
46. Carleton, *The Case of Madam Mary Carleton*, pp. 30–1.
47. *An Historicall Narrative of the German Princess*, p. 8.
48. *The Deportment and Carriage of the German Princess* and the *Memoires*, both published after Carleton's death.
49. *The Arraignment, Tryal and Examination of Mary Moders*, p. 2.
50. Wiener, 'Is a Spinster an Unmarried Woman?' See also Edwards, 'The Case of the Married Spinster'.
51. See Todd and Spearing, *Counterfeit Ladies*, p. xxviii. It was rumoured that Steadman had also married again, see *The Female Hector*, p. 4.
52. Ibid. p. 12.
53. Todd, *ODNB Online*, p. 104.
54. *The Arraignment, Tryal and Examination of Mary Moders*, p. 15.
55. *An Historicall Narrative of the German Princess*, p. 17.
56. Holden's play does not survive. Carleton claimed to have authored *An Historical Narrative* and the longer *Case of Madam Mary Carleton*, whilst her husband put his name to a pamphlet entitled *The Ultimum Vale of John Carleton of the Middle Temple, London, Gent*.
57. Carleton, *The Case of Madam Mary Carleton*, The Epistle Dedicatory.
58. Ibid.

59. *An Historicall Narrative of the German Princess*, p. 17.
60. Defoe, *Moll Flanders*, p. 1.
61. *Memoires of Mary Carleton*, pp. 60–1.
62. Kietzman, *Self-Fashioning of an Early Modern Englishwoman*, p. 197.
63. Ibid. p. 200.
64. See Introduction, n. 41 onwards.
65. London Metropolitan Archives, Middlesex Sessions, MJ GB 150/MJSR 1351/MJSR 1383.
66. Ibid. MJSR 1393.
67. *Calendar of State Papers Domestic: Charles II*, Entry Book 28, f. 42.
68. Defoe, *Moll Flanders*, p. 328. See also Kietzman, *Self-Fashioning*, p. 221.
69. Beattie, *Crime and the Courts*, p. 479.
70. Beckles, 'The Concept of "White Slavery"', p. 574.
71. Hinds (ed.), *CSP Venetian Series*, vol. 30, p. 309 (3 March 1656).
72. Beckles, 'The Concept of "White Slavery"', p. 573.
73. Grant, *Acts of the Privy Council*, p. 553.
74. Ibid. p. 480.
75. Jeaffreson, *A Young Squire*, vol. 2, p. 193.
76. Beattie, *Crime and the Courts*, p. 479.
77. London Metropolitan Archives, Middlesex Sessions, MJ SR 1411.
78. Coldham, *The Complete Book of Emigrants*, p. 186 (my italics).
79. Coldham, *More Emigrants in Bondage*.
80. Beattie, *Crime and the Courts*, p. 480. See also Smith, 'Transportation of Convicts', p. 242.
81. Kirkman, *The Counterfeit Lady Unveiled*, p. 12, p. 176.
82. Ibid. pp. 178–9.
83. Ibid. p. 180.
84. *News from Jamaica in a Letter from Port Royal Written by the German Princess to Her Fellow Collegiates and Friends in New-Gate* (London: 1671).
85. *Some Luck, Some Wit; Memories of the life of famous Madam Charlton*.
86. *Memoires of Mary Carleton*, p. 54.
87. Defoe, *Moll Flanders*, pp. 358–9.
88. Coldham, *Emigrants in Chains*, p. 63.
89. Herrup, 'Punishing Pardon', p. 131.
90. Ibid. p. 125.
91. Smith, 'Transportation of Convicts', p. 249 (my emphasis).
92. Atkinson, 'The Free-Born Englishman Transported', p. 89.
93. Ibid. p. 98.
94. Whistler, *Voyage to the West Indies*, f. 9.
95. Cormack, *A Power to Do Justice*, p. 230.
96. Ibid. p. 235.
97. *Memoires of Mary Carleton*, p. 62.
98. It is worth noting, however, that the failed Bill of 20 February 1663, 'for Transporting of Felons and Rogues into Foreign Plantations', *does* address this issue.
99. Smith, 'Transportation of Convicts', p. 238.
100. Ligon, *A True and Exact History of Barbados*, p. 59.
101. Beckles, 'The Concept of "White Slavery"', pp. 577–8.

102. *Journal of the House of Commons*, vol. 7: 1651–1660 (London: 1802), <http://www.british-history.ac.uk>(last accessed 24 November 2019), pp. 619–20.
103. Rivers and Foyle, *Englands Slavery, or Barbados Merchandize*, p. 6.
104. Ibid.
105. Stock (ed.), *Proceedings and Debates*, vol. 1, p. 258.
106. Morgan, 'Petitions Against Convict Transportation', p. 112.
107. Morgan and Rushton, 'Print Culture, Crime and Transportation', p. 57. See also Devereaux, 'Imposing the Royal Pardon', pp. 101–38.
108. Morgan and Rushton, 'Print Culture, Crime and Transportation', pp. 58–9.
109. *Memoires of Mary Carleton*, p. 57.
110. Ibid. p. 61.
111. Kietzman, *Self-Fashioning of an Early Modern Englishwoman*, p. 250.
112. Ibid. p. 250.
113. *Memoires of Mary Carleton*, pp. 57–9.
114. Ibid. p. 59.
115. *Poor Robin's jests*, p. 87.
116. Kirkman, *The Counterfeit Lady Unveiled*, p. 176.
117. Kietzman, *Self-Fashioning of an Early Modern Englishwoman*, p. 250.
118. See Todd, *ODNB Online*.
119. Dolan, *True Relations*, p. 19.
120. Kirkman, *The Counterfeit Lady Unveiled*, p. 195.
121. *London Gazette*, No. 742, 26 December 1672, p. 2.
122. Kirkman, *The Counterfeit Lady Unveiled*, pp. 182–3.
123. *An Exact and True Relation*, p. 6.
124. Ibid. p. 5.
125. Ibid. pp. 5–6.
126. Ibid. p. 7.
127. *Memoires of Mary Carleton*, p. 93.
128. Kirkman, *The Counterfeit Lady Unveiled*, p. 204.
129. *Memoires of Mary Carleton*, p. 94.
130. Case of Cecilie Labree, 26 April 1704, *OBP Online* (last accessed 14 January 2020) (o17040426-1).
131. See e.g. case of 11 July 1677, and *Ordinary's Account*, 23 January 1678 (OA16780123), *OBP Online* (last accessed 14 January 2020) (t16770711-8).
132. Hunter, 'New Light on the Drummer of Tedworth', pp. 311–53.
133. See *OBP Online*.
134. *Virginia Gazette*, 23 March 1739.
135. Morgan and Rushton, 'Print Culture, Crime and Transportation', p. 52.
136. Ibid. p. 53.
137. *An Exact and True Relation*, p. 7.
138. Kirkman, *The Counterfeit Lady Unveiled*, pp. 200–1.
139. Ibid.
140. *Memoires of Mary Carleton*, p. 121.
141. Kirkman, *The Counterfeit Lady Unveiled*, p. 209.
142. Ibid. p. 208.
143. *The Deportment and Carriage of the German Princess*, Wing/D1077A.
144. Ibid. p. 2.

145. Kirkman, *The Counterfeit Lady Unveiled*, p. 220; *The Deportment and Carriage of the German Princess*, p. 5.
146. *The Deportment and Carriage of the German Princess*, p. 4.
147. *The German Princess Revived*, Wing/G613.
148. Morgan and Rushton, 'Print Culture, Crime and Transportation', p. 50.
149. *The German Princess Revived*, p. 8.
150. Morgan and Rushton, 'Print Culture, Crime and Transportation', p. 50.
151. Ibid. p. 52.
152. *Newcastle Courant*, 30 December 1738.
153. Langbein, 'Historical Origins of the Sanction of Imprisonment', p. 55.
154. Rivers and Foyle, *Englands Slavery, or Barbados Merchandize*.
155. Defoe, *Moll Flanders*, p. 1.
156. Syme, *Theatre and Testimony*, p. 18.

Bibliography

Legal and Historical Sources

Bruce, John (ed.), *Calendar of State Papers Domestic: Charles I, 1629–31* (London, 1868).
Cockburn, J. S., *Calendar of Assize Records: Essex Indictments* (London: HMSO, 1980).
Cockburn, *Calendar of Assize Records: Home Circuit Indictments, Elizabeth I and James I*, (London: HMSO, 1985).
Cockburn, J. S., *Calendar of Assize Records: Kent Indictments* (London: HMSO, 1980).
Cockburn, J. S., *Calendar of Assize Records: Surrey Indictments* (London: HMSO, 1980).
Cockburn, J. S., *Calendar of Assize Records: Sussex Indictments* (London: HMSO, 1980).
Firth, C. H. and R. S. Rait (eds), *Acts and Ordinances of the Interregnum, 1642–1660* (London: History of Parliament Trust, 1911).
Grant, W. L. (ed.) *Acts of the Privy Council, Colonial Series 1615–1616* (Hereford: 1908).
Green, Mary Anne Everett, Francis Daniell and Francis Bickley (eds), *Calendar of State Papers Domestic: Charles II, 1660–61* (London: 1861).
Green, Mary Anne Everett, Francis Daniell and Francis Bickley (eds), *Calendar of State Papers Domestic: Charles II, 1661–62* (London: 1861).
Green, Mary Anne Everett, Francis Daniell and Francis Bickley (eds), *Calendar of State Papers Domestic: Charles II, 1664–65* (London: 1863).
Green, Mary Anne Everett, Francis Daniell and Francis Bickley (eds), *Calendar of State Papers Domestic: Charles II, Entry Book* (London: 1861).
Hinds, Allan B. (ed.), *Calendar of State Papers Venetian Series 1655–56* (London: 1930).
House of Commons Journal, British History Online: <http://www.british-history.ac.uk>
House of Lords Journal, British History Online: <http://www.british-history.ac.uk>
Hughes, Paul L. and James F. Larkin (eds), *Tudor Royal Proclamations, Volume II, The Later Tudors (1553–1587)* (New Haven and London: Yale University Press, 1969).

Jeaffreson, J. C. (ed.), *Middlesex county records: Volume 2: 1603–25* (London: 1887).
Jeaffreson, J. C. (ed.), *Middlesex county records: Volume 3: 1625–67* (London: 1888).
Larkin, James F. (ed.), *Stuart Royal Proclamations, Volume II, Royal Proclamations of King Charles I 1625–1646* (Oxford: Clarendon Press, 1983).
Larkin, James F. and Paul L. Hughes (eds), *Stuart Royal Proclamations, Volume I, Royal Proclamations of King James I 1603–1625* (Oxford: Clarendon Press, 1973).
Le Hardy, William (ed.), *Middlesex county records: Volume 1: 1612–14* (London: 1935).
Lemon, Robert (ed.), *Calendar of State Papers Domestic: Elizabeth, 1581–90*, (London: 1865).
London Metropolitan Archives, Middlesex Sessions, MJ GB 150/MJSR 1351/ MJSR 1383; MJ SR 1411.
Old Bailey Proceedings Online, <www.oldbaileyonline.org>, version 9.0.
Raithby, John (ed.), *Statutes of the Realm, Volume 4: 1547–1624* (London: 1819).
Raithby, John (ed.), *Statutes of the Realm, Volume 5: 1625–80* (London: 1819).
Sainsbury, W. N. (ed.), *Calendar of State Papers, Colonial Series: 1574–1660* (London: 1860).
State Papers Domestic: Charles I (London: National Archives).

Primary Sources

An Account of the sentence which past upon Titus Oates (upon conviction of horrid perjuries) at the Kings Bench-bar, Saturday May 16th, 1685 (London: 1685), Wing/A385.
The Arraignment, Tryal and Examination of Mary Moders, Otherwise Stedman, now Carleton, (Stiled, the German Princess), At the Sessions-House in the Old Bayly being brought Prisoner from the Gatehouse Westminster, for having two husbands (London: N. Brook, 1663), Wing/A3764.
Articles, whereupon it was agreed by the archbishoppes and bishoppes of both provinces, and the whole cleargie, in the Convocation holden at London in the yere of our Lorde God 1562 according to the computation of the Churche of Englande for the avoiding of the diversities of opinions, and for the stablyshing of consent touching true religion. Put foorth by the Queenes aucthoritie (London: Richard Jugge and John Cawood, 1571), STC (2nd ed.)/10038.9.
Bacon, Francis, *The Works of Sir Francis Bacon*, ed. James Spedding, Robert Leslie Ellis and Douglas Denon Heath, 15 vols (London: Longman & Co., 1857).
Bicknoll, Edmond, *A sword against swearers and blasph[e]mers shewing the lawfulness of the oath and how great a sinne it is to swear falsely, vainly or rashly* (London: Richard Watkins, 1579), STC (2nd ed.)/3049.
Birch, Thomas (ed.), *A Collection of the State Papers of John Thurloe* (London: Fletcher Gyles, 1742).
Blackstone, William, *Blackstone's Commentaries on the Laws of England*, ed. Wayne Morrison, 4 vols (London: Cavendish Publishing, [1765–9] 2001).

Bloody Newes from Dover (London: 1647) Wing (2nd ed.)/B3267.

Bullen, A. H. (ed.), *A Collection of Old English Plays*, vol. 3 (London: Wyman and Sons, 1882).

Burdet, William, *A Wonder of Wonders* (London: 1651), Wing (2nd ed.)/B5620.

Carleton, John, *The Ultimum Vale of John Carleton, of The Middle Temple, London, Gent. being a true description of that grand imposter, late a pretended Germane-lady* (London: 1663), Wing/C585A.

Carleton, Mary, *The Case of Madam Mary Carleton, lately stiled the German Princess, truely stated with an historical relation of her birth, education, and fortunes; in an appeal to his illustrious Highness Prince Rupert. By the said Mary Carleton* (London: 1663), Wing (CD-ROM, 1996)/C586A.

Carleton, Mary, *An Historicall Narrative of the German Princess containing All material Passages, from her first Arrivall at Graves-End, the 30th of March last past, untill she was discharged from her Imprisonment, June the sixth instant. Written by her self, for the satisfaction of the world, at the request of divers persons of honour* (London: 1663), Wing (2nd ed.)/H2106.

Caryll, John, *Naboth's Vineyard, or The Innocent Traytor*, in George de F. Lord (ed.), *Poems on Affairs of State: Augustan Satirical Verse, 1660–1714* (New Haven: Yale University Press, 1965), vol. 2, pp. 82–99.

Chapman, George, Ben Jonson and John Marston, *Eastward Hoe*, in *The Roaring Girl and Other City Comedies*, ed. James Knowles (Oxford: Oxford University Press, 2001), pp. 67–140.

Chidley, Samuel, *Retsah, a cry against a crying sinne* (London: 1652), Wing/C3838.

Clavell, John, *A recantation of an ill-led life* (London: 1628), STC (2nd ed.)/5369.2.

The Clipper's Execution. Or, Treason Justly Rewarded manifested in the fearful example of two women who were notorious offenders, and tryed at the Old-Bayly the 13th of this present April, 1678, for clipping and defacing His Majesties coyn . . . to the tune of In summer time (London: 1678), Wing/C4716.

Cobbett, William, *Cobbett's Complete Collection of State Trials and Proceedings for High Treason and other Crimes and Misdemeanours from the earliest period to the present time*, ed. T. B. Howell and T. J. Howell, 33 vols (London: R. Bagshaw, Longman & Co., 1809–26).

Coke, Edward, *The Second Part of the Institutes of the Lawes of England* (London: 1671).

Coke, Edward, *The Third Part of the Institutes of the Laws of England: Concerning High Treason, and other Pleas of the Crown, and Criminal Causes*, 4th ed. (London: 1669).

Cook, John, *Unum Necessarium: Or the Poore Mans Case being an expedient to make provision of all poore people in the Kingdome* (London: 1649), Wing (2nd ed.)/C6027.

Cosin, Richard, *An Apologie for Sundrie Proceedings by Jurisdiction Ecclesiasticall* (London: 1593), STC (2nd ed.)/5822.

Cranmer, Thomas, *Certayne sermons or homilies appoynted by the kynges Majestie, to be declared and redde, by all persones, vycars, or curates, every So[n]day in their churches, where they have cure* (London: Edwarde Whitchurche, 1547), STC (2nd ed.)/13641.

Croke, Sir George, *The second part of the reports of George Croke*, trans. Sir Harbottle Grimston (London: 1683).
Dalton, Michael, *The countrey justice conteyning the practise of the justices of the peace out of their sessions. Gathered for the better helpe of such justices of peace as have not beene much conversant in the studie of the lawes of this realme* (London: 1618), STC (2nd ed.)/6205 and (London: 1619), STC (2nd ed.)/6206.
A Declaration from Oxford (London: 1651), Wing (CD-ROM, 1996)/ D585A.
Deeds against Nature and Monsters by kinde (London: 1614), STC (2nd ed.)/809.
Defoe, Daniel, *Moll Flanders* (London: Penguin, [1722] 1987).
Defoe, Daniel, *Roxana: the fortunate mistress* (London: Penguin, [1724] 1982).
Dekker, Thomas and John Webster, *Northward Ho*, in *The Dramatic Works of Thomas Dekker*, ed. Fredson Bowers, 4 vols (Cambridge: Cambridge University Press, 1953), vol. 2, pp. 393–490.
Dekker, Thomas and John Webster, *Westward Ho*, in *The Dramatic Works of Thomas Dekker*, ed. Fredson Bowers, 4 vols (Cambridge: Cambridge University Press, 1953), vol. 2, pp. 313–92.
Dekker, Thomas, John Webster and Thomas Middleton, *The Roaring Girl*, in *The Roaring Girl and Other City Comedies*, ed. James Knowles (Oxford: Oxford University Press, 2001), pp. 225–310.
The Deportment and Carriage of the German Princess Immediately before her Execution: and Her last Speech at Tyburn (London: 1672), Wing/D1077A.
Derham, William, *Physico-Theology*, 12th ed. (Glasgow: Robert Urie, 1752).
de Voragine, Jacobus, *The Golden Legend: Readings on the Saints*, trans. W. G. Ryan, 2 vols (Princeton: Princeton University Press, 1993).
Discours d'une histoire et miracle advenu en la ville de Mont-fort cinq lieues près Rennes en Bretagne (Bibliothèque de l'Arsenal in Paris, shelfmark 8o J 5521), 5, octavo, 12 pp.
Discours miraculeux et véritable advenu nouvellement, en la personne d'une fille nommée Anne Belthumier, servant en l'Hostellerie du Pot d'Estain, en la Ville de Mont-fort entre Nantes et Rennes en Bretagne, laquelle a esté pendu III jours & 3. nuits sans mourir. Avec Confession de plusieurs dudit Mont-fort, comme l'on pourra voir par ce present discours (Bibliothèque Municipale de Douai, shelfmark 1589/4), octavo, 15pp.
Dod, John, *A treatise or exposition upon the Ten commandements grounded upon the Scriptures canonicall* (London: 1603), STC (2nd ed.)/6967.
Donne, John, 'The Bracelet', in *The Oxford Authors: John Donne*, ed. John Carey (Oxford: Oxford University Press, 1990).
Donne, John, *Sermon Preached upon Candlemas Day, 1623*, in *Sermons of John Donne*, ed. George Potter and Evelyn Simpson (Berkeley and Los Angeles: University of California Press, 1953–62).
Doolittle, Thomas, *The Swearer Silenced, or The evil and danger of prophane swearing and perjury demonstrated by many arguments and examples of God's dreadful judgments upon sinful swearers* (London: J. Astwood, 1689), Wing/D1898.
Drue, Thomas, *The Duchess of Suffolke*, ed. Richard Dutton and Steven K. Galbraith (Athens: Ohio University Press, 2015).

England's Complaint: Or the Nation's Abuse thro' Clipping and Coyning (London: 1692), Wing (CD-ROM, 1996)/E2952A.

Evelyn, John, *The Diary of John Evelyn*, ed. John Bowle (New York: Oxford University Press, 1983).

An Exact and True Relation of the Examination, Tryal and Condemnation of the German Princess (London: January 1672), Wing/E3619.

A fearefull example, shewed upon a perjured person (London: 1591), STC (2nd ed.)/19965.

The Female Hector, or the Germane Lady turn'd Mounsieur (London: 1663).

Finch, Henry, *Nomotechnia; cestascavoir, Un description del common leys dangleterre* (London: 1613), STC (2nd ed.)/10870.

Fitzherbert, Anthony, *L'Office et Auctorite de Justices de Peace* (London: 1538).

Fleetwood, William, *A Sermon against clipping, preached before the Right Honourable the Lord Mayor and the Court of Aldermen, at the Guild-Hall Chapel* (London: 1694), Wing/F1249.

Foster, Joseph, *Alumni Oxonienses: the members of the University of Oxford* (Oxford: Oxford University Press, 1891).

Foxe, John, *The actes and monuments of these latter and perilous days* (London: 1563), STC (2nd ed.)/11222.

Fulbecke, William, *A parallele or conference of the civil law, the canon law, and the common law of this realme of England. Wherein the agreement and disagreement of these three lawes, and the causes and reasons of the said agreement and disagreement, are opened and discussed* (London: 1601), STC (2nd ed.)/11415.

Fuller, Thomas, *The History of the Worthies of England* (London: 1662), Wing/F2441.

Fuller, Thomas, *Mixt Contemplations in Better Times* (London: 1660).

Gauden, John, *A discourse concerning publick oaths, and the lawfulness of swearing in judicial proceedings written by Dr. Gauden ... in order to answer the scruples of the Quakers* (London: 1662), Wing/G352.

The German Princess Revived: or The London Jilt: Being a True Account of the Life and Death of Jenney Voss (London: 1684), Wing/G613.

Gilbert, Jeffrey, *The Law of Evidence* (London: 1754).

Goodcole, Henry, *Nature's Cruell Step-Dames, or Matchlesse Monsters of the Female Sex* (London: 1637), STC (2nd ed.)/12012.

Hale, Matthew, *History of the Pleas of the Crown*, ed. S. Emlyn (London: 1736).

Heath, James, *A Chronicle of the Late Intestine War* (London: 1676), Wing/H1321.

Holinshed, Raphael, *Chronicles of England, Scotland and Ireland*, 6 vols (London: 1586).

James VI/I, *The True Lawe of Free Monarchies, or the Reciprock and Mutuall Dutie betwixt a Free King and his Naturall Suiects* (London: 1603), STC (2nd ed.)/14410.5.

Jeaffreson, John C. (ed.), *A Young Squire of the Seventeenth Century: Papers of Christopher Jeaffreson, 1676–1686*, 2 vols (London: 1878).

Jonson, Ben, *The Alchemist*, in *Three Comedies*, ed. Michael Jamieson (London: Penguin Classics, 1985), pp. 173–317.

Kelyng, Sir John, *A Report of Divers Cases in Pleas of the Crown, adjudged and determined in the reign of . . . Charles II* (London: 1796).
Kinney, Arthur (ed.), *Renaissance Drama: An Anthology of Plays and Entertainments* (Oxford: Blackwell Publishing, 2005).
Kirkman, Francis, *The Counterfeit Lady Unveiled. Being a full account of the birth, life, most remarkable actions, and untimely death of Mary Carleton, known by the name of the German Princess* (London: 1673), Wing (2nd ed.)/K630A.
Laconics: Or, new maxims of state and conversation relating to the affairs and manners of the present time (London: 1701).
Lambarde, William, *Eirenarcha: or of the office of the justices of peace in two books* (London: 1581), STC (2nd ed.)/15163.
The laws discovery: or a brief detection of sundry notorious errors and abuses contained in our English laws, whereby thousands are annually stript of their estates, and some of their lives. By a well-wisher to his country (London: 1653), Wing (2nd ed.)/F40.
The life and death of Jacke Straw (London: 1594), STC (2nd ed.)/23356.
Ligon, Richard, *A True and Exact History of Barbados* (London: 1657), Wing/L2075.
London Gazette, No. 742, December 26, 1672.
Maitland, F. W., *The Collected Papers of Frederick William Maitland*, ed. H. A. L. Fisher, 3 vols (Cambridge: Cambridge University Press, 1911).
Mandeville, Bernard, *The Fable of the Bees: Or, Private Vices, Publick Benefits*, ed. F. B. Kaye, 2 vols (Oxford: 1924).
Mankind, ed. Kathleen A. Ashley and Gerard NeCastro (Middle English Text Series Online) <https://d.lib.rochester.edu/teams/text/ashley-and-necastro-mankind>(last accessed 10 July 2020).
Manningham, John, *The Diary of John Manningham of the Middle Temple 1602–1603*, ed. Robert Parker Sorlien (Hanover, NH: University Press of New England, 1976).
'Martha Scambler's repentance', in *Deedes Against Nature and Monsters by Kinde* (London: 1614), STC/809.
The Memoires of Mary Carleton, Commonly Stiled the German Princess. Being a Narrative of Her Life and Death Interwoven with Many Strange and Pleasant Passages, from the Time of Her Birth to her Execution at Tyburn (London: 1673), Wing/G35B.
Memories of the life of famous Madam Charlton, commonly stiled the German Princess setting forth the whole series of her actions, with all their intrigues and subtile contrivances from her cradle to the fatal period of her raign at Tiburn: being an account of her penitent behavior, in her absteining from food and rest, in the prison of Newgate, from the time of her condemnation to her execution, January 23, 1672/taken from her own relation, whilst she was prisoner in the Marshalses, and other certain information; with her nativity astrologically handled, and an epitaph on her tomb (London: 1673), Wing/M1700.
Mercurius Politicus, No. 28 (12–19 December 1650).
Mercurius Politicus, No. 32 (9–16 January 1651).
Middleton, Thomas, *A Chaste Maid in Cheapside*, in *Women Beware Women and Other Plays*, ed. Richard Dutton (Oxford: Oxford University Press, 1999), pp. 1–72.

Middleton, Thomas, *The Revenger's Tragedy*, ed. R. A. Foakes (Manchester: Manchester University Press, 1996).
Morgan, Joseph, *Phoenix Britannicus, being a collection of scarce and curious tracts* (London: T. Edlin, 1731).
Munday, Anthony, *A View of sundry Examples. Reporting many straunge murthers, sundry persons perjured, Signes and tokens of Gods anger towards us* (London: William Wright, 1580), STC (2nd ed.)/18281.
The narrative of the sessions, February 26, 1678/9. With a particular account of the trial of the notorious coiners, that received sentence for treason (London: 1679), Wing (2nd ed.)/N224.
Nashe, Thomas, *The Works of Thomas Nashe*, ed. Ronald B. McKerrow, 5 vols (Oxford: Basil Blackwell, 1958).
News from Jamaica in a Letter from Port Royal Written by the German Princess to Her Fellow Collegiates and Friends in New-Gate (London: 1671), Wing (2nd ed.)/N976B.
Nourse, Timothy, *Campania Foelix. Or, A discourse of the benefits and improvements of husbandry containing directions for all manner of tillage, pasturage, and plantation* (London: 1700), Wing/N1416.
Onslowe's Case, Court of King's Bench, 1 January 1564. 73 E.R. 532; (1564) Dyer 242.
Overbury, Sir Thomas, *A True and Perfect Account of the Examination, Confession, Trial, Conviction and Execution of Joan Perry, and her two Sons, John and Richard Perry, for the supposed Murder of Will. Harrison, Gent Being one of the most remarkable occurrences which hath happened in the memory of man* (London: 1676), Wing (2nd ed.)/O614A.
Parker, Martin, *No Naturall Mother but a Monster* (London: 1634), in H. E. Rollins (ed.), *A Pepysian Garland* (Cambridge: Cambridge University Press, 1922), pp. 425–30.
Parker, Matthew, *The Holy Byble conteynyng the Olde and Newe Testament/set foorth by aucthoritie* (Bishops' Bible) (London: Richard Jugge, 1575), STC (2nd ed.)/2114.
Pears, Iain, *An Instance of the Fingerpost* (London: Jonathan Cape, 1997).
Pendred, William, *To His Excellencie, the Lord-general Cromwel. The humble remonstrance of many thousands in, and about the city of London, on the behalf of all the free-commoners of England* (London: 1653), Wing (2nd ed.)/T1353A.
Percival, Thomas, *Medical Ethics, or, a code of institutes and precepts adapted to the professional conduct of physicians and surgeons* (Manchester: 1803).
Peters, Hugh, *A Word for the Armie, and Two Words to the Kingdome. To cleare the one, and cure the other* (London: 1647), Wing (2nd ed.)/P1726.
Petty, William, *The Petty Papers: Some unpublished writings of Sir William Petty. Edited from the Bowood Papers by the Marquis of Lansdown*, 2 vols (London: Constable & Co. Ltd, 1927).
Plot, Robert, *The Natural History of Oxfordshire, being an essay towards a natural history of England* (Oxford: L. Lichfield, 1677).
Plowden, Edmund, *The Commentaries or Reports of Edmund Plowden of the Middle Temple, esq . . . in two parts* (London: S. Brooke, 1816).
Poor Robin's jests; or The compleat jester (London: 1667), Wing (2nd ed.)/W3075A.

Rayner, J. L. and G. T. Crook (eds), *The Complete Newgate Calendar*, 5 vols (London: Navarre Society, 1926).
A Review of the Universal Remedy for all Diseases Incident to Coin, With Application to Our Present Circumstances. In a Letter to Mr Locke (London: 1696), Wing/R1200.
Rivers, Marcellus and Oxenbridge Foyle, *Englands Slavery, or Barbados Merchandize; represented in a petition to the high court of Parliament, by Marcellus Rivers and Oxenbridge Foyle gentlemen, on behalf of themselves and three-score and ten more free-born Englishmen sold (uncondemned) into slavery: together with letters written to some honourable members of Parliament* (London: 1659), Wing (2nd ed.)/R1553.
Rowlands, Samuel, *The Betraying of Christ* (1598), STC (2nd ed.)/21365.
The Royal Regulation: Or, The King and Parliaments industrious Care in Regulating the State of the Coin of this Kingdom, for the Ease and Happiness of all loyal and loving Subjects (London: 1690s).
St German, Christopher, *The dyaloges in Englishe, betwene a Doctour of diuinitie, and a student in the lawes of Englande* (London: Richardi Totelli, 1565).
Shakespeare, William, *Cymbeline*, ed. J. M. Nosworthy (Walton-on-Thames: Cengage Learning, 2007).
Shakespeare, William, *Love's Labour's Lost*, ed. H. R. Woudhuysen (Walton-on-Thames: Cengage Learning, 1998).
Shakespeare, William, *Measure for Measure*, ed. A. R. Braunmuller and Robert N. Watson (London: Bloomsbury, 2020).
Shakespeare, William, *Richard II*, ed. Stanley Wells and Gary Taylor (Oxford: Oxford University Press, 2005).
Shakespeare, William, *Titus Andronicus*, ed. Stanley Wells and Gary Taylor (Oxford: Oxford University Press, 2005).
Shakespeare, William, *Troilus and Cressida*, ed. Stanley Wells and Gary Taylor (Oxford: Oxford University Press, 2005).
Sharp, Jane, *The Midwives Book, Or the Whole Art of Midwifry Discovered*, ed. Elaine Hobby (Oxford: Oxford University Press, 1999).
Smith, Thomas, *De Republica Anglorum: The maner of gouernement or policie of the realme of England* (London: 1583), STC (2nd ed.)/22857.
Some Luck, Some Wit, Being a Sonnet upon the Merry Life and Untimely Death of Mistriss Mary Carlton, Commonly Called the German Princess. To a New Tune, Called the German Princess Adieu (London: 1672), Wing (CD-ROM, 1996)/S4516.
Stock, Leo, ed., *Proceedings and Debates in the British Parliament Respecting North America* (Washington, DC: Carnegie Institution, 1924).
Strode, William, *A sermon concerning swearing preached before the King's Majesty in Christ-Church Oxon, May the 12, 1644* (Oxford: 1644), Wing/802:26.
Strype, J., *Annals of the Reformation and Establishment of Religion and other various occurrences in the Church of England, during Queen Elizabeth's happy reign* (Oxford: Clarendon Press, 1824).
The Third Commandment, an essay tending to prove that perjury deserves not only the pillory but a much severer punishment, occasioned by a reflection on the heinious [sic] sin and extream mischiefs of perjury and the great confusion into which this kingdom and Church of England have lately been brought by false oathes (London: 1685), Wing/T904.

T.I., *A world of wonders. A masse of murthers. A covie of cosonages Containing many of the moste notablest wonders, horrible murthers and detestable cosonages that have beene with in this land* (London: 1595), STC (2nd ed.)/14068.5.

Tillotson, John, *The lawfulness, and obligation of oaths a sermon preach'd at the assises held at Kingston upon Thames, July 21, 1681* (London: 1681), Wing/T1200.

Tomlinson, William, *Seven Particulars, containing as followeth, I. Against oppressors. II. Magistrates work and honor. III. A meditation for magistrates upon Dan. 12.4. IV. Of hanging for theft, filling the land with blood. V. To the high & lofty in the earth, who exalt themselves by discent or blood. VI. Of ministers maintenance, two extreams. VII. Of persecuting for speaking in the synagogues (by many called churches.) Given forth for publique service by W.T.* (London: 1658), Wing (2nd ed.)/T1851.

To the right honourable the Commons of England, in Parliament assembled, Humble petition of thousands wel-affected persons inhabiting the City of London, Westminster, the borough of Southwark, hamlets and places adjacent, September 11, 1648 (London: 1648), Wing (2nd ed.)/L2188.

Treason and murther discovered Being a true and perfect relation of the tryal & condemnation of James Alsop the father, and William Alsop his son for treason and murder; at the assises held at Chelmsford for the county of Essex, on Wednesday the 25th of March, 1674 . . . Written by a person who was present at the tryal (London: 1674), Wing (2nd ed.)/T2070.

The true narrative of the proceedings at the Sessions-House in the Old-Bayly which began on Wednesday the 13th of this instant April and ended on Thursday the 14th following (London: 1681), Wing (2nd ed.)/T2829.

A True Narrative of the Tryal of Titus Oates for Perjury, At the King's-Bench-Barr at Westminster On Friday the 8th of May 1685 (Dublin, reprinted: 1685), Wing (2nd ed.)/T2840AE.

A True Relation of Go[ds] Wonderfull Mercies in Preserving one Alive, which hanged five days, who was falsly accused (London: 1605), STC (2nd ed.)/14668.

The unhappy marksman. Or A perfect and impartial discovery of that late barbarous and unparallel'd murther committed by Mr. George Strangwayes (London: 1659), Wing (2nd ed.)/U68.

Vaughan, Rice, *A Discourse of Coin and Coinage* (London: 1675), Wing/V131.

Ventris, Sir Peyton, *The reports of Sir Peyton Ventris Kt., late one of the justices of the Common-pleas in two parts* (London: 1696), Wing/V235.

Virginia Gazette, 23 March 1739.

Ward, John, *The Lives of the Professors of Gresham College* (London: 1740).

Watkins, Richard, *Newes from the dead. Or a true and exact narration of the miraculous deliverance of Anne Greene, who being executed at Oxford Decemb. 14. 1650. afterwards revived and by the care of certain hysitians [sic] there, is now perfectly recovered* (Oxford: 1651), Wing (2nd ed.)/W1074.

Whetstone, George, *Promos and Cassandra* (London: 1578).

Whistler, Henry, *Voyage to the West Indies* (1654), Sloane MSS.3926.

Willughby, Percival, *Observations in Midwifery*, ed. H. Blenkinsop (Warwick: H. T. Cooke & Son, 1972).

Winstanley, Gerrard, *The New Law of Righteousness budding forth, in restoring the whole creation from the bondage of the curse. Or A glimpse of the*

new heaven, and new earth, wherein dwels righteousnes. (London: 1649), Wing (2nd ed.)/W3049.
Wood, Anthony, *Athenae Oxonienses: an Exact History of all the Writers and Bishops who have had their Education in the University of Oxford from 1500 to 1690*, ed. Philip Bliss (London: F. C. and J. Rivington, 1813–20).
Wood, Anthony, *The Life and Times of Anthony Wood, antiquary, of Oxford, 1632–1695, described by Himself*, ed. Andrew Clark (Oxford: Oxford Historical Society & Clarendon Press, 1891).

Secondary Sources

Agamben, Giorgio, *Homo Sacer: Sovereign Power and Bare Life*, trans. Daniel Heller-Roazen (Stanford: Stanford University Press, 1998).
Atkinson, Alan, 'The Free-Born Englishman Transported: Convict rights as a measure of eighteenth-century empire', *Past and Present*, 144.1 (1994), pp. 85–115.
Baker, J. H., *An Introduction to English Legal History* (London: Butterworths, 1990).
Baker, J. H., 'Coke's Notebooks and the Sources of his Reports', *Cambridge Law Journal*, 30 (1972), pp. 59–86.
Baker, J. H., 'Criminal Justice at Newgate 1616–1627: Some Manuscript Reports in the Harvard Law School', *Irish Jurist*, 8.2 (1973), pp. 307–22.
Baker, J. H., 'Review', *The American Journal of Legal History*, 22.4 (1978), pp. 337–40.
Bakewell, Peter (ed.), *Mines of Silver and Gold in the Americas* (Aldershot: Varorium, 1996).
Beattie, J. M., 'The Cabinet and the Management of Death at Tyburn after the Revolution of 1688–1689', in Lois G. Schwoerer (ed.), *The Revolution of 1688–1689* (Cambridge: Cambridge University Press, 2002), pp. 218–33.
Beattie, J. M., *Crime and the Courts in England 1660–1800* (Oxford: Clarendon Press, 1986).
Beattie, J. M., *Policing and Punishment in London, 1660–1750: Urban crime and the limits of terror* (Oxford: Oxford University Press, 2001).
Beattie, J. M., 'The Royal Pardon and Criminal Procedure in Early Modern England', *Historical Papers*, 22.1 (1987), pp. 9–22.
Beckles, Hilary, 'The Concept of "White Slavery" in the English Caribbean During the Early Seventeenth Century', in John Brewer and Susan Staves (eds), *Early Modern Conceptions of Property* (London and New York: Routledge, 1995), pp. 572–85.
Beckles, Hilary, *White Servitude and Black Slavery in Barbados, 1627–1715* (Knoxville: University of Tennessee Press, 1989).
Bellamy, John, *Criminal Law and Society in Late Medieval and Tudor England* (Gloucester: Alan Sutton, 1984).
Bernthal, Craig, 'Jack Cade's Legal Carnival', *Studies in English Literature*, 42.2 (2002), pp. 259–74.
Bernthal, Craig, 'Staging Justice: James I and the Trial Scenes of *Measure for Measure*', *Studies in English Literature*, 32.2 (1992), pp. 247–69.
Berry, Philippa, '"Salving the mail": Perjury, grace and the disorder of things

in *Love's Labour's Lost*', in Ewan Fernie (ed.), *Spiritual Shakespeares* (Abingdon: Routledge, 2005), pp. 94–108.

Bray, Gerald (ed.), *Tudor Church Reform: the Henrician Canons of 1535 and the 'Reformatio Legum Ecclesiasticarum'* (London: Boydell Press, Church of England Record Society, 2000).

Bridenbaugh, Carl, *Vexed and Troubled Englishmen* (Oxford: Oxford University Press, 1967).

Bridenbaugh, Carl and Roberta Bridenbaugh, *No Peace Beyond the Line: the English in the Caribbean 1624–1690* (Oxford: Oxford University Press, 1972).

Calderwood, James L., '*Love's Labour's Lost*: A Wantoning with Words', *Studies in English Literature*, 5.2 (1965), pp. 317–32.

Capp, Bernard, 'Bigamous Marriage in Early Modern England', *The Historical Journal*, 52.3 (2009), pp. 537–56.

Capp, Bernard, 'Life, Love and Litigation: Sileby in the 1630s', *Past and Present*, 182.1 (2004), pp. 55–83.

Carey, John, 'Donne and Coins', in John Carey (ed.), *English Renaissance Studies* (Oxford: Clarendon Press, 1980), pp. 151–63.

Challis, C. E., 'Spanish Bullion', *Journal of European Economic History*, 4.2 (1975), pp. 381–92.

Challis, C. E., *The Tudor Coinage* (Manchester: Manchester University Press, 1978).

Chartier, Roger, 'The Hanged Woman Miraculously Saved: An *occasionnel*', in Alain Boureau and Roger Chartier (eds), *The Culture of Print: Power and the Uses of Print in Early Modern Europe* (Oxford: Polity Press, 1989), pp. 59–91.

Clark, Sandra, *Women and Crime in the Street Literature of Early Modern England* (Basingstoke: Palgrave Macmillan, 2003).

Cockburn, J. S., *A History of English Assizes 1558–1714* (Cambridge: Cambridge University Press, 1972).

Cockburn, J. S., 'Patterns of Violence in English Society: Homicide in Kent 1560–1985', *Past and Present*, 130.1 (1991), pp. 70–106.

Cockburn, J. S., 'Trial by the Book? Fact and theory in the criminal process, 1558–1625', in J. H. Baker (ed.), *Legal Records and the Historian* (London: Royal Historical Society, 1978), pp. 67–79.

Cockburn, J. S. and Thomas A. Green (eds), *Twelve Good Men and True: The Criminal Trial Jury in England, 1200–1800* (Princeton: Princeton University Press, 1988).

Coldham, Peter Wilson, *The Complete Book of Emigrants 1607–1660* (Baltimore: Genealogical Publishing Co., 1987).

Coldham, Peter Wilson, *The Complete Book of Emigrants 1661–1699* (Baltimore: Genealogical Publishing Co., 1990).

Coldham, Peter Wilson, *The Complete Book of Emigrants in Bondage 1614–1775* (Baltimore: Genealogical Publishing Co., 1988).

Coldham, Peter Wilson, *Emigrants in Chains* (Stroud: Alan Sutton, 1992).

Coldham, Peter Wilson, *More Emigrants in Bondage 1614–1775* (Baltimore: Genealogical Publishing Co., 2002).

Condren, Conal, *Argument and Authority in Early Modern England* (Cambridge: Cambridge University Press, 2006).

Conklin, George, 'Witchcraft Trials in England: An Examination of Judicial Integrity', *American Bar Association Journal*, 45.9 (1959), pp. 938–40.
Cormack, Bradin, *A Power to Do Justice: Jurisdiction, English Literature and the Rise of Common Law, 1509–1625* (Chicago: University of Chicago Press, 2007).
Cornish, W. R., *The Jury* (London: Penguin, 1968).
Craig, Sir John, *The Mint, a History of the London Mint from A.D. 287 to 1948* (Cambridge: Cambridge University Press, 1953).
Crawford, Catherine, 'Legalizing Medicine', in Michael Clark and Catherine Crawford (eds), *Legal Medicine in History* (Cambridge: Cambridge University Press, 1994), pp. 89–116.
Crawford, Patricia, 'The Construction and Experience of Maternity in Seventeenth-Century England', in Valerie Fildes (ed.), *Women as Mothers in Pre-Industrial England* (London: Routledge, 1990), pp. 3–38.
Cressy, David, *Gypsies: An English History* (Oxford: Oxford University Press, 2018).
Cromartie, Alan, 'The Constitutionalist Revolution: The Transformation of Political Culture in Early Stuart England', *Past and Present*, 163.1 (1999), pp. 76–120.
Cromartie, Alan, '*Epieikeia* and Conscience', in Lorna Hutson (ed.), *The Oxford Handbook of English Law and Literature, 1500–1700* (Oxford: Oxford University Press, 2017), pp. 320–36.
Curran, Kevin (ed.), *Shakespeare and Judgment* (Edinburgh: Edinburgh University Press, 2017).
Davis, Natalie Zemon, *Fiction in the Archives: Pardon Tales and their Tellers in Sixteenth-Century France* (Stanford: Stanford University Press, 1987).
Devereaux, Simon, 'Imposing the Royal Pardon: Execution, Transportation and Convict Resistance in London, 1789', *Law and History Review*, 25.1 (2007), pp. 101–38.
Dickinson, J. R. and J. A. Sharpe, 'Infanticide in Early Modern England: the Court of Great Sessions at Chester, 1650–1800', in Mark Jackson (ed.), *Infanticide: Historical Perspectives on Child Murder and Concealment, 1550–2000* (Aldershot: Ashgate, 2002), pp. 35–51.
Dolan, Frances E., *Dangerous Familiars: Representations of Domestic Crime in England, 1550–1700* (Ithaca, NY: Cornell University Press, 1994).
Dolan, Frances E., *True Relations: Reading, Literature and Evidence in Seventeenth-Century England* (Philadelphia: University of Pennsylvania Press, 2013).
Dollimore, Jonathan, 'Transgression and Surveillance in *Measure for Measure*', in Jonathan Dollimore and Alan Sinfield (eds), *Political Shakespeares: New Essays in Cultural Materialism* (Manchester, Manchester University Press, 1985), pp. 72–87.
Dunne, Derek, *Shakespeare, Revenge Tragedy and Early Modern Law* (Basingstoke: Palgrave Macmillan, 2016).
Edwards, Edward, *The Life of Sir Walter Raleigh* (London: Macmillan, 1868).
Edwards, Valerie, 'The Case of the Married Spinster: An Alternative Explanation', *American Journal of Legal History*, 21.3 (1977), pp. 260–5.
Feavearyear, Sir Albert, *The Pound Sterling: A History of English Money* (Oxford: Clarendon Press, 1963).

Fischer, Sandra K., *Econolingua* (New Jersey: Associated University Presses, 1985).

Fisher, George, 'The Jury's Rise as Lie Detector', *Yale Law Journal*, 107.3 (1997), pp. 573–713.

Flanigan, Tom, '*Cymbeline* and the Sermons *Against Strife and Contention* and *Against Swearing and Perjury*: an Intertextual Reading', *Journal of the Wooden O Symposium*, 2 (2002), pp. 89–103.

Forman, Valerie, 'Marked Angels: Counterfeits, Commodities and *The Roaring Girl*', *Renaissance Quarterly*, 54.4 (2001), pp. 1531–60.

Foucault, Michel, *Discipline and Punish*, trans. Alan Sheridan (London: Penguin, 1977).

Freeman, Thomas S., 'Fate, Faction, and Fiction in Foxe's Book of Martyrs', *Historical Journal*, 43.3 (2000), pp. 601–23.

Gabel, Leona, *Benefit of Clergy in England in the Later Middle Ages* (Northampton: Smith College Studies in History, vol. 14, 1928–9).

Gaskill, Malcolm, *Crime and Mentalities in Early Modern England* (Cambridge: Cambridge University Press, 2000).

Geng, Penelope, 'Before the Right to Remain Silent: The Examinations of Anne Askew and Elizabeth Young', *Sixteenth Century Journal*, XLIII.3 (2012), pp. 667–79.

Goodrich, Peter, 'Endnote: Untoward', in Patrick Hanafin, Adam Geary and Joseph Brooker (eds), *Law and Literature* (Oxford: Blackwell Publishing, 2004), pp. 159–62.

Gordon, Michael D., 'The Invention of a Common Law Crime: Perjury and the Elizabethan Courts', *American Journal of Legal History*, 24.2 (1980), pp. 145–70.

Gordon, Michael D., 'The Perjury Statute of 1563: A Case History of Confusion', *Proceedings of the American Philosophical Society*, 124.6 (1980), pp. 438–54.

Gowing, Laura, *Common Bodies: Women, Touch and Power in Seventeenth-Century England* (New Haven and London: Yale University Press, 2003).

Gowing, Laura, *Domestic Dangers: Women, Words and Sex in Early Modern London* (Oxford: Clarendon Press, 1996).

Gowing, Laura, 'Secret Births and Infanticide in Seventeenth-Century England', *Past and Present*, 156.1 (1997), pp. 87–115.

Green, Thomas Andrew, *Verdict According to Conscience: Perspectives on the English Criminal Jury, 1200–1800* (Chicago and London: University of Chicago Press, 1985).

Greenblatt, Stephen, 'The History of Literature', *Critical Inquiry*, 23.3 (1997), pp. 460–81.

Griffiths, Paul, 'Politics made visible: order, residence and uniformity in Cheapside, 1600–45', in Paul Griffiths and Mark S. R. Jenner (eds), *Londonopolis: Essays in the Cultural and Social History of Early Modern London* (Manchester: Manchester University Press, 2000), pp. 176–97.

Grupp, Stanley, 'Some Historical Aspects of the Pardon in England', *American Journal of Legal History*, 7.1 (1963), pp. 51–62.

Hadfield, Andrew, *Lying in Early Modern English Culture* (Oxford: Oxford University Press, 2017).

Hay, Douglas, 'Property, Authority and the Criminal Law', in Douglas Hay, Peter Linebaugh, John G. Rule, E. P. Thompson and Cal Winslow (eds),

Albion's Fatal Tree: Crime and Society in Eighteenth-Century England (New York: Random House, 1975), pp. 17–64.
Hayne, Victoria, 'Performing Social Practice: The Example of *Measure for Measure*', *Shakespeare Quarterly*, 44.1 (1993), pp. 1–29.
Helmholz, R. H., *Roman Canon Law in Reformation England* (Cambridge: Cambridge University Press, 1990).
Herrup, Cynthia, *The Common Peace: Participation and the Criminal Law in Seventeenth-Century England* (Cambridge: Cambridge University Press, 1987).
Herrup, Cynthia, *A House in Gross Disorder; Sex, Law and the 2nd Earl of Castlehaven* (Oxford: Oxford University Press, 1999).
Herrup, Cynthia, 'Negotiating Grace', in Thomas Cogswell, Richard Cust and Peter Lake (eds), *Politics, Religion and Popularity in Early Stuart Britain* (Cambridge: Cambridge University Press, 2002), pp. 124–40.
Herrup, Cynthia, 'Punishing Pardon: Some Thoughts on the Origins of Penal Transportation', in Simon Devereaux and Paul Griffiths (eds), *Penal Practice and Culture 1500–1700* (Basingstoke: Palgrave Macmillan, 2004), pp. 121–7.
Higgins, John C., 'Justice, Mercy and Dialectical Genres in *Measure for Measure* and *Promos and Cassandra*', *English Literary Renaissance*, 42.2 (2012), pp. 258–93.
Hindle, Steve, *The State and Social Change in Early Modern England, c.1550–1640* (Basingstoke: Palgrave Macmillan, 2000).
Hoffer, Peter C. and N. E. H. Hull, *Murdering Mothers: Infanticide in England and New England 1558–1803* (New York: New York University Press, 1984).
Hudson, Judith, '"The nine-liv'd Sex": women and justice in seventeenth-century popular poetry', in Susan Wiseman (ed.), *Early Modern Women and the Poem* (Manchester: Manchester University Press, 2013), pp. 201–19.
Hudson, Judith, 'Seventeenth-century legal fictions: the case of John Perry', *The Seventeenth Century*, 32.3 (2017), pp. 297–320.
Hunter, Michael, 'New Light on the Drummer of Tedworth: conflicting narratives of witchcraft in Restoration England', *Historical Research*, 78.201 (2005), pp. 311–53.
Hutson, Lorna, 'From Penitent to Suspect: Law, Purgatory and Renaissance Drama', *Huntington Library Quarterly*, 65.3/4 (2002), pp. 215–319.
Hutson, Lorna, 'Imagining Justice: Kantorowicz and Shakespeare', *Representations*, 106.1 (2009), pp. 118–14.
Hutson, Lorna, *The Invention of Suspicion: Law and Mimesis in Shakespeare and Renaissance Drama* (Oxford: Oxford University Press, 2007).
Hutson, Lorna, 'Noises Off: Participatory Justice in *2 Henry VI*', in Constance Jordan and Karen Cunningham (eds), *The Law in Shakespeare* (Basingstoke: Palgrave Macmillan, 2007), pp. 143–66.
Hutson, Lorna (ed.), *The Oxford Handbook of English Law and Literature, 1500–1700* (Oxford: Oxford University Press, 2017).
Hutson, Lorna and Victoria Kahn (eds), *Rhetoric and Law in Early Modern Europe* (New Haven and London: Yale University Press, 2001).
Ingram, Martin, *Church Courts, Sex and Marriage in England 1570–1640* (Cambridge: Cambridge University Press, 1987).
Jackson, Mark (ed.), *Infanticide: Historical Perspectives on Child Murder and Concealment, 1550–2000* (Aldershot: Ashgate, 2002).

Jackson, Mark, *New-Born Child Murder: Women, Illegitimacy and the Courts in Eighteenth-Century England* (Manchester: Manchester University Press, 1996).

Jackson, Mark, 'Suspicious Infant Deaths: the statute of 1624 and medical evidence at coroners' inquests', in Michael Clark and Catherine Crawford (eds), *Legal Medicine in History* (Cambridge: Cambridge University Press, 1994), pp. 64–86.

Jordan, Constance, 'Interpreting Statute in *Measure for Measure*', in Bradin Cormack, Martha C. Nussbaum and Richard Strier (eds), *Shakespeare and the Law: A Conversation Among Disciplines and Professions* (Chicago: University of Chicago Press, 2013), pp. 101–20.

Kent, Joan, 'Attitudes of Members of the House of Commons to the Regulation of "Personal Conduct" in Late Elizabethan and Early Stuart England', *Bulletin of the Institute of Historical Research*, 46.113 (1973), pp. 41–71.

Kerrigan, John, *Shakespeare's Binding Language* (Oxford: Oxford University Press, 2016).

Kesselring, K. J., 'A Draft of the 1531 "Acte for Poysoning"', *The English Historical Review*, 116.468 (2001), pp. 894–9.

Kesselring, K. J., *Mercy and Authority in the Tudor State* (Cambridge: Cambridge University Press, 2003).

Kietzman, Mary Jo, 'Defoe Masters the Serial Subject', *ELH*, 66.3 (1999), pp. 677–705.

Kietzman, Mary Jo, *The Self-Fashioning of an Early Modern Englishwoman: Mary Carleton's Lives* (Aldershot: Ashgate, 2004).

Klerman, Daniel, 'Was the Jury Ever Self-Informing?', *Southern California Law Review*, 77.1 (2003), pp. 123–50.

Knafla, Louis A., '"John at Love Killed Her": The Assizes and Criminal Law in Early Modern England', *The University of Toronto Law Journal*, 35.3 (1985), pp. 305–20.

Knowles, Ronald, 'The Farce of History: Miracle, Combat and Rebellion in 2 Henry VI', *Yearbook of English Studies*, 21 (1991), pp. 168–86.

Lake, Peter and Michael Questier, *The Trials of Margaret Clitherow: Persecution, Martyrdom and the Politics of Sanctity in Elizabethan England* (London: Bloomsbury, 2011).

Langbein, John H., 'Albion's Fatal Flaws', *Past and Present*, 98.1 (1983), pp. 96–120.

Langbein, John H., 'The Criminal Trial before the Lawyers', *University of Chicago Law Review*, 45.2 (1978), pp. 263–316.

Langbein, John H., 'The Historical Origins of the Sanction of Imprisonment for Serious Crime', *Journal of Legal Studies*, 5.1 (1976), pp. 35–60.

Langbein, John H., *Prosecuting Crime in the Renaissance* (Cambridge, MA: Harvard University Press, 1974).

Leslie, Marina, 'Representing Anne Green: Historical and Literary Form and the Scenes of the Crime in Oxford, 1651', in Alison LaCroix, Richard McAdams and Martha Nussbaum (eds), *Fatal Fictions: Crime and Investigation in Law and Literature* (Oxford: Oxford University Press, 2015), pp. 89–110.

Linebaugh, Peter, *The London Hanged: Crime and Civil Society in the Eighteenth Century* (London: Verso, 2003).

Macdonald, Michael and Terence R. Murphy, *Sleepless Souls: Suicide in Early Modern England* (Oxford: Clarendon Press, 1990).
Macfarlane, Alan, *The Justice and the Mare's Ale: Law and Disorder in Seventeenth-Century England* (Oxford: Oxford University Press, 1981).
Macfarlane, Alan, *Witchcraft in Tudor and Stuart England: A Regional and Comparative Study* (London: Routledge, 1970).
MacKay, Lynn, 'Refusing the Royal Pardon: London Capital Convicts and the Reactions of the Courts and Press, 1789', *The London Journal*, 28.2 (2003), pp. 21–40.
McAlindon, Tom, 'Swearing and Forswearing in Shakespeare's Histories: The Playwright as Contra-Machiavel', *Review of English Studies*, 51.202 (2000), pp. 208–29.
McKenzie, Andrea, '"This Death Some Strong and Stout-Hearted Man Doth Choose": The Practice of Peine Forte et Dure in Seventeenth- and Eighteenth-Century England', *Law and History Review*, 23 (2005), pp. 279–313.
McKenzie, Andrea, *Tyburn's Martyrs: Execution in England 1675–1775* (London: Hambledon Continuum, 2007).
McNeill, Fiona, *Poor Women in Shakespeare* (Cambridge: Cambridge University Press, 2007).
Majeske, Andrew, 'Equity's absence: the extremity of Claudio's prosecution and Barnardine's pardon in Shakespeare's *Measure for Measure*', *Law and Literature*, 21.2 (2009), pp. 169–84.
Marcus, Leah, *Puzzling Shakespeare: Local Reading and its Discontents* (Berkeley: University of California Press, 1988).
Martin, Randall, *Women, Murder and Equity in Early Modern England* (New York: Routledge, 2007).
Mead, Stephen X., '"Thou art chang'd": public value and personal identity in *Troilus and Cressida*', *Journal of Medieval and Renaissance Studies*, 22.1 (1992), pp. 237–59.
Milligan, Burton, 'Counterfeiters and Coin-clippers in the Sixteenth and Seventeenth Centuries', *Notes and Queries*, 182 (1942), pp. 100–05.
Mitnick, John Marshall, 'From Neighbor-Witness to Judge of Proofs: The Transformation of the English Civil Juror', *American Journal of Legal History*, 32.3 (1988), pp. 201–35.
Morgan, Gwenda and Peter Rushton, 'Print Culture, Crime and Transportation in the Criminal Atlantic', *Continuity and Change*, 22.1 (2007), pp. 49–72.
Morgan, Kenneth, 'Petitions Against Convict Transportation, 1725–1735', *The English Historical Review*, 104.410 (1989), pp. 110–13.
Mozley, J. F., *John Foxe and his Book* (London: S.P.C.K., 1940).
Mukherji, Subha, *Law and Representation in Early Modern Drama* (Cambridge: Cambridge University Press, 2006).
Mukherji, Subha, '"Understood Relations": Law and Literature in Early Modern Studies', *Literature Compass*, 6.3 (2009), pp. 706–25.
Muldrew, Craig, *The Economy of Obligation: The Culture of Credit and Social Relations in Early Modern England* (Basingstoke: Macmillan, 1998).
Murphy, Theresa, *The Old Bailey* (Edinburgh: Mainstream Publishing, 1999).
Mush, John, 'The Life of Margaret Clitherow', in John Morris (ed.), *The Troubles of our Catholic Forefathers Related by Themselves* (London: Burns and Oates, 1877), pp. 331–433.

Neill, Michael, 'Bastardy, Counterfeiting and Misogyny in *The Revenger's Tragedy*', *Studies in English Literature, 1500–1900*, 36.2 (1996), pp. 397–408.
Newman, Karen, '"Goldsmith's ware": Equivalence in *A Chaste Maid in Cheapside*', *Huntingdon Library Quarterly*, 71.1 (2008), pp. 97–113.
Peters, Julie Stone, 'Law, Literature and the Vanishing Real: On the Future of an Interdisciplinary Illusion', *PMLA*, 120.2 (2005), pp. 442–53.
Phan, Marie-Claude, 'Les déclarations de grossesse en France (XVIe–XVIIIe siècles) Essai institutionnel', *Revue d'Historie modern et contemporaine* (1975), pp. 61–88.
Posner, Richard, *Law and Literature: A Misunderstood Relation* (Cambridge, MA: Harvard University Press, 1988).
Prest, Wilfrid R., 'The Art of Law and the Law of God: Sir Henry Finch (1558–1625)', in Donald Pennington and Keith Thomas (eds), *Puritans and Revolutionaries: Essays in Seventeenth-Century History presented to Christopher Hill* (Oxford: Clarendon Press, 1978), pp. 94–117.
Raymond, Joad (ed.), *Making the News: An Anthology of the Newsbooks of Revolutionary England 1641–1660* (Moreton-in-Marsh: The Windrush Press, 1993).
Sarat, Austin and Nasser Hussain (eds), *Forgiveness, Mercy and Clemency* (Stanford: Stanford University Press, 2007).
Sawday, Jonathan, *The Body Emblazoned: Dissection and the Human Body in Renaissance Culture* (London: Routledge, 1995).
Schmitt, Carl, *Political theology: Four chapters on the concept of sovereignty*, trans. George Schwab (Cambridge, MA: MIT Press, 1985).
Shabeen, Naseeb, 'Shakespeare and the Bishops' Bible', *Notes and Queries*, 47.1 (2000), pp. 94–7.
Shagan, Ethan, 'The Ecclesiastical Polity', in Lorna Hutson (ed.), *The Oxford Handbook of English Law and Literature, 1500–1700* (Oxford: Oxford University Press, 2017), pp. 336–52.
Shapiro, Barbara, *A Culture of Fact: England 1550–1720* (New York: Cornell University Press, 2000).
Shapiro, Barbara, *'Beyond Reasonable Doubt' and 'Probable Cause': Historical Perspectives on the Anglo-American Law of Evidence* (Berkeley: University of California Press, 1991).
Shapiro, Barbara, 'Law and the Evidentiary Environment', in Lorna Hutson (ed.), *The Oxford Handbook of English Law and Literature, 1500–1700* (Oxford: Oxford University Press, 2017), pp. 257–76.
Shapiro, Barbara, 'Law Reform in Seventeenth-Century England', *The American Journal of Legal History*, 19 (1975), pp. 280–312.
Sharpe, J. A., *Crime in Early Modern England 1550–1750* (Harlow: Longman, 1984).
Sharpe, J. A., *Crime in Seventeenth-Century England: A County Study* (Cambridge: Cambridge University Press, 1983).
Sharpe, J. A., *Defamation and Sexual Slander in Early Modern England: The Church Courts at York* (York: York University Press, 1980).
Sharpe, J. A., 'Domestic Homicide in Early Modern England', *Historical Journal*, 24 (1981), pp. 29–48.
Sharpe, J. A., '"Last Dying Speeches": Religion, Ideology and Public Execution in Seventeenth-Century England', *Past and Present*, 107 (1985), pp. 144–67.

Sheen, Erica and Lorna Hutson, *Literature, Politics and Law in Renaissance England* (Palgrave Macmillan: Basingstoke, 2005).
Shirley, Frances, *Swearing and Perjury in Shakespeare's Plays* (London: George Allen & Unwin, 1979).
Shuger, Debora, *Political Theologies in Shakespeare's England: The Sacred and the State in* Measure for Measure (Basingstoke: Palgrave, 2001).
Skulsky, Harold, 'Pain, Law and Conscience in *Measure for Measure*', *Journal of the History of Ideas*, 25.2 (1964), pp. 147–68.
Smith, Abbot Emerson, 'The Transportation of Convicts to the American Colonies in the Seventeenth Century', *The American Historical Review*, 39.2 (1934), pp. 232–49.
Smith, Rosalind, 'A "goodly sample": exemplarity, female complaint and early modern women's poetry', in Susan Wiseman (ed.), *Early Modern Women and Poetry* (Manchester: Manchester University Press, 2013), pp. 181–200.
Spalding, James C., 'The *Reformatio Legum Ecclesiasticarum* and the Furthering of Discipline in England', *Church History*, 39.2 (1970), pp. 162–71.
Spurr, John, 'A Profane History of Early Modern Oaths', *Transactions of the Royal Historical Society* (Sixth Series), 11 (2001), pp. 37–63.
Stacey, Richard, '"The Vow is Made": Communal Swearing in *Titus Andronicus*', *Forum for Modern Language Studies*, 54.1 (2018), pp. 60–72.
Staub, Susan C., 'Early Modern Medea: Representations of Child Murder in the Street Literature of Seventeenth-Century England', in Naomi J. Miller and Naomi Yavneh (eds), *Maternal Measures: Figuring Caregiving in the Early Modern Period* (Aldershot: Ashgate, 2000), pp. 333–47.
Staub, Susan C., '"A Wench Re-Woman'd": The Miraculous Recovery of Anne Greene', *Renaissance Papers* (1997), pp. 101–12.
Stone, Lawrence, 'The Educational Revolution in England 1560–1640', *Past and Present*, 28.1 (1964), pp. 41–80.
Strain, Virginia Lee, *Law Reform in English Renaissance Literature* (Edinburgh, Edinburgh University Press, 2018).
Strain, Virginia Lee, 'The "Snared Subject" and the General Pardon Statute in Late Elizabethan Coterie Literature', in Donald Beecher, Travis DeCook, Andrew Wallace and Grant Williams (eds), *Taking Exception to the Law: Materializing Injustice in Early Modern English Literature* (Toronto: University of Toronto Press, 2015), pp. 100–19.
Streete, Adrian, 'Charity and Law in Love's Labour's Lost: A Calvinist Analogue', *Notes and Queries*, 49.2 (2002), pp. 224–5.
Styles, John, '"Our traitorous money-makers": the Yorkshire coiners and the law, 1760–83', in John Brewer and John Styles (eds), *An Ungovernable People: the English and their law in the seventeenth and eighteenth centuries* (New Jersey: Rutgers University Press, 1983), pp. 172–254.
Stymeist, David, 'Criminal Biography in Early Modern News Pamphlets', in Donald Beecher, Travis DeCook, Andrew Wallace and Grant Williams (eds), *Taking Exception to the Law: Materializing Injustice in Early Modern English Literature* (Toronto: University of Toronto Press, 2015), pp. 137–61.
Suarez, Michael, 'A Crisis in English Public Life: The Popish Plot, *Naboth's Vineyard* (1679), and Mock-Biblical Satire's Exemplary Redress', *Huntingdon Library Quarterly*, 67.4 (2004), pp. 529–54.

Sullivan, Ceri, *The Rhetoric of Credit: Merchants in early modern writing* (London: Associated University Presses, 2002).
Summerson, H. R. T., 'The Early Development of the Peine Forte et Dure', in E. W. Ives and A. H. Manchester (eds), *Law, Litigants and the Legal Profession* (London: Royal Historical Society, 1983), pp. 116–25.
Suzuki, Mihoko, 'The Case of Mary Carleton: Representing the Female Subject, 1663–73', *Tulsa Studies in Women's Literature*, 12.1 (1993), pp. 61–83.
Syme, Holger Schott, *Theatre and Testimony in Shakespeare's England: A Culture of Mediation* (Cambridge: Cambridge University Press, 2011).
Tawney, R. H. and E. Power (eds), *Tudor Economic Documents*, 3 vols (London: Longman, 1924).
Thomas, Keith, 'The Puritans and Adultery: The Act of 1650 Reconsidered', in Donald Pennington and Keith Thomas (eds), *Puritans and Revolutionaries: Essays in Seventeenth-Century History presented to Christopher Hill* (Oxford: Clarendon Press, 1978), pp. 257–82.
Todd, Janet, 'Mary Carleton', *Oxford Dictionary of National Biography Online*, <http://www.oxforddnb.com>(accessed 12 May 2008).
Todd, Janet and Elizabeth Spearing (eds), *Counterfeit Ladies* (London: William Pickering, 1994).
Veall, D., *The Popular Movement for Law Reform 1640–1660* (Oxford: Clarendon Press, 1970).
Walker, Garthine, *Crime, Gender and Social Order in Early Modern England* (Cambridge: Cambridge University Press, 2003).
Walsham, Alexandra, *Providence in Early Modern England* (Oxford: Oxford University Press, 1999).
Watt, Tessa, *Cheap Print and Popular Piety, 1550–1640* (Cambridge: Cambridge University Press, 1991).
Weber, Annette, 'The Hanged Judas of Freiburg Cathedral', in Eva Frojmovic (ed.), *Imagining the Self, Imagining the Other: Visual Representation and Jewish-Christian Dynamics in the Middle Ages and Early Modern Period* (Leiden: Brill, 2002), pp. 165–88.
Wiener, Carol Z., 'Is a Spinster an Unmarried Woman?', *American Journal of Legal History*, 20.1 (1976), pp. 27–31.
Witmore, Michael, *Pretty Creatures: Children and Fiction in the English Renaissance* (Ithaca: Cornell University Press, 2007).
Wolfe, Don, *Leveller Manifestoes of the Puritan Revolution* (New York: Thomas Nelson & Sons, 1944).
Wordie, J. R., 'Deflationary factors in the Tudor Price Rise', *Past and Present*, 154.1 (1997), pp. 49–61.
Wrightson, Keith, 'Infanticide in European History', *Criminal Justice History*, 3 (1982), pp. 430–36.
Wrightson, Keith, 'Two Concepts of Order: Justices, constables and jurymen in seventeenth-century England', in John Brewer and John Styles (eds), *An Ungovernable People: The English and their law in the seventeenth and eighteenth centuries* (New Brunswick: Rutgers University Press, 1980), pp. 21–46.
Wrotham, Simon, 'Sovereign Counterfeits: The Trial of the Pyx', *Renaissance Quarterly*, 49.2 (1996), pp. 334–59.
Zaller, Robert, 'The Debate on Capital Punishment during the English Revolution', *The American Journal of Legal History*, 31.2 (1987), pp. 126–44.

Index

abjuration of the realm, 130
adultery
  1650 Act, 117, 148
  coining imagery, 74–6, 79
Agamben, Giorgio, 16, 27, 42, 52
'angels', 62, 68
Arraignment, Tryal and Examination of Mary Moders, The, 177, 184, 196
Articles of Church of England, 29, 34
assizes, 5, 10, 134
  Act of Oblivion, 138
  benefit of clergy cases, 153–4
  clergy rolls, 152
  coining cases, 62–5, 69, 71–3, 83, 85, 88–9
  infanticide cases, 103
  maiden assizes, 137
  Measure for Measure, 144–5
  pardons ('circuit') 142–5
  return from transportation case, 194
  sermons, 29
  transportation, reprieve for, 173
Atkinson, Alan, 186

Bacon, Francis, 3, 100
Baker, J. H.
  benefit of clergy, 153
  Coke, Edward, 4
  documentation of law, 6
  legal fictions, 3
  peine forte et dure, 160–1
ballads
  coining and clipping, 87–90
  infanticide, 104–6
Barbados, 172–3, 182–3, 185, 187

Beard, Thomas, *Theatre of God's Judgements*, 41
Beattie, J. M., 17, 180
  execution statistics, 134
  jurors, 10, 180
  pardon, 140, 143
  pillory, 39
  theft, 175, 180
  transportation, 173, 175, 182–3
Beckles, Hilary, 182
benefit of clergy, 9, 20, 130–1, 150–7, 159, 161–3
  abolition, 157
  branding, 151–2
  coining, 85
  definition, 150
  history, 150–2, 157
  reading test, 150–1, 153–4
  scope, 152
  statutes, 151–2, 174
  transportation, 174
  women, 119, 152, 177
Bernthal, Craig, 133 n.11, 155
Berry, Philippa, 54
Bicknoll, Edmund, *A Sword Agaynst Swearing*, 31, 40–6
  Anne Averies case, 42
  Father Lea case, 43
  Grimwood case, 45
bigamy
  benefit of clergy for, 154
  Mary Carleton, 176–9
Blackstone, William, *Commentaries on the Laws of England*, 111, 132, 159–60

Blondeau, Pierre, 72
Bloody Newes from Dover, 104
Bloudy Mother, The, 99
Bridenbaugh, Carl, 172
Burdet, William, *A Wonder of Wonders*, 98, 107, 112–14
 critique of law, 114, 119, 122
 Leveller interests, 113
 pardon, 112
 providence, 114, 118

Calderwood, James, 51
canon law *see* church courts, jurisdiction
capital punishment
 application of, 9, 125, 169, 174, 180
 debate around, 10–14, 21, 198–9
 drama, 75–6, 81, 147
 execution statistics, 103, 134
 offences, 9, 18–21, 37, 47, 63–4, 65 n.9, 67, 69–74, 84–5, 100, 102, 134–5, 154, 177, 194
 see also benefit of clergy; pardon; *peine forte et dure;* sanction
Capp, Bernard, 154
Carey, John, 70
Carleton, John, 168, 176–9, 196
Carleton, Mary, 21, 168–203
 aliases, 179–83, 190
 bigamy charges, 176–9
 Case of Madam Mary Carleton, The, 177, 189
 death, 196
 'Discovery', 193
 feme covert, 169, 177, 179
 'German Princess', 168–9, 176–9, 189–191, 195, 197
 Historicall Narrative of the German Princess, An, 177
 Kirkman biography, 169, 176, 184, 190, 193
 Letter from Port Royal ('News from Jamaica'), 168, 179, 184–5, 187, 188–92, 193, 198
 life, 176–9
 pamphlets, 168
 petitions, 181
 plays, 178, 190
 pleading the belly, 181, 194
 return from transportation, 168, 173, 175, 192–6
 theft charges, 180–3, 192, 195
 transportation records, 182, 183–4, 189–92
Caryll, John, *Naboth's Vineyard, or The Innocent Traytor*, 49–50
 Popish Plot references, 49–50
 subornment of perjury, 49
Challis, C. E., 66
Chapman, George (with Jonson and Marston), *Eastward Hoe*, 77
Chartier, Roger
 French *occasionnels*, 120–4
Charles I
 pardons, 137, 141
Charles II
 1660 Act of Oblivion, 135, 139
 mechanisation of Royal Mint, 90
 transportation proclamation, 13, 174
Chaste Maid in Cheapside, A (Middleton), 19, 64, 71, 77–82
 adultery, 79
 Cheapside, 77–8
 closed-economy coining, 78–80
 goldsmiths, 77
 Promoters' scene, 79
Chidley, Samuel, *A Cry Against a Crying Sinne*, 12
church courts, 6–7, 26–8, 35, 38–9, 55, 79, 148–54; *see also* jurisdiction
Clarke, John, 97
Clavell, John, *A recantation of an ill-led life*, 137
clemency *see* pardon
clipping, 65
 circumcision images, 72–3
 coining and clipping rings, 63, 72
 offenders, 72, 76–7
 planting clippings, 68
 prosecution, 82–87
 treason designation, 63, 67, 85–7
 see also coining
Clitherow, Margaret, 160
Cobbett, William, *State Trials*,
 Ann Price case, 50–1
Cockburn, J. S.
 benefit of clergy, 154

coining cases, 85
execution statistics, 134
infanticide prosecutions, 118
pardons, 136, 143
peine forte et dure, 160
coinage
 debasement, 66
 foreign coins in circulation, 70
 gold/silver ratio, 66
 image of monarch, 70–1
 intrinsic worth, 65
 types of coins, 70
coining, 62–96
 alchemy associations, 83
 cases, 62–96
 clipping, 65
 closed-economy coining, 72, 78–80
 coining and clipping rings, 63, 72
 defamation suit, 92
 economic impact, 71–2, 87
 image of monarch, 70–1
 juror sympathy, 84–5
 Lancashire, 63
 language of coins, 68–9, 72, 74, 92
 law, association with, 76–7
 offenders, 72, 76–7
 penalties, 62, 82, 85–7
 prosecution, 82–87
 Royal Mint, 66, 72, 90
 statutes, 65, 66, 71
 support for coiners, 87
 sweating, 65
 treason designation, 63, 69–73, 85–7, 91
 uttering, 65, 69
 washing, 65, 77, 83
 'yellow trade', 63
 Yorkshire, 63, 72
 see also counterfeiting; clipping
Coke, Edward, 4, 36–7
 coining penalties, 68, 85–6
 Grimwood case, 46
 Institutes, 4, 55
 pardons, 135, 137
 peine forte et dure, 160
Coldham, Peter Wilson, 172, 183
commandments, 37
 third, 31
 fifth, 71
 seventh, 74
 ninth, 31
common law, 2–3, 5–8, 15, 19, 25–8, 33–8, 46, 55–6, 66, 86, 100, 117, 132, 144, 149, 150; *see also* jurisdiction
compurgation, 111, 120
Condren, Conal, 35
Conklin, George, 160
consequence *see* capital punishment; sanction
Cook, John, 13
Cormack, Bradin, 6, 15, 28, 38, 57, 63, 170, 186
counterfeiting, 1, 18, 62–96; *see also* coining
Cranmer, Thomas, 8; see also *Homily Against Swearing and Perjury*
Crawford, Catherine, 101, 117
Cressy, David, 141, 162
criminal biographies, 188
Cromwell, Oliver, 13
Cymbeline (Shakespeare)
 Iachimo as perjurer, 54

Dalton, Michael, *The Countrey Justice,* 36–7
Davis, Natalie Zemon, 140
Decalogue, 19, 27, 31, 37, 69, 71, 74; *see also* commandments
Declaration from Oxford, A, 98, 112–14
 critique of law, 114, 119
 Leveller interests, 113
 providence, 114, 118
 vision scene, 113, 124
Deeds against nature and Monsters by kinde, 105–6
Defoe, Daniel, 185
 Moll Flanders, 175, 179, 181, 185, 198
 Roxana, 175
Dekker, Thomas
 Northward Ho, 64
 The Roaring Girl, 62
 Westward Ho, 64
Deportment and Carriage of the German Princess Immediately before her Execution, The, 196

Derham, William, *Physico-Theology*, 98
Derrida, Jacques, 132
Devereaux, Simon, 157
de Voragine, Jacobus, *Legenda Aurea*, 44, 123
dissection, 108–9
Dolan, Frances, 100, 104, 120, 124, 191
Donne, John
  'The Bracelet', 73
  Sermon Preached Upon Candlemas Day, 71
Doolittle, Thomas, *The Swearer Silenc'd*, 42, 48
Drue, Thomas, *The Duchess of Suffolk*, 155
Dunne, Derek, 17, 76, 145

Edwards, Valerie, 161
Elizabeth I
  benefit of clergy statistics, 154
  coinage reforms, 2, 19, 66–7, 71
  pardons, 136, 138, 149
  peine forte et dure, 160
equity, 5
Evelyn, John, 87
  Diary, 98, 110, 123
Exact and True Relation of the Examination, Tryal and Condemnation of the German Princess, An, 192–3, 195
execution statistics, 103, 134
exile, 130

felony *see* capital punishment, offences
feme covert, 161, 169, 177, 179; *see also* spinster
Finch, Henry, *Nomotechnia*, 11–12, 138
Fisher, George, 34
Fitzherbert, Anthony, *L'Office et Auctorite de Justices de Peace*, 101
Flanigan, Tom, 55
Fleetwood, William, *Sermon Against Clipping*, 19, 70–1, 73, 84
Forman, Valerie, 65

Foucault, Michel, 8–9
Foxe, John, *Acts and Monuments*, 33
  Grimwood case, 45–6
Freeman, Thomas S., 45–6
French infanticide pamphlets *see occasionnels*
Fulbecke, William, 6, 66
Fuller, Thomas, *History of the Worthies of England*, 111

Gabel, Leona, 150, 153
galley service, 130, 171
Garnet, Henry
  trial, 56
Gaskill, Malcolm
  coining, 63, 69, 84, 87
  clipping, 68
  'mentalities', 16
Gauden, John, 30
'German Princess' *see* Carleton, Mary
German Princess Revived, The, 197
Gesta Grayorum, 138
goldsmiths, 77
Goodrich, Peter, 14–15
Gordon, Michael D., 34–6
Gowing, Laura, 6, 98
  infanticide cases, 100, 103, 111
  legal testimony, 17
  servants, 114
Greenblatt, Stephen, 153
Greene, Anne, 19, 97–129
  concealment of child, 115–16
  medical evidence, 106–12, 115, 120
  parallel case, 118
  pardon, 112, 116, 125, 139
  rape, 111
  recovery, 107–11
  spectacle, 109, 139–40
  trial, 115
  vision, 113
Gresham, Thomas, 66
Grimwood, William, 45–6
Grupp, Stanley, 151

Haddon, Walter, 33
Hadfield, Andrew, 40
Hale, Matthew, 4
  benefit of clergy, 151–2
  coining case, 86

Hale Commission, 2
Hay, Douglas, 133
Heath, James, *Brief Chronicle of the Intestine War*, 98
Helmholz, R. M., 149
Henry VI, Part 2 (Shakespeare),
  Clerk of Chartam trial, 156
  Jack Cade, 155–6
  Lord Saye trial, 155
Herrup, Cynthia
  communal justice, 8, 134
  pardons, 136, 139, 163, 185–6
  pleading the belly, 131
  verdicts, 17
Higgins, John, 134
Hindle, Steve, 134
Hoffer, Peter C., 101, 103
Homily Against Swearing and Perjury, 8, 26, 28, 30–3, 37, 52
Hull, N. E. H, 101, 103
Hussain, Nasser, 132
Hutson, Lorna, 5
  benefit of clergy, 154
  communal justice, 8–9, 134
  providence, 9, 124
  and Sheen, Erica, 14–15

indentured servitude, 171, 185–8
infanticide, 10, 19, 97–129
  1624 Act, 100–3, 114–15
  Carolina Code, 101
  concealment, 101–3, 115
  European prosecutions, 100, 122
  evidence, rules of 100–1
  prosecutions, 111
  statistics, 101, 103
Ingram, Martin, 6
Interregnum
  capital punishment, 13
  pardons, 137

Jackson, Mark, 103–4
Jamaica (Port Royal), 168, 179, 184–5, 193
James I
  coinage policy, 66–7
  Coronation pardon, 135
  infanticide policy, 102–3
  Measure for Measure, 131, 142
  pardon of Ralegh, Markham, Cobham, Grey, 133
  perjury statutes, 55
  statute pardons, 137, 149
  transportation Commission, 171
  True Law of Free Monarchies, 142
Jeaffreson, Christopher, 174, 182–3
Jezebel
  as suborner of perjury, 49–50
Jonson, Ben,
  Alchemist, The, 83
  (with Chapman and Marston)
  Eastward Hoe, 77
Jordan, Constance, 142, 149
Judas Iscariot
  hanged Judas iconography, 44–5
  as perjurer, 43, 49
judges
  benefit of clergy, 151–4, 177–8
  coining cases, 86
  Europe, 100
  infanticide cases, 115, 116, 122–3
  pardons, 136, 139, 141, 142–5
  peine forte et dure, 157, 159–61
  perjury, 35–6
  role, 6, 9, 100, 175, 180
  transportation, 13, 173, 175, 192–4
juries
  coining cases, 84, 92
  infanticide cases, 100
  juror nullification, 9
  'partial' verdicts, 9
  role under common law, 100
  'self-informing', 19
jurisdiction
  benefit of clergy, 151
  canon law, 6–7, 26–8, 35, 38–9, 55, 79, 148–54; *see also* church courts
  common law, 2–3, 5, 6–8, 15, 19, 25–8, 33–8, 46, 55–6, 66, 86, 100, 117, 132, 144, 149, 150
  transported felons, 186–8
Justices of the Peace, 8, 101, 114, 119, 134, 144–5

Kelyng, John, 115
Kent, Joan, 148
Kerrigan, John, 32, 51

Kesselring, K. J., 132, 135 n.21, 152 n.90, n.95
  jurisdiction of pardons, 149
  purchasers of pardons, 136
Kietzman, Mary Jo, 175, 180, 189–90
Kirkman, Francis, 169, 176–7, 184, 190–3, 196
Klerman, Daniel, 36

Lake, Peter,
  and Michael Questier, 160
Lambarde, William, *Eirenarcha*, 144–5
Langbein, John, 7, 10, 17, 171 n.10, 172, 180
law
  communal participation, 6, 8–9, 16, 99–100, 134, 162–3, 173
  dramatic form, 15
  legal fictions, 3
  and literature, 14–18
  see also common law; jurisdiction
Laws discovery, The, 156
Leslie, Marina, 110, 113
Levellers, 3, 11, 13
  Agreement of the People, 11
  Anne Greene pamphlets, 113
  Humble Petition of Thousands wel-affected Persons, 11
  Large Petition, 11
lex talionis, 7, 12, 161
Lichfield, Leonard, 97
Life and Death of Jack Straw, The, 153, 155
Ligon, Richard, 187
Linebaugh, Peter, 104
Locke, John, 90
London Gazette, 192, 198
Love's Labour's Lost (Shakespeare), 14, 18, 25–7, 29, 51–4
  Berowne, 14, 25, 29, 40, 47, 52–4
  Costard, 52, 57
  forfeiture, 40, 54
  King, 32, 37, 47, 51–4
  Nine Worthies masque, 53, 57
  oaths and vows, 29, 37, 39
  plague, 32
  Princess, 32, 37, 39–40, 47, 51–4

punishment of perjury, 25, 47, 52
Rosaline, 39, 40, 54
subornment of perjury, 47–8

McAlindon, Tom, 25
Macfarlane, Alan, 63, 99
MacKay, Lynn, 157
McKenzie, Andrea, 130, 133, 153, 159
McNeill, Fiona, 131
Majeske, Andrew, 131, 147
Mandeville, Bernard, *Fable of the Bees*, 117
Mankind, 154
Manningham, John, *Diary*, 77
manslaughter, 10, 139–40
Marcus, Leah, 142
Marston, John (with Chapman and Jonson), *Eastward Hoe*, 77
Maryland, 172, 182, 183
Mead, Stephen, 69, 91
Measure for Measure (Shakespeare), 20, 130–67
  Angelo, 141, 142, 143–5, 146–9
  Barnardine, 130, 139–40, 146–8, 150, 162
  Claudio, 142, 147, 149, 162–3
  Duke, 144, 147, 149–50, 157, 162
  James I, 131, 142
  legal system, 138, 144–5
  Lucio, 141, 144, 147, 149, 157, 160
  marriages, 149–50
  pardons, 131–2, 141, 144–5, 157
  Provost, 132, 134, 142, 145–7, 163
  sexual offences, 148–50
  state clemency, 131, 138
medical witnesses, 117
Memoires of Mary Carleton, 184, 185, 189, 193, 196 n.140
Memories of the Famous Madam Charlton, 185
Mercurius Politicus, 97, 123
mercy *see* pardon
Mestrell, Eloy, 72
Middleton, Thomas, 62
  A Yorkshire Tragedy, 160
  see also A Chaste Maid in Cheapside,

The Revenger's Tragedy, The Roaring Girl
midwives
  coining case, 84
  infanticide cases, 116–17, 122
military service, 130
miscarriage of justice, 19
  Anne Greene, 97–129
  pardons, 140
Morgan, Gwenda
  and Peter Rushton, 188, 195, 197
Mukherji, Subha, 15, 89, 98
Muldrew, Craig, 66
Munday, Anthony, *A View of sundry Examples*, 41–6
  Anne Averies case, 42
  Father Lea case, 43
murder, 10
Murphy, Theresa, 104

Naboth's Vineyard (Biblical episode), 48–9
narrative theory, 16, 100
Nature's Cruell Step-Dames, 104
Neill, Michael, 74–5
Newes from Jamaica see Carleton, Mary
Newes from the Dead, 98, 106–11, 112–16, 119–20, 124–5
  genre, 104, 106, 124–5
  poems, 97–8, 106–7, 110–2, 119–20, 125
  see also Watkins, Richard
Newgate Calendar, 175
Newman, Karen, 78

Oates, Titus *see also* Popish Plot, 26–7, 31, 48
oaths
  assertory oath-taking, 30
  lawful oaths, 29–32
  oaths of passage, 35
occasionnels, 120–4
  Anne Belthumier, 120–4
  Anne des Grez, 121–4
Onslowe's Case, 35–6, 48
Oxford
  infanticide case, 118
  law in, 119
  printers, 98
  University, 97, 110–11, 114
  see also Greene, Anne

pamphlets
  botched hangings, 104, 123
  Carleton, Mary, 168–203
  coining and clipping, 87–90
  infanticide, 99, 104–5, 111, 120–4; *see also* Burdet, William; *A Declaration from Oxford*; Watkins, Richard
  occasionnels, 120–4
  peine forte et dure, 159
  perjury, 40–6
pardon, 130–50, 157–63
  1660 Act of Oblivion, 135, 138–9
  administration, 136, 139, 143
  circuit pardon, 142–5
  conditional, 133, 141, 143, 157, 158, 173–5, 185–6
  Coronation pardons, 135–6
  definition and language, 131
  disruptive, 132
  fees, 136–7, 139
  general (royal) pardon, 20, 134–9
  gloves, 137
  'mock' pardon, 138
  petitions, 140–1
  purchasers of pardons, 136
  refusing pardon, 157–8, 188
  special (individual) pardon, 139–42
  statute pardons, 135–9
Parker, Martin, *No Naturall Mother but a Monster*, 105–6
peine forte et dure, 20, 131, 157–63
  abolition, 162
  Clitherow, Margaret, 160
  history, 157–8
  pamphlets, 159
  pleading the belly, 160
  prison forte et dure, 159
  reasons for refusing to plead, 160–2
  reluctance to impose, 159, 161–2
  statistics, 160
Percival, Thomas, 117
perjury, 1, 18, 25–61
  1563 Act, 8, 18, 25, 33–40, 55
  forfeiture, 38–40, 54

perjury (cont.)
  Homily Against see Homily Against Swearing and Perjury
  Judas imagery see Judas Iscariot
  oath of perjurer, 39
  perjurium, 38
  punishment of, 38–40
  subornment of, 39, 47–51
Peters, Hugh, 11
Peters, Julie Stone, 14
Petty, William, 97–8, 107–11, 114, 120
  Petty Papers, The, 115–16, 123
pillory, 25, 27, 38
pleading the belly, 131, 160, 181, 194
Plot, Robert, *Natural History of Oxfordshire*, 98
Plowden, Edmund, 5
Poor Laws, 102
Popish plot
  Titus Oates, 26–7, 31, 48
  trials, 2, 18, 48
Posner, Richard, 14
pregnancy plea see pleading the belly
providence, 9
  coining and clipping, 63, 89–90, 92
  infanticide, 20, 97, 100–1, 104–6, 107, 113–4, 118, 124–5
  perjury, 26–8, 40–6, 48, 56
punishment
  proportionable, 1, 3, 7, 11–12, 18–19, 26, 43, 47–8, 50, 161, 169
  see also sanction
Puritan politicians, 103

Questier, Michael, and Peter Lake, 160

Ralegh, Walter, 133
Raymond, Joad, 110, 123
Reformatio Legum Ecclesiasticarum, 33
reprieve, 130, 137, 143
  Anne Greene, 98, 111–12, 118, 140
  Measure for Measure, 140, 141–2, 145, 147
  pleading the belly, 84, 131
  transportation as, 13, 21, 156, 168–203
  see also benefit of clergy; pardon; transportation, reprieve for

Revenger's Tragedy, The (Middleton), 19, 64, 77, 81–2
  coining and adultery, 73–6
  law as corrupt, 75
  rhetoric, forensic, 16
Rivers, Marcellus and Oxenbridge Foyle case, 187
Roaring Girl, The (Middleton and Dekker), 19, 62, 75, 80–2
  entrapment, 62, 68, 73
  law as corrupt, 68, 81
  Moll Cutpurse, 62, 80–2
  'thief-whore' image, 73
Royal Mint, 66, 72
  mechanisation, 90
Rushton, Peter
  and Gwenda Morgan, 188, 195, 197

St Christopher, colony of, 172
St German, Christopher, 5
sanction
  abjuration of the realm, 130
  execution see capital punishment
  exile, 130
  galley service, 130, 171
  military service, 130
  pillory, 25, 27, 38
  proportionable, 1, 3, 7, 11–12, 18–19, 26, 43, 47–8, 50, 161, 169
  transportation see transportation, reprieve for
  treason, 63, 67, 85–7
sanctuary, 130
Sarat, Austin, 132
Sawday, Jonathan, 109
Schmitt, Carl, 27, 52
Scripture-based legal system, 7, 12
Shagan, Ethan, 6, 28
Shakespeare, William
  Richard II, 160
  Troilus and Cressida, 159–60
  see also *Cymbeline*; *Henry IV, Part 2*; *Love's Labour's Lost*; *Measure for Measure*
Shapiro, Barbara, 8, 12, 14, 19, 37, 111
Sharpe, J. A.
  benefit of clergy, 152–3

church courts, 6
execution statistics, 134
infanticide prosecutions, 103
Shirley, Frances, 31, 37
Skulsky, Harold, 162
Smith, Abbot Emerson, 9, 172, 173, 184, 186
Smith, Rosalind, 106
Smith, Thomas, *De Republica Anglorum*, 158
Smith, Sir Thomas, 171, 173
spinster, 161, 169, 177, 179
Spurr, John, 30
Star Chamber, 34–5
statute law, 1, 6–7
   Bacon, Francis, 3
   equity, 5
   interpretation, 7–8
Staub, Susan, 104, 108
Stone, Lawrence, 151
Strain, Virginia Lee, 17
   general pardons, 138
   Measure for Measure, 144
Strode, William, 30
Strype, J. 138
Styles, John, 63
Stymeist, David, 99
Sullivan, Ceri, 70
Summerson, H. R. T., 158
Suzuki, Mihoko, 168
Syme, Holger Schott, 2, 4, 198

theft, 9, 175, 180, 192
Thomas, Keith, 148
Tillotson, John, 29
Todd, Janet, 169, 177
Tomlinson, William, *Seven Particulars*, 1, 11
transportation, reprieve for, 13, 130, 156, 168–203
   1718 Act, 13, 21, 170
   benefit of clergy, 174–5
   Charles II proclamation, 13, 174
   destinations, 172, 182
   East India Company, 171
   European approaches, 171
   female convicts, 182–3
   history, 170–5

indentured servitude, 171, 185–8
James I Commission, 171
jurisdiction, 186–8
refusal of, 157–8, 188
rehabilitation, 174
return from, 21, 170, 173 192–6
uncertainty, 169–70, 191–2
see also pardon, conditional
treason, 63
   penalties for, 67, 85–7

Unhappy Marksman, The, 159, 161

Vaughan, Rice, 71
Verney, Thomas, 172, 182
Virginia, 172, 182
Virginia Gazette, 194
Voss, Jenney, 196

Walker, Garthine, 103, 106, 119
Walsham, Alexandra, 41, 98–9, 111, 118
Ward, John, *Lives of the Professors of Gresham College*, 98
Watkins, Richard, 107
   Newes from the Dead, 98, 106–11, 112–16, 119–20, 124–5
Watt, Tessa, 98
Webster, John
   Westward Ho, 64
   Northward Ho, 64
Whetstone, George, *Promos and Cassandra*, 145
Whistler, Henry, 173, 186
Wiener, Carol, 177
Wilkins, George, *Miseries of Enforced Marriage, The*, 160
Wilkins, John, 109
Willughby, Percival, 115
Wood, Anthony, 5, 46, 118
   poem, 98, 119
Wren, Christopher, 98
Wrightson, Keith, 118

Yarington, Robert, *Two Lamentable Tragedies*, 151–2

Zaller, Robert, 12–13

EU representative:
Easy Access System Europe
Mustamäe tee 50, 10621 Tallinn, Estonia
Gpsr.requests@easproject.com